ALIENS, ANGELS, & DEMONS

ALIENS, ANGELS, & DEMONS

Extraterrestrial Life in Judaism/Kabbalah & its Vital Relevance for Modern Times

R. Ariel B. Tzadok

Also by R. Ariel B. Tzadok:

WALKING IN THE FIRE

> *Classical Torah/Kabbalistic*
> *Meditations, Practices & Prayers.*
> ISBN 978-0-9791601-0-3

PROTECTION FROM EVIL

> *Exposing & neutralizing*
> *harmful spiritual forces.*
> ISBN 979-8-554-63579-3

VISIONS OF THE END OF DAYS

> *A Kabbalistic View of the Book of Daniel*
> *With a Guide to Dream Interpretations*
> ISBN 979-8-554-64539-6

Available on Amazon.com

Check out our courses in all areas of study

Available at **www.koshertorah.com**

YouTube: **KosherTorah School of Rabbi Ariel Bar Tzadok**

Aliens, Angels, & Demons

Extraterrestrial Life in Judaism/Kabbalah & its Vital Relevance for Modern Times

The KosherTorah School
for Biblical, Judaic & Spiritual Studies
www.koshertorah.com
arieltzadok@gmail.com

ISBN: 979-8-557-29557-4

Layout, graphic and cover design by: Dovid S. Brandes
Kabbalistic artwork for sale at *www.brandesart.com*

PROUDLY PRINTED IN THE USA

Giving is such a great thing.

One who gives of one's heart, and one's wealth is doubly blessed.
It is said that the Hand of G-d will never leave such a one
until he is blessed not just double, but seven-fold.

This book is dedicated to the many students
of the KosherTorah School
who contributed their support towards its publication.

Special thanks are due to Sherri Daniels, Rene Lerma, Felix Palacio
Romero, Rachel Shifren and many other anonymous donors.

Special thanks are due to Michael Alter
for all his generous help in editing and reviewing the text,
and to Dovid Brandes for his designs, formatting, and artwork.

"The secrets of forbidden relationships
must not be taught before (more) than three.
Nor the (secrets) of creation before (more) than two.
Nor the (secrets) of the chariot before one
unless that one is a sage and can understand on one's own."

Mishna Hagigah 2

This is the ancient law by which I am bound.
What I reveal in this book
is not meant to be spelled out step by step with ease.
In this book, I provide you with
all the building blocks with which to build,
and all the instructions to follow.
I cannot build for you.
You will have to build for yourself.
I will not tell you what to believe
You will have to decide this for yourself.

Use your wisdom, and understanding.
Combine them with your knowledge.
If you put all the pieces together properly,
you will then see that which the ancients long ago referred to as
the "work of creation" (ma'aseh bereshit) and
the "work of the chariot" (ma'aseh merkava).
You will then be able to understand
the mysteries of the past, and the secrets of the present.
You will even be able to gaze into tomorrow,
and see what is coming.

In the end, if you are wise,
you will gaze upon the wondrous palace
that your own hands have built.

So, build with wisdom, build in peace,
and make Heaven
(and those who dwell there)
proud of you.

TABLE OF CONTENTS

PART THREE
G-D, ANGELS ,& HUMANITY

<u>PART FOUR</u>
THE DISCLOSURE ESSAYS

In the Temple, in ancient Jerusalem:

"On the 21st day of the month of Iyar, a certain great and incredible phenomenon appeared: I suppose the account of it would seem to be a fable, were it not related by those who saw it... for before sunset, **chariots and troops of soldiers in their armor were seen running about among the clouds**... Moreover, at... Shavuot, as the priests were going about... as was their custom... they said that... they felt a quaking, and heard a great noise, and after that they heard a sound as of a great multitude, saying, 'Let us remove from here.'"

(Josephus, The Jewish War, Book 6, Chapter 5:3)

"As for the existence of angels, there is no necessity to cite any proof from Scripture, where the fact is frequently mentioned".

(Maimonides, Guide 2:6)

"Every act of G-d is described as being performed by angels.
But 'angel' means 'messenger';
hence every one that is entrusted with a certain mission is an angel".

(Maimonides, Guide 2:6)

"We have already explained that the term "angel" is a homonym, and is used of the intellectual beings, the spheres, and the elements: for all these are engaged in performing a divine command".

(Maimonides, Guide 2:7)

Foreward

Over the many years that I have served as the rabbi of the KosherTorah School, I have been asked many bizarre questions. Some questions deal with straightforward religious topics. Other questions seem to come from either the *Twilight Zone*, or the *X-Files*. I usually manage to both surprise and educate those who inquire of me.

Most people today, including many of my fellow rabbis, have no idea about what Judaism, over the many centuries of its existence, actually has to say about other-worldly revelations, and "close-encounter" experiences. It is safe and politically correct to address commonly accepted religious topics. Yet, Jewish beliefs, explorations, and experiences of higher realities was never what one could call "safe," politically correct, or commonly accepted.

Since ancient times, Judaism and its practitioners have long delved into the mysterious, the mystical, and the metaphysical. What was found there, first by the biblical prophets, and later by the prophetic Kabbalists, was considered so threatening to the common, everyday person, that an entire block of Torah teaching became restricted to the public. Thus was born, the *Sitrei Torah*, the secrets of the Torah/Jewish path. Over many centuries this body of knowledge grew. It came to incorporate many things, only one of them being that which became known as the Kabbalah.

Those who inherited the system and the practices of the biblical prophets, and the later Kabbalists alongside them, all shared one common secret. They all knew that we are not alone, not in our universe, and not even on our own planet. There are many other beings that G-d created alongside human beings. Some of them have been traditionally called angels. Others have been called demons. Most recently these other beings have become known to us as extraterrestrials, and aliens. Identities can be a funny thing, in that they can be so fluid, and transparent.

For the most part, not too many researchers scour the ancient records to compare the old stories of encounters, with the new ones. This lack of investigation leaves many old secrets undisturbed. Yet, some of what is taught in the *Sitrei Torah* involve matters very relevant to the modern day, and thus should no longer be kept secret.

The book that you are about to read will introduce you to many of the ideas, and beliefs, that the *Sitrei Torah* tradition in Judaism has long taught, but few have learned. In light of modern times, it is now appropriate, if not necessary, to open the closed curtain that conceals the secrets, and to reveal, at least a bit

Introduction

Do you believe in angels? How about demons? Their existence and presence is a given in many of the world's religions. Yet, do these entities exist only in the realms of religion, legend, folklore, and/or psychology, or is it possible that there is more to them than meets the eye?

Wouldn't it be interesting if they were indeed real sentient beings, and not mere byproducts of the mind? In light of our modern scientific understanding of the world around us, we would have to explore what would be the real place of these beings of ancient lore in the reality in which we live. The identities of these ancient beings, if they are indeed as real as religious literature insists that they are, might need to be reevaluated in light of our evolution beyond religious myths.

We are all familiar with the popular modern beliefs about UFOs and alien beings. Our movies and television programs are filled with such stories. Science fiction lovers consist of a very large global audience. But is there any truth behind these modern urban legends? Many people really want to believe in extraterrestrial life, and that we are being visited by beings from other worlds. But in a world inundated with an avalanche of information and misinformation, knowing what to believe today becomes a more and more difficult task.

Aliens, like angels and demons, may be very real. To some these entities have been with us since ancient times. Many believe that the aliens, angels, and demons of the past have gone away long ago, with only the memory of them still haunting the shadows of our collective subconscious. But maybe they have never gone away. Maybe they are still here. Maybe they have always been here, but as our society has changed over the years and decades, so too has the appearances of these otherworldly beings. Maybe, as we change, they change, taking on a new guise and form in which they can pass among us unrecognizable. Is any of this real? Is this all imaginary? How are we to know? What are we to believe? And does any of it matter anyway?

Angels, demons, and now aliens; human history is full of stories of encounters with beings not of this Earth. Some believe, others disbelieve. Even if proof exists, the nature of proof itself is subject to interpretation. So until some major, earth-shattering, history-altering event occurs, we are left to ponder, to contemplate, and even to argue about our beliefs. Maybe such an event will occur in our future. Religious writings seem to indicate this. Of course, this event, usually given a messianic perspective is perceived to be religious. But if such an event were to actually occur, I do not believe that the global media covering the event would be describing it in religious terms. And yet, around the world, the faithful of many religions are waiting.

In biblical, and later Judaic and Kabbalistic literature, there is a long-documented record of encounters with entities not of this Earth. These stories, when subject to religious interpretation, needless to say, take on a religious, moralistic overtone. We end up talking about angels and demons, and how they relate to good and evil. Yet, in light of years of modern UFO sightings, and numerous claims of extraterrestrial encounters, many of which echo ancient encounters, both the secular and religious are beginning to ask, is there a connection between our modern stories, and those of the past?

Is there a connection between angels, demons, and extraterrestrial aliens? And if there is such a connection what does this reveal to us about religion?

The book that you are about to read will outline and document for you the teachings of the Bible, Judaism, and the Kabbalah about extraterrestrial life. This includes ancient legends about angels, and demons, as well as modern legends about aliens, and UFOs. We will attempt to investigate the question: aliens, angels, and demons; is there a connection?

Now, from the outset, I must confess that I personally have never been to Outer Space, and to the best of my knowledge I have never met a real extraterrestrial of any kind. Therefore, what I have gathered here in this book is not to tell you "what's out there," but rather to expose you to the literature that claims to know what is out there. I will let the sources speak for themselves.

Faith is a very personal matter. What an individual wishes to believe, or chooses to believe is their choice. My job is not to tell one what to believe. My job is to provide information so that the reader can choose for him/herself what to believe (or not to believe).

The essays chosen for this book are a compilation of materials that have been written (and published) over a period of twenty-five years. Most of what I have written was designed for my Orthodox Jewish readership. However over the many years it became very apparent that what I was writing attracted a far greater audience.

A number of years ago, I was approached by the Hollywood production company Prometheus Entertainment, and invited to serve as a guest speaker on their popular television program, "Ancient Aliens". I thought the offer rather strange that a popular television program would be interested in the ideas and views of an Orthodox rabbi, representing Orthodox Judaism. Nevertheless, I accepted their invitation, and appeared on their program. Little did I realize just how many out there in the television audience were interested in what I had to say. Since my initial appearance I have been featured on the show in a number of episodes over a number of years. I am always surprised to discover just how much interest in this topic there is out there.

"Ancient Aliens" is a successful television program focused on public entertainment. Apparently, the show is doing an excellent job at doing just that. At the time of this writing, I believe that they are starting their tenth season. The reason why the show has been so popular is because there is a large audience of people out there, who sincerely believe that we are not alone here on our Earth, or in our universe, and they are more than just curious to find out about just who else is out there, and more so, what their relationship to us really is.

"Ancient Aliens" has served a very interesting public service in that the show not only entertains its audience, but raises many questions about our human past, and an alleged extraterrestrial presence. The television audience wants answered. But, alas, *"Ancient Aliens"* is a TV show about questions, good ones, bad ones, and others in between. While the show does a good job at researching many mysteries and asking many pertinent questions, answers to our most pressing questions are not always forthcoming.

I am only a minor voice among many others on the show. In spite of hours of interviews, my on-air time is naturally reduced to minutes. The full message that I represent, of what the Bible, Judaism, and especially the Kabbalah teach never gets the airtime that I believe it rightfully deserves. Therefore, I felt it necessary to compile my many years of writings on the subject and present them here to the public.

Much of the Judaic material that I reveal in this book is presented here for the very first time in English translation. Many of the teachings are unknown, or ignored by many in the religious community. In my opinion, this is all the more reason to make them available, and accessible to the public. Moshe told Pharaoh, "let my people go". While I am certainly no Moshe, I say, "let my people know!"

The ancient teachings found in Judaism and the Kabbalah about extraterrestrial life, in my opinion, shine a great deal of light onto the modern mystery of UFOs. I believe that we need to come to the material with an open mind, and an open eye. Indeed, for those who believe in an imminent messianic intervention in human history, an overhaul of our knowledge about angels is imperative.

The material that you are about the read has been divided into three divisions. The first part of this book is a collection of my individual essays on the subject. Each one was written independently, and are presented here topically, not sequentially in order of publication. You will see that in some essays I hint to certain things, that in other essays I elaborate more fully. I could have streamlined the style for editorial reasons but chose not to. I wanted to present to you the materials in their original forms for the highest levels of honesty, and integrity.

The second and third parts of this book deal with the subject matter in a deeper, more religious and mystical manner. For those who have never before delved deep into the metaphysical teachings of the Kabbalah, this exposure should be most enlightening.

PART ONE

GENERAL ESSAYS

Chapter 1

A Glimpse Into the Secrets of Genesis

Our modern tradition is that on the *Shabbat* following the Jewish High Holidays we begin again the cycle of Torah readings, beginning with Genesis/Bereshit. In this Torah portion, which we read in the Synagogue over a period of about 45 minutes, we cover the first six chapters of Genesis. These chapters chronicle the first few thousand years of human history, from Adam until Noah. I am always overwhelmed when it comes to writing anything about these chapters, for nothing that I have taught on these subjects over the last twenty years has ever been short and simple.

Granted, we can learn moral pointers and all our fairy tales about what we believe creation is all about. In the end, with all the nice, politically correct religious teachings about Genesis, none of us have even scratched the surface as to what these vital and essential chapters really mean.

Is it not amazing that even after thousands of years of Torah commentaries, there are still numerous Orthodox Jews who believe that the creation story in Genesis is literal and must be accepted and embraced only in the form in which they understand it. How these so-called religious folks can call themselves "learned in Torah" is one of the glaring contradictions in modern-day religion. Fundamentalism is a dangerous thing in that by definition it blocks out both rational thinking and intuitive/mystical experience.

Fundamentalists of all sorts are like horses wearing blinders. They are trained to look in only one way and no other. Deviations are to be severely punished. Maybe this is necessary for horses, but to the best of my recollection, Genesis has taught that we human beings are created in the Divine Image and endowed with nishmat hayim (the spirit of life), a level of sentience and consciousness not found in other animal species.

Dolphins, whales and other land mammals have been shown to have great intelligence, some of which can even be compared to that of a young human child. This fact should not surprise us. After all, like us, members of the animal kingdom are created by the Divine Hand and contain within them the Divine Pattern. Torah Law for both Jews and Gentiles requires of us to show the utmost respect for animal life. While we are permitted to eat the flesh of permissible animals, we are still obligated at the same time never to inflict pain on any living creature. Tza'ar ba'alei hayim (inflicting pain upon animals) is a terrible evil that is punished directly by the Hand of Heaven.

That said, with the intelligence of animals and the respect due them duly noted, still when was the last time anyone ever had an intelligent conversation with a member of the animal kingdom about abstract art, science or philosophy? Obviously never! Granted, presently we have a language barrier, but let us put that aside and say, that maybe someday those barriers will be breached. On the day when we can talk openly with all members of the animal kingdom, what will they have to say?

We may communicate with them about basic needs, maybe even learn from them about adaptations to certain environments. However, will we be able to discuss with them the beauty of a DaVinci or of Mozart? Granted they will acknowledge the existence and presence of such works, but do they have the component of consciousness that can peer into such works and extract from them the experiences of emotion, awe, beauty and wonder? I believe that we will find when the day comes, animals; however smart they may be lack a certain component of sentient thought that we humans take for granted. This component is the Divine Image within us.

We are all part of the natural order and yet there is a part of us that is above it. This idea is what the creation story of Adam teaches. There are two creation accounts of Adam, one in chapter one of Genesis and the second in chapter two. Most scholars, Jewish and Christian, religious and secular jump through their scholarly hoops trying to prove that the two stories are one and that they are just two different ways of describing the same event. However, this unified narrative is not what all Torah commentaries have taught!

A solid body of Torah commentaries on Genesis exists dating back over centuries that clearly state that the two stories are speaking about two different creations of humanity. These authoritative Torah commentators clearly state that the Adam in Genesis was not the first human being created; rather that he was the first human to have achieved a higher status of humanity.

Authoritative Torah teachings from every genre, from Talmud to Kabbalah, candidly discuss pre-Adamic humanity. Many of these teachings go so far as to state that pre-Adamic humanity was by no means primitive cave-men, but rather a well advanced technologically sophisticated society. Historical and archaeological records from around the world also indicate the truth of these teachings. However, such revelations terrify modern day fundamentalists of both the religious and the secular camps. The religious do not want to budge from their literal readings of Genesis and the secular equally do not want to budge from their myth that modern man evolved from cave men and apes, only recently achieving sentience.

It is ever so clear how stubborn fundamentalists of all kinds can be. Whether one is religious or secular, the fundamentalist is one who is so emotionally entrenched within his/her own opinion that there is no further room for any rational discussion, or tolerance of alternate viewpoints. Yes indeed, fundamentalism is as stubborn as stubborn can be. No one wants to listen; no one wants to learn; no one seeks truth and by all means, no one wants to change! So, as sophisticated as we have become technologically, we are at the same time falling back into a pit of mental darkness, similar to the Dark Ages. Elements within secular atheism have set themselves up to become a new world religion as fundamentalist, dogmatic and anti-scientific as all the fundamentalist movements before it. With relentless vigor it denies the old truths of religion while at the same time it proclaims as "self-evident" the truths of its own making. Never has blind faith led anyone into the light. All that blind faith does is to lead one into the darkness of denial. This is not the way to find G-d, or to discover G-d's truths.

So, the social war between old-time bible-based religion and new-time secular atheist religion battles on. As Solomon said so long ago, *"there is nothing new under the sun"* (Eccl 1:9). Narrow-mindedness, and stubbornness seem to go hand in hand. Together, they appear to be the greatest scourge ever to inflict humankind throughout history. I wonder if the members of the animal kingdom have to suffer with stubborn misguided members of their own flocks. We humans are, after all, supposed to be the wisest of species here on Earth. In this, I believe that we have failed miserably. I believe that our greater intelligence which has enabled us to build human civilization is also enabling us to destroy both it, and ourselves. I have never seen wars fought in the animal kingdom similar in magnitude to human wars with genocide and mass destruction, with destruction, for its own sake, being the goal. Is this our future? Was it already in our past?

Ancient Torah teachings reveal that pre-Adamic humanity rose to great heights and then fell from those heights almost destroying itself completely. The Kabbalah teaches us that this did not only happen once, but on a number of occasions. Ancient legends from around the world and ancient archeology may indeed substantiate these claims. But, who can say for sure? After all, in a hundred (or more) years from now, humanity may be recovering from a nuclear World War III (or IV) and the survivors in this future day may look back upon our modern society in the same way that we today tell tales of ancient Atlantis.

Torah teaches us that this cyclical rise and fall of technological achievement has indeed occurred. These teachings are a portion of what is concealed in the Torah portion of Genesis. Maybe I have aroused your interest and curiosity in these matters. To discuss them in the details they deserve would require a large volume of research, the likes of which I cannot provide here and now.

Torah is not a history book. It is not even a religious document. Torah came down to us from Heaven. It was revealed to us and given to us from beyond our Earth. This is a fundamental belief of Torah Judaism. Yet, do you understand the ramifications of this statement? Torah is from Heaven, true, but just what exactly is Heaven and where exactly is it? It may be another world in our universe or as most popularly conceived Heaven is another dimensional plane, one overwhelmingly different from our own. So, Torah from Heaven, by definition, means that Torah is extraterrestrial. It is not of this Earth.

An extraterrestrial Torah; now that is something to upset all fundamentalists, religious and secular alike. That word "extraterrestrial" is used only to describe the make-believe stories about flying saucers and little green men from Mars, but never in relationship to something religious. Well, maybe we all need to become a little less fundamentalist. Torah and most other religious systems speak about angels. Angels are said to come from Heaven and visit us here on Earth; that sounds rather extraterrestrial to me!

Genesis 6 speaks about certain "sons of G-d" who came and took the daughters of men for wives. Many Torah commentaries say that these "sons of G-d" were angels who came down from Heaven to take wives. Now, that is a close encounter! One leading Torah Sage of the 20th century even claimed that these "sons of G-d" were humanoid extraterrestrials who came to Earth from Outer Space, basing the theory on a 9th century Torah commentary! Genesis, chapters 1-6 contains many mysteries. This section of Torah is known in the Mishna as Ma'aseh Bereshit (the work of creation).

Ma'aseh Bereshit is one of the three classical schools of ancient Kabbalistic learning. These teachings are no longer taught in the popular Kabbalah philosophies prominent today. However, as ignored as these teachings may be, they are still nonetheless there and they will not go away. There is much more to Torah than any fundamentalist will ever be able to see.

It is amazing what we can discover if only we make the effort to look. But beware: you may not like what you find! Torah is extraterrestrial and what it really contains truly defines what is "out of this world". And once you gaze "out of this world" you gaze into the next world, the one the religious call Heaven. And once you gaze into Heaven, also called in Torah the Garden of Eden no vision of life here on Earth will ever be the same. This is the sweetness of Torah and the destiny and salvation for humanity.

Chapter 2

The Rabbinic-Kabbalistic Teachings
On Extraterrestrial Life Forms

I most certainly am not the first Rabbi to reveal material concerning life on other planets. Other Kabbalistic Rabbis before me have written books revealing some of the best-kept secrets in the world. We will discuss just a few of them here.

The late 18th century was a turbulent time for Jews living in Europe. The so-called age of "enlightenment and science" was spreading even into Jewish circles. This new religion of science sneered at the valued teachings of the Bible and sought in every way to contradict them, to "prove them wrong scientifically". One of the great Kabbalistic Sages of Eastern Europe, Rabbi Pinchas Eliyahu Horowitz of Vilna, arose to meet this challenge. He authored a monumental work on Kabbalah and science the likes of which has not been duplicated to this day.

In 1797, Rabbi Horowitz published his monumental work *Sefer HaBrit*, The book of the Covenant. The work begins by discussing the order of the physical universe, the stars, planets, and the like. He continues to discuss the physical world and finishes with long, rich metaphysical discourses on the nature of man, consciousness, and prophecy. The scope of the text is far too great to do it appropriate justice here. I must limit myself to our topic and Rabbi Horowitz's most striking revelations about it. It seems that even in Rabbi Horowitz's days there was interest and speculation about life on other planets. In Section 1, Lecture 3, Chapters 3 and 4, Rabbi Horowitz responds to the so-called scientific theories of his day regarding life on other planets and proceeds to enumerate from authoritative Jewish sources what the Torah teaches about this subject.

In Kabbalistic literature it is taught that the Holy One, blessed be He, has created an infinite number of worlds. Most commentators on these Kabbalistic texts will state that the worlds being spoken of are spiritual worlds. In other words, the Kabbalah is speaking about an infinite inter-dimensional quantum reality. There are four general dimensions or worlds in the Kabbalistic panorama; the three highest of these dimensions/worlds are Atzilut, Beriah, and Yetzirah. These correspond to the dimensions of Spirit, Mind, and Emotion respectively. Therefore, any worlds manifesting these realities are not going to be physical, as we understand the meaning of physical.

Rabbi Horowitz now steps in with a significant point. In Chapter 3 he asks why should the number of worlds in the fourth Kabbalistic level, Asiyah, corresponding to the physical realm, be any less than the infinite number of worlds in the supernal realms above it. He continues by quoting the holy Zohar "in many places" and the Mishna that in the future the Holy One, blessed be He, is to place each and every righteous person as a governor over 310 worlds. Rabbi Horowitz emphasizes that these are physical worlds in outer space. The future being spoken of is the time after the Messianic age and the resurrection of the dead. The reward of the righteous is that they are to ascend to the stars and rule sections of the galaxy as the regents of the Holy One, blessed be He.

He continues to bring evidence of other worlds from the Bible itself. With these proof texts, he not only claims to prove that there are other worlds, but that they are also inhabited by beings. Rabbi Horowitz quotes from Judges 5:23, *"cursed be Maroz, cursed be those who dwell there".* The Talmud (b. M. Kat. 16a) records an opinion that Maroz is the name of a planet. And the verse says, *"cursed be those who dwell there".* This seems to imply that the planet Maroz is inhabited. Rabbi Horowitz concludes Chapter 3 with the words, *"According to my opinion, there are inhabited planets [in outer space] and this is also implied in the Tikunei Zohar".*

Accepting the given fact of other inhabited worlds, Rabbi Horowitz now addresses the issue of what type of beings are on these other planets. He begins by criticizing those who are of the opinion that the other planets are just like ours, with similar people of free will, similar animals, plant life and the like. He calls these beliefs *"lies and a waste".* Those who believe them, Rabbi Horowitz says, are *"simpletons who will believe anything".*

Rabbi Horowitz asks why so many planets would be needed just for our forms of life. Certainly, our planet is large enough to hold us all. Being that these planets are so numerous and distant from one another they must also be very different. No two can be exactly alike; each one is different from the other both generally and specifically.

Rabbi Horowitz also says it is a fallacy to think that the planets are formed of the same types of matter as is ours. He gives an example of the sun (which in Judaism is also considered a planet). Can someone dwell on the Sun and not be burned, he asks? Would not the brilliant light blind a person? In addition, as an example, on Saturn he asks, would not a person freeze to death there due to its cold nature? To again prove the point of the varying types of life that are in outer space, Rabbi Horowitz uses the example of the ocean, saying that just as sea creatures differ tremendously from land creatures due to the different nature of their environments, so do the inhabitants of the other planets differ from us.

He then follows with one of his most important points. He acknowledges that these extraterrestrial beings are *"ba'alei sekhel u'madah"* (masters of intelligence and science). Yet, with all their intellectual potentials, Rabbi Horowitz claims that all extraterrestrials will lack one essential component that will forever set them apart from the human race. They lack *"behirah"*, the ability of free will. Free will separates mankind from any and every other species. It is free will that is the G-d given spiritual component that separates the human race from being just another animal species.

The definition of free will is too involved to be comprehensively covered at this time. For now, understand that free will is not just the ability to think for yourself and choose between this and that direction. Free will is something far more than the discretionary ability of determination that is to be found within most all species of life. Free will is the spiritual ability to raise consciousness above the control of the forces of time and space. Free will is the ability of an entity to evolve at the spiritual level.

The universe, that which is seen and unseen, as we know from Genesis 1:1, was created by Elohim, i.e. G-d. Our Sages reveal to us that the Name of G-d, Elohim, is the impersonal Name of G-d, His "*Katnut*" (smallness), the Name that expresses only the outermost expressions of the Divine. The Name Elohim in Gematria (Hebrew numerology) is equal to the word "*HaTeva*" which means "nature," and it is a reference to the laws of nature, i.e., the natural universe. It is the Name that corresponds to the second letter of the Hebrew alphabet Bet, the letter that begins the Torah.

The Kabbalistic Sages also reveal to us that just as there is the letter Alef before the letter Bet, so is there an entirely different level of reality underlying the manifest and un-manifest universe. In this universe of Alef, the Holy One's, blessed be He, true essence is revealed. Here is G-d known by the holy four-letter Name YHWH that is so holy that it is never spoken aloud. It is pronounced *Adonai* in prayer and as HaShem in everyday speech.

The level of YHWH is above the level of Elohim as the Heavens are above the Earth. Under the Name Elohim, all is subject to the laws of the natural universe, no matter how sublime and concealed these laws are. There is the universal pattern of operations and when these are discovered, technologies can be developed to manipulate them. All of this constitutes the universe within which we reside, and includes all that we will ever know of it. This is the universe created by Elohim, as it is written, *"In the beginning Elohim created."* (Gen 1:1). Elohim is referred to as the "Left Hand of G-d," the source of Divine restriction and judgment.

Yet, there is a power above and beyond the universe. This power led by the direction of the Divine Will, may, for reasons known to Itself, supersede the laws of nature, be they revealed or concealed. This power is called the "Right Hand of G-d" that intervenes in His universe. This is the Name YHWH. This is the Alef level.

The YHWH/Alef level of the universe is by definition above and beyond the laws of the universe. It is a law unto itself, the true eternal Law. In order for it to be revealed, experienced, and expressed within our universe of time and space, YHWH had to cloak Himself in an appropriate garment that could contain Him. This garment, which exists in time and space, is the house where the spirit of YHWH dwells. This garment, this house, is the holy Torah. The Torah is the exclusive domain and inheritance of Israel, the people of this planet, given to us by YHWH at Mount Sinai. The Torah only takes the form of a book as it is revealed in this world. Similar to man, whose body is only the shell of the true human, so the book of the Torah serves to encase its soul, which is YHWH. From such a high source, the Torah reveals to the Jew many things beyond the limitations of our planet and our corporeal existence.

As a Sage of the Torah, Rabbi Horowitz's view (which was also shared by the late Lubavitcher Rebbe) is that there are a countless number of inhabited planets in outer space, many of which may very well have highly advanced technological societies. Nonetheless, none of them have the potential of the spiritual heights unique to the human race, created in the image of G-d.

While the Torah does acknowledge the existence of other planets and of extraterrestrial beings, there is no direct mention of these beings having a technology capable of allowing them to visit the Earth. Nonetheless, the author of *Sefer HaBrit* does ascribe to them those abilities.

Another modern author who has written on the topic of extraterrestrials from a Torah point of view is Rabbi Aryeh Kaplan. His works are numerous and his Kabbalistic texts are now classics in English Judaica. The following is my translation of an excerpt from his Hebrew book *Moreh Ohr* (Moznaim, Jerusalem 1992) which clearly shows that the topic of extraterrestrials is of interest in Orthodox Jewish circles.

Sefer Moreh Ohr, **The Human Species**

Now we must contemplate whether the human species alone is the [exclusive] purpose in creation or whether there are other species that have been created for this purpose. Also, are there worlds other than this one? The ancients have already spoken [of these matters]. In Sefer Ohr HaShem (Ma'amar 4, Drash 2) it is explored whether it is possible that there is one world or many worlds. It says, now there are many who say that the great number of worlds does not harm the complete unity that there is in this world. They emanated for the purpose of improvement and favor. Now there is not a shortage of those who receive improvement. He concludes that there is no proof from this view, rather that nothing is proved or disproved, only there is the possibility.

After this he mentions what our Sages have said in the Talmud (b. A.Z. 3b), that [HaShem] placed 18,000 worlds [in the firmament]. However, truthfully this is not evidence. Perhaps these worlds are spiritual [in nature] and not physical. We already know that there are an infinite number of spiritual worlds, as the Ari'zal stated in Sefer Etz Haim, (Sha'ar 3, Chap. 1). One might be able to bring evidence from the verse in Psalms 145:13, "Your Kingdom is the Kingdom of all the worlds," which the Targum translates as "Your Kingdom is the Kingdom IN all the worlds". However, here too, one can say that the verse is speaking of spiritual worlds and not physical ones.

Following the views of Sefer Ohr HaShem is [the author's] student, the author of the Ikkarim, who is quoted in Sefer HaBrit (1:3:1), "It is not said whether there are other worlds; because there could not be free will there. They would not have Torah or any Divine service. Therefore we do not touch this issue". It appears that this view is also accepted by others.

There seems to be some minor evidence to support this view from the Talmud (b. Ber. 31a) where it states that all land that mankind was commanded to inhabit, was inhabited and that all land that mankind was not commanded to inhabit, has not been inhabited. However, truly there is no proof from this for it is possible that this is speaking only of the land on this planet, and not of other worlds.

Reference what is said regarding this in Sefer Kol Yehuda, commentary to the Kuzari (2, 82, 34a).

That which comes and unites these two opinions is the Sefer HaBrit (1:3:3) which states that the stars are really worlds, and that they each have a place of habitation. Also, [it is stated] that the 18,000 worlds [referenced above] are physical planets.

He brings evidence from the [Bible, quoting the] verse from Shoftim [Judg 5:23], "cursed be Maroz, cursed be those who dwell there". According to what is written in [Talmud b.] Moed Katan 16a, Maroz is the name of a planet. And the verse says, "cursed be those who dwell there". This clearly implies that there are those who dwell in the stars. However, this too can be refuted. We can say that this verse speaks of the hosts of the star (i.e. the surrounding stars), as it is written in the Zohar (V'et'hanan 269a [29a]) relating to this verse. There it refers to the stars' assistants. However, according to the plain meaning of the matter, the view of the Sefer HaBrit seems clear. There in chapter 4, he writes about the stars, whether they are worlds, and if they are all equal to one another, and if creation there is as creation here. He brings down the example of the ocean, and points out how different life in the ocean is from life on the land.

He also writes there, "There is no doubt that there are no other people in our image and likeness who have free will, even if they are very smart and intelligent. For it is already known that it is impossible for there to be free will other than with the species of man who inhabits this Earth". There is no place for Torah or Divine service other than in this world. Review there in depth. He brings his evidence from [Talmud b.] Berakhot that is mentioned above, that all the stars were created for the sake of Israel.

What he has written that the dwellers in the stars have no free will presents a difficulty from the same place that he uses to bring his evidence. It says, "Cursed be Maroz, cursed be those who dwell there". However, if they have no free will, how could they be subject to punishment and cursing? This needs investigation. We can dismiss this by saying that it is possible that they are like the angels, who do not have free will, yet we see that they can be punished. Reference Sefer Hasidim (530).

There in Sefer HaBrit it is written that there is evidence of inhabitants on the stars from the Tikunei Zohar. However, he does not state the source. It appears to me, however, that his source is in the introduction to Tikkun 7 (14b), on the verse (Songs 6:5), "worlds without end". If there are worlds without end, the stars too are infinite. For each star is called an individual world. Moreover, the worlds have no end.

It is written there in the Tikunei Zohar that every righteous person has his own star; therefore each has his own [private] world. This is written in the Midrash (Shemot Rabbah 52:3) that each righteous person has his own world. It appears, according to this that the 18,000 worlds spoken of in [Talmud b.] Avodah Zarah correspond to the 18,000 righteous hinted to in Ezek 48:35, "surrounded by 18,000," as is mentioned also in [Talmud b.] Suk. 48b. Truly this is what is written in Sefer Iyun Ya'akov, commentary to Ayn Ya'akov on Avodah Zarah, Siman 5.

According to this, it appears that the stars were created to become the place of habitation of the righteous in the future. This is a profound thing! This implies that in the World to Come that comes after the resurrection, we will be traveling to the stars, in order that each and every righteous person will rule over his own planet. This also seems to be supported by what is written in [Talmud b. Sanh. 92b, on Isaiah 40:31, "They shall rise like the eagle," meaning that the Holy One, blessed be He, will give wings to the righteous. It is also written in the Introduction to the Zohar 12b that in the future the Holy One, blessed be He, will give them wings to fly over the entire world.

To return to our subject, in truth, there is great support for the views of the Sefer HaBrit from what is written in the Pardes, Sha'ar 2, Ch. 7, "we will ask one question that has confounded a number of the investigators of wisdom... being that it is [G-d's] way to radiate His good upon others, why then did He not create millions and billions of worlds, being that He is able... and create a number of worlds similar to our own. At first, this question will trouble the eyes of the enlightened, and they will be silenced. In truth, this is a really good question. It took a profound mind to even formulate this question". He there explains his reasons how it is impossible to have more than one order of supernal worlds. Being that the order for all the supernal worlds is for the sake of the human species, according to the secret meaning of the verse (Ber. 1:26), "Let us make man in our own image". All this is so that He can guide mankind and to enable them to receive reward and punishment. Therefore, if there is no more than one order to the supernal worlds, there can be no more than one species that possess free will and are subject to reward and punishment. In addition, it would not be appropriate for the creator to have more than one purpose. See what the Shefa Tal 1:3 has written on this.

The Rabbis and Kabbalists have never come out and directly said that they were in communication with beings from the stars. Therefore, Jewish literature while full of otherworldly encounters, does not ascribe any of them as being overtly extraterrestrial.

Just because the Rabbinic/Kabbalistic authorities acknowledge that there are beings on other worlds, this does not necessarily conclude that it is these beings and their spaceships that are being seen by millions of people worldwide. Other possible identities can be given to our visitors.

In religious literature, there is a long history of recorded interactions with otherworldly beings. Religiously, these being are identified as angels and demons. I believe that the time has come to further investigate the true identities of these otherworldly beings, to ascertain if indeed they play any part in modern extraterrestrial encounters.

Chapter 3

What Are Angels?

What is an angel? What type of life form is it? Being that angels are considered something religious, most definitions and discussions about them are religious. But what do these religious people really know about them? All they have are ancient texts, and later interpretations of those texts, usually based on one sort of philosophy or another. Essentially, there is a lot of talk about angels, but very little understanding.

If there is anything real about angels, if there are really actually life forms out there that we call angels, then the one thing about them that we can say for certain is that they are from out of this world. And, whether we like it or not, the proper term to refer to life forms that are not of this Earth, is "extraterrestrial".

So, mythology and prejudice aside, if we wish to entertain the reality of angels, then we must delve into the exploration of the extraterrestrial, with all the implications in light of modern science and discovery.

Ezekiel saw a group of different types of angels together that formed what we call the *Merkava* (chariot). Regardless of all the philosophical, religious explanations of what the *Merkava* actually was (is), one thing the Bible makes clear is that it is some sort of a transportation device.

Unlike G-d, angels are not omnipresent. Angels, like all other life forms, need some form of transport to travel from point A to point B. In all due respect to their wings, angels apparently need more than just their wings to get around.

Apparently, angels seem to struggle with one another in ways that seem very human. When Daniel recites his prayer to G-d (ref. Dan 10:12,13), the angel in charge of delivering the answer is held up by another angel refusing him passage. The angel sent to answer Daniel's prayer has to call for angelic backup in order to get through to accomplish his mission. Why is it that the angel in question simply did not invoke the name and authority of G-d in order to secure his passage? With such authority, how could he have been challenged by another angel? How otherworldly are they, if indeed they can act so humanlike, so confrontational? They obviously are not human, then again, neither is acting very "angelic".

Angels are portrayed throughout the Bible as being both human in form, and completely otherworldly. The philosophic interpretations loudly proclaim angels to be completely non-corporeal, and any appearance that they make take is only symbolic, or exclusively in the mind of the beholder. Yet, the non-philosophical camp, which includes many who still practice the ancient traditions of communicating with angels say something very different. For those who, even today, descend before the *Merkava*, angels are real. Some of them are corporeal beings, not too different from human beings, whereas others are life forms that would require modern science to expand the definitions of life itself.

One way or another, those who wish to dismiss the reality of angels have nothing to contribute to this discussion. In contrast, those of us who do believe in angels have a lot of questions that require exploration, even though definitive answers may not be forthcoming without some outside help.

So, what is an angel? Where do they come from? What are their indigenous forms in the home worlds that they naturally inhabit? The Hebrew term for angel is *"malakh,"* which means messenger.

What then is the angelic message? What is their mission and purpose? Why are they coming here?

We say that angels come from "Heaven," but what exactly is Heaven, and where exactly is it? If it is a parallel dimension, then, if I were standing in Heaven, and looked up, would I see a sky? If I looked down, would I see ground under my feet?

If Heaven is a real place, then just what kind of place is it? If angels truly reside there, then what are they doing other than delivering messages for G-d and standing around singing all day.

Indeed, if Heaven is real, is there even day or night there? In that place is there any concept of time, as we know it? If Heaven is a parallel dimension, then what are the laws of nature that govern that domain, and what is the relationship between that dimension and our own?

As we see, there are many questions to ask by those who truly wish to strip religion of mythology and restore the ancient experiences to the realms of reality and science where they rightfully belong.

If angels are real, then there is no greater example of extraterrestrial involvement with humanity than this. Who are they? What are they? Why are they here? I believe that rather than turn to religious doctrine, dogma, and theology we should instead turn to science, experience, and exploration into areas which many might find uncomfortable, if not outright frightening.

But, if we are ever to grow as a united race of sentient beings (human beings), then, in my opinion, we should seek out those others, not of this world, who are out there and possibly "closer" to G-d than we. If we can find them and verify their reality, we might find that our first contact with this (these) extraterrestrial race(s) might not be first contact after all.

We should be looking for them! Maybe, they are waiting for us! Either way, they are here!

Chapter 4

Telepathic Communication With Real Angels

Centuries of experiential detachment and baseless philosophical speculations have taken our understanding about angels from the realm of reality and placed it squarely into the realm of fantasy and myth.

Yes, we do believe in angels, but what exactly is it that we believe about them? Nowadays most fantasize about angels in the most unrealistic ways, totally oblivious to the reality of their being and the true purpose of their existence and presence.

There are many who claim that they talk with angels. Yet, most today do not know how to communicate with angels, and those who claim they do, for the most part, are in actuality in touch with something very different. If these same individuals were to be placed under psychological review, it might be revealed just how much of their so-called "communication" is simple "wishful thinking," archetypal projection, or serious dissociated delusions.

Unlike the images that proliferate in modern culture, real angels are not human beings, and rarely when they are experienced for real do they ever bother to present themselves as such. We should, therefore, not expect them to look human or to act human. Yet, like human beings, they are intelligent sentient life forms, even though their actual forms are radically different from our own. As intelligent beings of an alien species, however different from us, the common denominator between us is our ability to think.

Therefore, the best form of communications between species as divergent as ours, is through a form of thought-based communications; the medium of mind-to-mind communication. This is the projection of thoughts and concepts as expressed through mental images, and not through words of any verbal language.

Mental images can have universally consistent meanings. This was why such images are called archetypes of the collective unconscious. When one entity projects mental imagery to another, with the intent of communicating a message and/or information; this is telepathy. According to the Bible, this is how angels, and even G-d, Himself, has communicated with human beings, since the dawn of creation.

One thing is clear in both the Bible and later Judaic literature: there exist many different types of angels. Today, rather than use the generic word, "type," to describe angelic differences, it is more appropriate to speak about different "species" or "races". One thing all "angels" have in common is that they are not homo-sapien (human) life forms, indigenous to our Earth. This, by definition, makes every one of them to be "extraterrestrial".

Using the modern term, "extraterrestrial," conjures up in our minds images of flying saucers and little gray creatures that crash at Roswell, New Mexico or abduct people from their beds in the middle of the night. What the truth is about such things is not our concern here. Rather than focus on the Grays and their saucers, our focus is on other races of extraterrestrials referred to in the Bible.

The Bible mentions numerous types of angels, which, in Hebrew are referred to as *Ofanim, Hayot, Cherubim*, and *Seraphim*. Humanoid figures are also described, but in ways that distinctly make them non-human. Then again, there are angels who appear completely human in every sense, interact with human beings in a normal manner, and then, some of them, disappear in a "puff" of smoke. Whether or not such disappearing acts reveal them to be non-human, or just in possession of some matter transference transportation device, we cannot, at this time, say with certainty.

We know that certain types of angels use transportation devices. This is clear from the episodes recorded of Elijah being taken to Heaven in some sort of craft, described as a chariot. Then, there is the more famous example of Ezekiel's chariot, which some modern authors go so far as to suggest that maybe it was some form of spaceship. In both of these cases, we cannot say for sure what either vehicle actually was. All we can say for sure is that the Bible represents these extraterrestrial (angelic) entities as traveling, and using some means of transportation device to get from point A, to point B.

Extraterrestrial encounters have been part and parcel of the human experience since the beginning of our recorded history. These encounters are best understood by those who have experience with them, as opposed to those who just speculate as to what they were really all about.

Essentially, those who know, know; whereas those who don't know, don't know. And, in spite of all their speculations and proclamations of religious beliefs or doctrines, those without direct experience don't know. This lack of first-hand experience puts all their speculations and beliefs into the realms of theory and myth, and outside the realm of reality.

Seeking out and experiencing an extraterrestrial encounter might not be as exotic and unheard of as many might think. Indeed, there is an entire body of meditative literature which provides detailed instructions about how actual contact is to be made. However, the nature of this contact is often misunderstood.

While many under the influence of Hollywood, science fiction and fantasy, seek entertaining sound and light shows similar to those presented in movies, actual close encounters between non-human extraterrestrials and their human contacts are, for the most part, are of a radically different nature. Most actual contact between humans and extraterrestrials is telepathic.

Telepathic communications transcend physicality, occur within the dimensions of the mind, and travel at the speed of thought. This is the most efficient way of establishing, and maintaining contact. The problem with it is that most human beings are not well endowed telepathically. Even when actual contact is made, people often do not recognize it, confuse it for something else, or otherwise discard it because it is not the entertaining sound and light show that they were led to believe should instead occur.

Telepathic communication is how any advanced race of beings would communicate over vast distances in space, time, and possibly dimensions.

When we here on Earth experience any kind of religious vision it is usually something internal, within the mind. Angelic entities have long been called "separate intelligences" (*sekhelim nivdalim*), and this has given rise to the doctrine and theology that angels are completely non-corporeal beings. In reality it might be when the angel is perceived in the vision all that is being received is a mental message, one that is able to create a visual image in the mind, along with clearly understood interpretations, or instructions.

Therefore, an angelic entity can be in its body (of whatever form in matter or energy), in its natural habitat (whatever, wherever that may be), and then simply telepathically project its message across space, time, and dimension directly into the mind of the receiver. When the entity thus channels its message into the mind of a human being, the entity is acting as a messenger (from the source of the message). The messenger entity is thus what we call a *Malakh*, an angel.

Any human being could thus receive a message, have an experience, and not even understanding the actual nature of the communication. One could think that the telepathically received visual image is the actual form of the entity in the message. But, nothing could be further from the truth. All telepathic messages are transmitted in a code that is understood at the deepest levels of the unconscious mind, whereas at the same time, this code is completely misunderstood by the conscious mind. Telepathic communications thus act in the mind along the same patterns as do dreams.

Dreams and visions have always been the forms of communication through which man speaks to, or hears from, Heaven, be it prophecy directly from G-d, or a message passed through one of the messengers (angels). This fact is clear throughout all biblical and later Torah literature.

As mentioned above, there exists, to this day, textual instructions that explain in decent detail how to expand human consciousness to become receptive to these psychic communications. While the process of training is long and arduous, it is still nevertheless, available to those who wish to invest the time, and effort to achieve the results promised therein.

Once actual and verifiable communication is made with otherworldly entities, it becomes vital for the human recipient to ascertain the authentic source of where such contact is coming from. Not all entities "out-there" are benign and/or benevolent. This too, we know from biblical texts. The dangers of contact with others not concerned with human safety, or human life, is a real threat. For this reason Torah law prohibited the practice of many occult rituals and techniques. These laws were instituted for human safety.

It is a given that our planet and universe is under the control of G-d's messengers (angels). They execute the Divine plan in accordance with the authority granted them. Yet, we should never think that as different as they may be from us, that they have no flaws or faults.

We should also keep in mind that there are angelic races that are more similar to human beings than others. This similarity can be a mixed blessing in that ancient records show that many of their number left their homes in the Upper World and came to Earth. Upon arriving here, they could not properly adjust, and thus became subject to natural Earthly forces that they were not designed to face. Many ended up taking human wives, bearing hybrid children, and creating such a state of unbalance that Heaven was forced to intervene with the ancient terrible flood.

Angels are not human and, therefore, will never fulfill human definitions of perfection. Indeed, real angels may not even meet the human definition for being either benign or benevolent. Angels are radically different from us and they fulfill their Divinely ordained governorship of our planet in accordance to their own ways and laws. This distinction is a clear and definitive biblical teaching.

There is a plan for humanity; an agenda since the beginning, and it will stay this way until the end is achieved! This is not a modern day conspiracy theory. This is one of the most ancient teachings of the Bible!

The Bible and the religions that have sprung up from it, teach us that G-d created humanity and that G-d has a plan for humanity. The Bible makes it quite clear that heavenly beings intervene and interact with human beings, on both the personal and collective level, on a regular basis.

However, as much as we individually wish to believe that we are masters of our own fates, the biblical message is that our arena of free choice is very much limited in its application. In reality, very little is in our hands.

While we may not be able to change the course of human events, we can still become aware of what some of these future events may be. While very little may actually be in our hands, nevertheless, there still exists some power in our hands. There is that which we can do. As such, we do have power, but this power is of the mind, not of the hand. We can therefore develop our latent mind powers and reach out and commune with the many others that surround us but are invisible to our sight.

Granted, this course may be very dangerous, but what path of growth, maturity, and ascent is ever safe? We can communicate when we first learn how to do it properly. Telepathic communication with extraterrestrial entities is an ancient practice still observed by those "in the know". To those who seek to join them, the path is open and welcoming.

Chapter 5

Identifying the "Sons of G-d" in Genesis 6

"The sons of G-d saw that the daughters of man were good, and they took themselves wives from whomever they chose... the Nefilim (fallen ones) were on the Earth in those days... The sons of G-d had come to the daughters of man and had fathered them. [The Nefilim] were the mightiest ones who ever existed, men of renown".
(Genesis 6:2, 4)

It is very interesting to note that with regards to understanding the identity of these "sons of G-d"(Benei Elohim), there exists in Torah tradition two almost parallel, and possibly mutually exclusive points of view.

The classical commentators traditionally identify these "sons of G-d" as a specific category of human beings, who are given this title for various reasons. Most of them only scarcely mention another sacred tradition that has been recorded for centuries before any of their works were ever written. Yet, just because the classical commentators may not elaborate on specific traditions does not mean that these traditions are any less equally authoritative. Remember this: the classical commentators were writing for the common person. I believe it is possible that they intentionally picked the simpler interpretation of these verses so as not to arouse any unnecessary curiosity and alarm on behalf of the greater public.

This being said, it is clear that most if not all the classical sources, dating back to Talmudic times, knew very well that the identity of these "sons of G-d" may be something very different than commonly described. One needs only to look at Rashi's commentary to these verses in Genesis and see how it compares with his Talmudic commentary to tractate Yoma (16b). The classical commentators knew very well that they were keeping a secret.

To offer us another identification of the "sons of G-d" we only need to return to the Bible. The very same Hebrew term "Benei Elohim" is used in the book of Job (1:6), where it states, "Now it fell upon a day, that the sons of G-d came to present themselves before HaShem". The day in question has traditionally been understood as Rosh HaShana and the sons of G-d here are clearly a race of entities we have come to call angels. Indeed, RaMBaM in his law code the Mishneh Torah, in the Laws of Torah Foundations (2:7) lists the Benei Elohim as one of the ten races of angels.

The Zohar (1:23a; 1:25a; ZH Ruth 99a) goes even further and in like kind to the ancient Sefer Hanokh (Enoch 7), one of the most ancient and intact sources of Torah legends known to us, the identity of these angels and their saga is revealed. According to these most ancient of sources, recorded by numerous later Torah authorities, there was a band of angels, Benei Elohim, who stood by at the original creation of Adam and resisted his creation and the authority given to him by G-d (ibid).

Legend tells us that they complained to G-d saying why should Adam be given so much authority and power over them seeing that he is destined to come to Earth, sin and fall. G-d replies to these angels that if they were ever to descend to Earth, their fall would be even worse (Zohar 1:9b, 37a). Such is the power and pull of physical attractions here on Earth.

The Zohar states that wanting to prove G-d wrong, two leading angels, Aza and Azael gathered together a band of two hundred of their brothers and together made a vow that they would descend to Earth and show the rest of Heaven that they unlike Adam could and would resist Earthly living and physical temptations, thus proving themselves to be superior. Their descent to Earth is what is recorded in Genesis 6 (1:23a; 1:25a; ZH Ruth 99a). Enoch 7 tells a similar story but with different and more detailed angelic names.

As we see immediately, G-d was proven right and these fallen angels were proven deadly wrong. Once they came to Earth they were overcome by physical sexual desires, which was a totally new and unknown sensation for them. Like Adam and Eve before them, they succumbed to the same fall.

The children of these mix-breed entities were not fully human and not fully angelic. They bore the humanity of their mothers and still maintained the superiority of their fathers. These hybrid humans, the Malbim commentary to this section of Genesis tells us, were the source for the ancient myths and legends of the ancient world. The ancient stories of the Greek gods of Olympus and the Norse gods of Asgard might very well have been founded upon the deeds and wanton behaviors of these fallen angels and their hybrid human children.

Granted the stories bestowed divinity upon these entities, but Malbim makes the emphatic point that such attributions are entirely false. Granted these entities did exist and that they were in comparison to us superhuman. Still, nonetheless, while being hybrid humans, there was nothing divine about them at all.

Now, I wish to delve further into the identity of these Benei Elohim (sons of G-d). Many modern Rabbis follow the opinion expressed by the RaMBaM (MT, Y.T. 2:5) that all angels are completely non-physical spiritual entities. However, many modern Rabbis do not devote study to angels and certainly have not had any direct exposure to them. One need just read the commentaries to RaMBaM's Torah foundations on the above quoted section about angels to see that there were many who disagreed with the RaMBaM about all angels being totally incorporeal.

Many of the Torah Sages stated emphatically (Perush RaMBaM HaMeir quoting the Yabetz and Rabi Shem Tov Ben Shem Tov; Ohel Moed 8 and others) that there are certain angels who have a sense of corporeality to them. In other words, these Benei Elohim might have been physical beings after all.

To give added credence to this opinion, I am aware that the late Rav Aharon Soloveitchik of Chicago was of the opinion that these Benei Elohim spoken of in Genesis 6 were actually very physical, humanoid extraterrestrials, who came to Earth. I had seen this opinion of his quoted in the Jewish newspaper, The Forward. I could not believe that one of the generation's leading Rabbis would believe such a radical thought and I was certain that the leftist leaning newspaper certainly misquoted the Rabbi with the intent to discredit him.

Living as I did at the time in Chicago and knowing the Rabbi's son well, I asked him personally if his father actually said these words, and if he actually believed them. His son, an esteemed Rabbi in his own right, personally confirmed to me in the affirmative on both counts and that he himself knew of the 9th century text from which his esteemed father had learned this.

Compiling then from the sources I have quoted, in ancient times there was a band of humanoid extraterrestrial entities who were originally in the service of Heaven but who rebelled. They came down here to Earth with good intent but succumbed to the overwhelming temptations of physical sensations and thus fell. They became entrapped here, not being able to return to their home in another dimension or possibly on another planet in this dimension. They bore their fate and started families, mingling their genetics with human genetics. This polluted the human gene pool thwarting the directives and intent of Heaven. The reaction from Heaven was swift and harsh. Being that the entire human gene pool as well as that of the animal kingdom had become contaminated, a comprehensive cleansing was needed. As we know, the flood soon followed.

More than just polluting the human gene pool, these fallen angels are also recorded to have taught pre-flood humanity what the literature calls treasures of wisdom (Enoch 8). When one reviews the list of the subjects that the fallen angels taught to humanity, we today would call these subjects technology. Apparently, the fallen angels brought to Earth a technological boom. In a short time, humanity jumped forward centuries with new technological developments. In the literature of the time, obviously the term technology was neither used nor known. Instead they referred to these special powers by the Hebrew term Kishufim (Zohar 1:126b), which today we translate as magic.

Indeed, the technology of the fallen angels was magic; just like our modern technology would be considered magic to those who never conceived of such things existing. Throughout human history every culture around the world has had a history and connection to the magical. The prevailing rationalist ideology of today dismisses magic as primitive and a fantasy. Yet, Torah sources state the complete opposite.

Magic, Kishufim, is quite real. There are numerous references to it in the Bible and throughout Torah literature. Indeed, there is even an entire chapter dedicated to dealing with it in the Shulkhan Arukh (Code of Jewish Law, Y.D. 179).

Magic operates in accordance to its own laws of nature and physics. In truth, Kishufim and magic are not magical at all; they are merely technological operations, mostly using the latent psychic powers of the mind. This was one area of technology that the fallen angels taught ancient man, how to use some the powers latent within them, placed there by G-d the Creator.

The flood was said to wipe out all traces of the fallen ones from the surface of the Earth. Whether some might have survived in another place is considered by some (e.g. the Zohar belief of an Inner Earth). While the surface of the Earth was supposedly cleansed of them, we find that a later generation, that of the Tower of Babel, discovered one of their lost technologies.

According to Rabbi Eliezer Ben David in his book, Out of the Iron Furnace (page 49), quoting and interpreting the Zohar, states that the biblical story of the builders of the Tower of Babel finding a valley and burning bricks therein is the Torah's way of saying that what the builders actually rediscovered was the secrets of nuclear energy.

Indeed, was the Tower of Babel nuclear powered? Legend tells us that the builders wanted to build the Tower high into the Heavens with the intent of attacking it as revenge for sending the flood. This might sound like a primitive myth, yet Rabbi Yonatan Eybeschutz commenting on this story states that the builders were planning to somehow build a fire under the Tower and thus launch it into Heaven.

If we place Rabbi Ben David's insights alongside those of Rabbi Eybeschutz we could understand the Tower of Babel as actually being the creation of a nuclear powered spacecraft intended to go to the stars, possibly to the home of the Benei Elohim to assault them there? As we can see, there is much more to Torah stories than the mere moralistic tales told by the classical commentators.

In the late 19th century archaeologists discovered in the deserts of what is now Iraq an ancient Ziggurat pyramid-like structure. Some at the time claimed that it was the remnant of the Tower of Babel. I have heard it said (but never saw accurate scientific confirmation) that digging down under the base of this monument they found that the sand underneath it had become petrified, as if it was turned into a large sea of glass. A find of this nature would be highly unusual and could be explained especially if there was any kind of nuclear history there. I apologize that I do not have access to the facts on this matter. Nonetheless, I present the story as is.

Stories of ancient nuclear wars should not be so readily dismissed. Torah sources are not the only ones to suggest such a strange possibility. The ancient Indian writings of the Mahabharata are also today understood as suggesting that there was an ancient pre-historic nuclear war. Of course, such things fly in the face of modern secular science, which arrogantly wants to proclaim itself supreme. However, legends from around the world, in every culture since the dawn of time have spoken of the wisdom of the ancients. The archaeological remnants from those days certainly testify to us today that we do not know as much as we may think. And certainly the ancients knew a lot more than we give them credit for.

Did the ancients have an extraterrestrial connection, one that led to their ultimate destruction? Not only Torah sources suggest this idea; there are many parallel stories told throughout the world. There exists much about our past than we know about today.

Rumor has it that our ancient and forgotten past has come back to haunt us. Modern stories of UFOs, extraterrestrial encounters, technological advancements supposedly reversed engineered from captured (or received) alien technologies, alien abductions and secret government conspiracies all are popularly believed and adamantly denied by all official sources. Even the modern State of Israel has been a hotbed of UFOs and alien sightings. So, who knows?

We do know this: legend tells us that before the coming of Mashiah the fallen angels would again intervene in human affairs triggering yet another apocalyptic intervention by Heaven. Only this time, the intervention will be that of Mashiah and his armada of angels (Zech 14:5). Judging from the opinion of Rabbi Soloveitchik that the "sons of G-d" might be the Benei Elohim angels and that these, in reality, might be humanoid extraterrestrials; could the army of angels accompanying Mashiah also be such? Would the coming of Mashiah therefore be understood by the world watching this event unfold on TV as an extraterrestrial invasion from Outer Space? Could the coming of Mashiah actually be such a thing?

Certainly we have gone outside the pale of traditional and comfortable biblical commentary. Yet, just because we have done so does not mean that we have erred from truth! As the old saying goes, "truth is stranger than fiction".

What we know and what we don't know about Torah, our own human past and our future human destiny should cause us to pause for a moment to contemplate these great things.

Chapter 6

Was Babel Nuclear Powered?
Was the Tower a Spaceship?

You might be surprised to know just how advanced-thinking our Sages were centuries ago. The older Kabbalists concealed in their words numerous profound secrets that many in modern times still do not understand what was written centuries ago.

Although the majority of modern Kabbalists are merely philosophers who only know how to read books, there are still a few who practice the more ancient traditions. They learn how to unlock the secret codes that most modern mystical philosophers do not even know exist.

With regards to the Tower and Babel we have to pay careful attention to the words used to describe the incident in the Torah text. We must pay equal attention to the words used in the ancient Kabbalistic commentaries. When we pay attention to the details we are able to unlock many shocking secrets.

In the Torah the *pasuk* (verse) states, *"And it came to pass when they traveled from the east, that they found a valley in the land of Shinar and settled there"* (Gen 11:2). "They traveled from the east" has a coded meaning, but so do the words, "they found a valley".

It is almost impossible to recognize the secret codes and their messages without knowledge of the original Hebrew. The traveling from the east (*m'kedem*) is understood as a movement away from something, as opposed to being a move towards something. They were traveling away from the *"kedem".* This name is related to the word Kadmon and means ancient. The "traveling" of the people was specifically their distancing themselves from G-d, and their attempt to remove themselves from divinely ordained natural order. Their intent was to create an environment immune from natural law, and all its destructive powers, as was recently seen by the flood.

In order to enable them to accomplish this formidable task, they would need some type of power, or energy, that could create for them an artificial environment, and endow it with the power to withstand natural forces. Numerous Midrashic literatures, including the Zohar, state that they discovered this ability secretly buried in the sands, concealed by members of the pre-flood generation for discovery later.

According to Rabbi Eliezer Ben David in his book, *"Out of the Iron Furnace",* they did not find a valley, a Bik'a; but rather they found a Bik'ia. This word Bik'ia means an opening or a discovery. The Zohar and others state that what they found was the ancient technology of the pre-flood generation.

The Hebrew word Bik'ia also means nuclear fission. Both the Torah text and our Sages commentaries seem to imply that the ancient technology hidden by the members of the generation of the flood, and later discovered by the builders of Babel, was nothing other than the secrets of nuclear technology. As incredible as this claim might sound, when we look into the ancient literature and see how the Sages describe the builders of Babel, and their intentions, we discover that this might not be so wild, and unbelievable, as we might initially think.

Rabbi Yitzhak D'min Acco writes in his *Mari'yat Ayin* how the generation of Babel had expert knowledge of both natural law and what he refers to there, using the ancient term, the Shiur Komah (the measurement of the stature). These "measurements" are symbolic numbers that were the first form used to house Kabbalistic secrets. The Shiur Komah school of Kabbalah is its oldest form with literature dating back to Temple times and included within it are actual sections of Scripture itself.

The "measurements" were by no means the mystical philosophy of the later Kabbalah schools. The Shiur Komah often included in-depth details about natural law, as it pertains to the universe, and strange and bizarre information about supernatural realities. The meanings of these secrets, while known to the Shiur Komah insiders, are still a baffling mystery to all outsiders and later generations. Most of these teachings were not speculations, but rather outright revelations given over to an individual, from either one or a number of angelic entities.

Rabbi Yitzhak discusses in detail how the generation of Babel had access to all this knowledge, and used it to build their city and their tower *"as a miniature in accordance to the supernal pattern".* Now, let us dismiss the mythology of such beliefs and understand it for what it really means. The people of the Generation of Babel were not holy mystics. They were grounded, down-to-Earth and by our definition, scientific. However, their science was far more advanced than our own.

Their intent to create an environment as a *"miniature of the supernal pattern"* meant that it was supposed to be complete and perfect, without any need of anything external, including power or spiritual connection to anything outside. Essentially they were trying to create a shielded bubble, without any openings to the outside. Nothing was to be able to enter, nothing physical, and nothing spiritual. They were even generating their own "life-force" energy, and sought to be disconnected from the universal flow. They wanted to have the laws of natural physics dominate, and exclude any other power, especially spiritual or psychic powers, like those that they held to be responsible for the flood.

Essentially the intent of the people of the Generation of Babel was to "tie G-d's Hands behind his back". They wanted to disable the power that caused the flood, and prevent it from every having the ability to again cause such destruction. This intent is what united them all.

It was considered to be the ultimate act of rebellion against Divine Authority, and essentially, it was considered, in the words of Midrashic literature, a declaration of war on Heaven. This is the meaning of the verse (Gen 11:4) that states, *"Come, let us build ourselves a city and a tower with its top in the heavens, and let us make ourselves a name"*. As incredible as this may sound, the Generation of Babel had the ancient technology to accomplish this task, and as the verse (Gen 11:6) says, *"nothing they plan to do will be unattainable for them!"*

Creating an environment so insular and disconnected from all outside influences is one thing. This may indeed be interpreted as an act of rebellion against living under Divine Authority. However, the intent of the Generation of Babel did not end here. The Torah text makes it very clear that they were building both a "tower" and a "city". The mention of both constructions implies a dual intent. Each project was different and served its own purpose. The "city" was to be the place from insular defensive protection. But the "tower" had a more nefarious purpose to fulfill.

According to Midrashic sources, including the Zohar, the Generation of Babel wanted to use the "tower" as their launching pad for a military retaliatory strike on Heaven. They were not just preparing defensively to protect themselves from future Divine wrath; they were also preparing to launch a major military offensive.

Again, to those who interpret Heaven as being just some ethereal, non-physical, spiritual "whatever" place somewhere "over the rainbow," such intent would be considered the heights of primitive stupidity. But remember who we are dealing with.

We are not dealing with ancient primitives who believed fairy tales about spiritual realities in the same way as is done today. These people had a vastly different experience and knew all too well that the domain that we call Heaven is far from imaginary or just being a non-physical spiritual domain.

They knew very well that the power that brought the flood emanated from the domain of a certain collective of angels. They knew that these same angels, as ethereal as they may be, still had a home in this universe. The generation of the flood knew where these angels came from. They recognized it as a planet somewhere out there in outer space.

According to Rabbi Eliezer Ben David in his *"Out Of the Iron Furnace"* (page 50), quoting the authority of the great Sage Rabbi Yonatan Eyebeshutz, the Tower had fire coming out of its bottom and was meant to be launched into space.

According to this opinion, the war that the Generation of Babel was planning was not merely spiritual, but physical. They had the ability and the plans to launch a nuclear powered spacecraft to fight an intergalactic war against a known and clear extraterrestrial threat.

In their eyes, this war had already begun with the extraterrestrials (angels) taking the first "shot". They blamed these intervening angels for creating the circumstances that brought on the flood. Now, it was payback time. And like the verse (Gen 11:6) quoted above stated, *"nothing they plan to do will be unattainable for them!"*

Their plan was formidable and their abilities powerful. Something had to be done to thwart their plans, without having to utterly destroy them. Thus the Torah continues to relate what happened next. Gen 11:7 clearly states, *"Come, let us descend".* The powers (in plural) came down to Earth clandestinely and invisibly and launched their own attack.

These powers are later identified in Daniel 4:14 as being the Watcher angels. Their chosen method of attack, as we have seen numerous times through Scripture is not to attack the body, or other physical forces, but rather to attack the individual mind.

These Watcher entities can telepathically and psychically either build or destroy the human mind. We see this clearly revealed in the book of Daniel where it was ordained that a future King of this same Babel (later Babylon), Nebuchadnezzar, was to be punished "for his sins" not with a lighting strike from Heaven, but rather with a "strike" against his mind. Nebuchadnezzar developed a severe mental illness that literally overnight turned him from a clear headed wise ruler and into a psychotic lunatic.

This is the technique of how the Watchers battle. They are the angels of the L-rd. As they did centuries later to Nebuchadnezzar so too did they do now to the members of the Generation of Babel. They confused their minds by creating disharmony between them, referred to in the text as the "confusion of speech".

As we all know, "united we stand and divided we fall". By sowing dissension among the ranks, the Watchers effectively destroyed their united intent, and thus brought about an end to their plans. For the Watchers, it was "mission accomplished". But there are still some loose ends that we need to follow.

United humanity was spread over the face of the Earth, to be divided into nations, each to face their future destiny. We learn of humanity's dispersal but what happened to the city, the tower and the ancient technologies used to build them?

Ancient legend teaches us that the Watchers destroyed part of the Tower, and left part of it intact to serve as a lesson to future generations. Some modern archaeologists believe that they have found the location of ancient Babel, and the remnant of the Tower. They claim to also have found evidence of some strange type of nuclear presence there that cannot be explained. As for the location of the ancient secret technology that enabled them to travel to the stars; the possibility of this surviving to modern days brings us into the midst of some of the more outrageous current conspiracy theories.

As society becomes more and more secular and scientific, UFO stories are growing more and more sophisticated. Yet, it is an unfortunate and sad fact that a part of the UFO conspiracy crowd has over the years transformed to become yet another haven for insane anti-Semitic fairy tales and lies. New UFO myths state the ridiculous, slanderous lie that Jews are the descendants of reptilian extraterrestrials seeking to take over the world and who suck the blood out of innocent Gentiles who discover their plans (a modern rendition of age-old stupidities). However, aside from getting Jews falsely involved in the nefarious, conspiratorial thick of things, other new conspiracy theories have arisen to describe certain current events.

UFO conspirators claim that the reason why the United States invaded Iraq was not to depose Saddam Hussein or to grab Iraqi oil. These conspirators claim that the real reason was because Saddam Hussein had discovered the ancient Babel "star-gate". Western Powers wanted it wrested from his hands before he learned how to use it, access extraterrestrial help and thus conquer the world as the expected anti-Christ.

Now, maybe you are like me and you get a good chuckle out of this type of story. However, as nonsensical as modern UFO conspiracies may be, it does not mean that everything claimed has to be false simply because it is attached to things stupid and prejudiced. Those who claim that Jews are blood sucking aliens are the same ones who believe that Jews put blood in Passover matzah and then claim the Holocaust never happened. What a great way to discredit anything real, however bizarre, by attaching it to psychotic ideas and racial prejudice.

According to our Torah traditions there very well is (or was) something buried in the Iraqi (Babylonian) desert which had tremendous power, and if understood could bestow that power upon its discoverers. While Torah does suggest this possibility, nonetheless it does not give credence to the conspiracy theory that the Iraqi war was a cover-up for the exploration and exploitation of such a "star-gate". Granted we may be quick to dismiss this as nonsense, let us at the same time remember that history documents Adolph Hitler having a great interest in the occult. As portrayed in many Hollywood films and documentaries, he did send out expeditions to find ancient, lost artifacts for their occult powers.

So, while we rightfully should dismiss most UFO conspiracies having any legitimacy, nonetheless, maybe not everything they say is completely false. As with anything else involved in a cover-up, the truth may never be known.

All that can be said for sure is that our modern society is radically changing. It is turning into the type of society that existed in ancient Babel. Modern technology is clearly a new Babel and a new tower. More and more society is turning away from the natural order of things and turning into something strange and bizarre. Indeed, science today has become the new religion; it alone claims to hold the keys to all supreme truths. Science and technology are the gods of the modern religion of hedonist atheism.

We think that we are emancipating ourselves from the authority of Heaven by proclaiming our new found scientifically based atheism. This is exactly what the Builders of Babel did a long time ago. We know what happened to them. Yet, today we deny the reality of ancient Babel so that we may also deny the moral of that lesson. We say that what happened to them will not happen to us. And why? Because Babel is only a story and it never really happened. As such the Babel myth is only a scare tactic and should not be considered or taken seriously. These are the conclusions of the modern secular atheist. If he is right, then so be it. But if he is wrong, and both history and archaeology do suggest it is dead wrong, then what?

Are we only fooling ourselves by trying to convince ourselves that Babel was a myth and that there is no lesson to be learned? If indeed Babel was real, then we become subject to the dire words of Albert Einstein. He said that the definition of insanity is repeating the same events and expecting different outcomes. If we are repeating the mistakes of the Builders of Babel, will we not also arouse the interest of "those above" who will have to "descend" among us to observe and to judge.

Are we any different from the Builders of the Babel? Will we suffer their fate of division? In this regard, I think not, because there is no unity today to suffer from division. Maybe today we would be subject to the very fate that the Tower Builders themselves had feared. If there is any truth to modern conspiracy theories about a world-wide cover-up of involvement with entities that are known in the biblical traditions as "the bad guys" we might be bringing down upon our own heads another intervention the likes of which we cannot possibly imagine. In light of what is happening in the world today, I do pause and wonder.

Chapter 7

The Virtual Reality of Alien Angels

I know many will question why I use the term "aliens" with regards to angels. Yet, I made this deliberate choice to make a statement about the actual nature of those entities that we call angelic beings.

Torah tradition does not need to wait for modern science to discover other forms of life in our universe. We have ancient knowledge dating back thousands of years that not only are we not alone in our universe; we are also not alone on our own planet. Before we discuss the Torah story of Avraham's three visiting guests, recorded in Genesis 18, chapter 6 previously mentions how certain "sons of G-d" came (down from Heaven) and took for themselves wives from the daughters of men. These sons of G-d are identified in Midrashic literature as being fallen angels. They were at one time far above human life and then came down here to stay. Now again, in Avraham's day, we are told by Midrashic tradition that his three guests are visiting angels.

Now, herein lies a disagreement amongst Torah commentators. Some say that the entire episode of the three visitors was nothing more than a prophetic vision; all happening in Avraham's mind. The second opinion however states that this was an actual event and that three angels physically appeared in the flesh and sat and dined with Avraham. Of course, the question is asked how angels can eat. The answer given is that they only appeared to be eating but that they actually did not.

Why would it be a problem for angels to eat? This is because most Sages are under the impression that angels are totally incorporeal beings, made up entirely of energy with no physical mass. While this is the majority accepted opinion, not all Sages agreed. Some were of the opinion that certain lower races of angels were somehow corporeal. Therefore, according to the opinion that states angels are incorporeal then they only appeared to be eating food (and possibly were only there in Avraham's vision). According to the other opinion, these angels took on flesh and dwelt amongst us. As such, they could eat, drink and in any other way appear totally human.

So then, what exactly are angels? According to both the Zohar and RaMBaM there are ten known species of angels, each being rather different from the other. Although RaMBaM is of the opinion all races of angels are ethereal, non-corporeal entities, Kabbalistic literature is split on the matter. Higher angelic races are considered to be ethereal in nature; whereas certain "lower" angelic races might have some sort of physical side to them.

In one ancient teaching, recorded in *Avot D'Rabbi Natan* there is discussion about another alien race of beings that we refer to as demonic. It is taught that these demonic entities share similar characteristics with both humans and angels. These entities like angels can be invisible, fly, and have prescient knowledge of the future. Like humans, these entities eat and drink, sexually procreate, and die. Now, how can something ethereal and non-corporeal eat and drink, have sex and die, unless there is a definite physical component to them? Now let us extrapolate from what we do know on to what we want to know. If these demonic entities are the fallen angels, spoken of in Genesis 6 and they can eat, drink, sexually procreate and die, does this mean that their non-fallen compatriots can do the same?

Interesting question, is it not? For those who believe angels are totally non-corporeal, this is not even a possibility. Yet, for those who believe otherwise, it certainly is. Moreover, for those who hold angels to be non-corporeal, then how did a collection of them become corporeal and thus subject to physical natural laws?

Now, in light of these two opinions we can review the episode of Avraham's three guests in two different ways. Was it a vision or was it physical? From all appearances, it was certainly physical, although physical appearance can be deceiving. The Torah reports that two of these entities left Avraham and headed towards Sodom, there to rescue Lot and to destroy the city. Now, certainly Lot and the men of Sodom were not having any type of vision of visitors. The two angels were clearly seen by Lot, his family, and the men of the city who even attempted to homosexually rape them. Hard as one may try, one cannot rape a vision. The clear physicality of these two entities gives credence and support to them also being physical in their visit with Avraham.

This episode in the life of Avraham seeing and actually interacting with corporeal angels, appearing as human, is not an isolated incident in the Torah, or in later biblical literature. The appearance of angels, then and now, might have a very real physical component to them. While knowledge of this as applied to understanding the Bible is nice, it is still only academic. Yet, angelic intervention among human beings never ended with the close of the biblical canon. Angels continue to intervene among us to this day. Countless stories, from around the world, have been told for centuries how this or that Rabbi met with Eliyahu HaNavi or some other Heavenly entity. The one thing these stories have in common is that the angel in question always comes in a physical form and always appears in the disguise of being simply human.

Now we can ask the question; how many times have angels come in modern times, performed their work and gone their way, without ever being recognized for who they truly are? The story of Avraham's three guests indicates to us the methods of angelic operations. How many of us have had a stranger suddenly appear in our lives at a strategic and critical moment; helped us with something and then disappear just as quickly? I myself have personally experienced this phenomenon and judging from the many conversations I have had with people all around the world, many others have also experienced this bizarre occurrence. Who can say who among us has actually interacted with an angel and did not recognize it as it was happening?

Now that I have laid the foundation for us to understand how angels can actually be amongst us, let us now ask a difficult, if not impossible to answer question. If angels come down and dwell among us, from where did they come and to where do they return? We can also inquire as to the methods of their travel and we might discover that what they do and how they do it might not be so incomprehensible now in light of our modern understandings of physics and technology.

There are many races of angels. Angels are messengers; their job is to serve. Some serve in one way, in one place and others in a different place and manner. In order for us to understand anything about angelic matters going on around us, both on and off our world, we must begin with an understanding of just what type of entity the angel that interacts with us is. What is an angel made of? If they can be corporeal, how is that possible? In order to understand the physics of an angel, we must first understand something about the physics of the universe at large.

According to ancient understanding, our physical world is formed with four elements, these being fire, air, water, and Earth. These elements are merely metaphors for the four forms of matter that we know as energy (fire/plasma), gas (air), liquid (water), and solid (Earth). Human anatomy is said to be made of all four elements. Angelic anatomy, however, includes only two elements, those of fire and air. These angels in question therefore have a form consisting of energy/plasma and possibly gas. Is it possible for sentient consciousness to inhabit a form of pure energy or something as ethereal as a gas? According to the ancients the answer is a definitive yes.

Sentient consciousness is a funny thing. Modern science wants to speak about and look for life as we understand it, a carbon based physical form. Yet, even scientists, I believe will admit that there may be forms of life so radically different from what we presently understand that we might not even recognize it as a sentient life form. This then describes the nature of one such race of beings, a specific race whose role it is to interact with humanity in some form of guardianship. In Hebrew they are called Malakhim which in English should be properly translated as messengers. The term angel is nebulous at best and does not properly characterize the race to which the term is applied.

These entities in their original indigenous state, consist of bodies of energy (and possibly gas). They then have some ability to congeal into a physical form, consisting of liquid and solid components, like us. Now, here is where we can use concepts of modern science to hypothesize just how they might be doing this.

Consider this: we are familiar with computer games and we are familiar with virtual reality. Let us say that I can put on a VR headset and enter into the computer program to play the game. From the point of view of the characters in the game I am actually one of them, however, the rules of the program affect me differently than them.

If, for example, I am playing a war game, the computer characters can get shot and die, never to return to active play. I, on the other hand, can reset the playing mode and get shot numerous times, die numerous times, and still come back every time to continue playing. I know what I am doing is not abnormal, and there certainly is nothing miraculous about it. However, if an in-game character was generated with artificial intelligence and could view itself as a sentient being (however artificial), it would view me and my so-called powers as nothing short of miraculous, or semi-Divine.

It is possible that from the "angelic" point of view, our world is nothing more than a virtual reality simulation, and we are each but players. The difference between the angels and us is that they are aware that they are playing a game, and that the game is not reality, whereas we have become entrapped in the game, and consider there to be no other reality. They thus come into and out of the game at will to try to reach us and get us to take off our "headsets" to remember the greater outside world.

While in the game they would appear as physical as we are. Yet, they would come and go according to the rules governing higher-level users of the computer program. We, who are stuck in the game, unable to access these special user privileges, witness their comings and goings and interpret these beings as being something totally alien; life forms radically different from our own, possibly beings of pure energy, with nothing more than a form lighter than a gas.

I have just now described to you how the angelic visitors came to Avraham and had a meal with him. They were actually physically there, if we can apply the term physical to them, any more than we can to a virtual character in a computer game. From the point of view of the technology underlying the game, all characters in it (those visiting and those stuck within it) are nothing more than packets of electrical energy. Yet, to those characters playing the game, their virtual reality is the only reality there is. By design, there appears to be no computer, no technology, no energy or the like. There is only the program, which the players interpret to be reality. This is the definition of a virtual reality; it is a convincing matrix and subjectively real to those therein.

Therefore, the two opinions of our Sages are both correct. Angels are both corporeal and non-corporeal entities simultaneously. It all depends upon how we are viewing the entity at the moment, as either being inside or outside the program.

For that matter, we human beings ourselves are also inside and outside the program simultaneously. That is why our human minds are split between what we psychologically refer to as the conscious and unconscious parts of the mind. The conscious part exists within the virtual reality of our present matrix. Our unconscious part exists in an entirely different dimensional plane; one so foreign to our conscious minds, that we cannot experience it and what little that is experienced is totally confusing.

The only way out of virtual reality is obviously to connect to that part of us that is outside of it. Yet, that part of our minds has the virtual reality headset on it, and the virtual signal deters our mental focus. Due to the nature of the game, we may not be able to remove our virtual helmets, but even while wearing them, we can remember that we are actually game players sitting in place somewhere very far away. If we remember who we really are, then we can activate all the extra rules designed for aware players. We can cease being mere computer characters of artificial intelligence and awaken to become actual players subject to using the controls of the game. Avraham was such an awakened player, so was Moshe *Rabbeynu*, Eliyahu HaNavi and many others. They knew the game codes and had the "hacks".

So, the next time we talk about angels, we should recognize how simple we may sound, talking about a reality that is anything other than simple. We do not have to concern ourselves whether or not angels actually have wings, multiple faces or the like. Who cares what they (and we) actually look like without the virtual "skin"? All we need to understand is that they are here with us, right here and now. They can pop in on us just as we can pop into our favorite computer game. They can come and go in time and space, with what for them is nothing more than a click of the mouse. The great revelation here is that we can do the same, if only we wake up and properly play the game.

Chapter 8

Angelic Virtual Reality, Human Visions or Actual Close Encounters

The Torah relates an episode that Avraham is visited by three guests. The text and later commentaries make it clear that these guests are most unusual and extraordinary. They are not human beings although they appear to be such in every which way. Yet, in spite of appearances they are not human. They are angels.

Now, here is where our inquiry must begin. The Hebrew word for "angel" is Malakh. It simply means messenger. Anyone can be a messenger be it from G-d or from a mortal human. These Malakhim are G-d's personal envoys. Yet, just who and what they are and where they come from is the topic of much discussion in religious, theological literature. Religious philosophers are at their preposterous best when they try to speak with authority about the existence and nature of a group of entities with which they have absolutely no firsthand information or experience whatsoever.

Talk about Malakhim abound, but is any of it real? Just because a teaching can be found in a book; does this make the teaching to be correct? Would it not be better to learn about a subject from one who has actual hands-on knowledge and experience with it? What do religious thinkers know about the actual nature of G-d's messengers? What can they tell us; what do they really know and how did they come about to know these things?

For centuries since biblical times, there has long been a tradition passed down through the prophetic, and then later Merkava and Kabbalistic schools teaching how to commune directly with G-d's messengers, the Malakhim. Those who have access to these teachings and who make use of them discover that they can indeed commune with the Malakhim today just as the ancients did a long time ago.

Modern Kabbalistic literature goes to extremes to define and describe the various classes of angels. One mystically philosophical opinion rigidly held to today (that actually stems from Greek philosophy) is that angels are entirely non-corporeal entities with absolutely no physical substance whatsoever. They are thought to be entirely cerebral entities with no type of body at all. When they would make their appearance to the likes of Avraham they merely cloaked themselves in a body for the moment and then upon completion of their mission, disrobe and return to their natural non-corporeal matter-less "non-forms".

While the description here of how these entities appear corporeal and then seem to disappear is accurate, we still have to understand what exactly it is that they are doing, not in light of the modern beliefs, which are philosophically base, but rather upon older beliefs which are based on much more experiential knowledge.

The older Kabbalists did not teach that angels are completely non-corporeal. Most of them understood that angels also had material bodies, but not of any material that we may recognize. According to ancient beliefs, all matter was divided into the four elements of fire, air, water, and Earth. We knows these forms by their modern names as state of matter, Earth=physical, water=liquid, air=gaseous and fire=plasma. The old literature states that while we human beings inhabit bodies made of all four types of matter, angels inhabit forms made up of only the air and fire forms. In other words, sentient "angelic" life forms inhabited bodies made of gaseous and plasmic elements. This would be a life-form totally different from our own and totally inconceivable according to standards of modern science.

A sentient energy or sentient gas would have to be composed of a molecular structure far beyond our present limited understanding of subatomic physics. What kind of gas or plasma would their "bodies" consist of we cannot even begin to guess. All we can say, at least what we think we can say, is that their forms are not constructed from any atomic material or molecular forms of which we are not presently aware.

Science now considers the existence of parallel universes to be a reality. It is believed that these alternate universes may be in inhabited by beings of unknown composition. Torah has long ago acknowledged this reality. What science discovers Torah reveals. Science is (believed to be) discovered by humanity; Torah is revealed to humanity from beyond the present confines of our humanity.

Whether we speak from a scientific or Torah point of view, one thing is certain; we are not alone! Whether it is in other places in our universe, or in a parallel universe, there are other entities out there. While science postulates their existence, Torah proclaims it. More than just this, Torah teaches us that these beings regularly travel between parallel worlds and come to Earth. In fact, our Torah itself comes from one of these parallel worlds, and these beings are its deliverers. They are the Angels of the Torah.

These parallel-world entities travel back and forth to our world using whatever forms of technology known to them that work under the natural laws that govern their domain. Angels just do not pop in and out by magic. They are not omnipresent and omniscient like G-d is. If an angel has to get around it has to use some means of transport. Just what kind of vehicle this may be we should not jump to conclusions just because we presume to understand it. After all, there are all too many movies and television programs made about topics like these, with each one presenting the imagination of its writers. Yet, these Hollywood fantasies only detract our minds from understanding the true awesome and ominous reality that surrounds us.

In modern times Ezekiel's chariot and the horse drawn chariot that took Eliyahu to Heaven are both considered to be symbolic imagery describing a wholly spiritual reality without any corporeal essence to it. However, as we have learned above, not everyone agrees with this rather didactic position.

Angels require some mechanism for transport because they are not omnipresent. It is possible to suggest and to consider that maybe Ezekiel's chariot and the chariot of Eliyahu are actual transportation devices and not mere symbolism or imagery. Granted, they do not have to be flying saucers or other types of space ships as many have suggested. However, just because these chariots are not flying saucers piloted by little green men from outer space does not mean that they are not another form of vehicle for either galactic or inter-dimensional transportation.

Just because we do not understand a thing does not give us the right to condemn it or preclude the possibility of its existence. Prejudice is akin to willful ignorance; both block the mind from integrating unfamiliar concepts. The biblical record is clear that angels travel through some means of transportation. Just what this means is anyone's guess. But no one should be so quick to dismiss the possibility of them possessing some highly advanced space/time transportation device. Yet, just what kind of mechanism would be utilized by beings whose makeup is only of gaseous material and plasma is beyond our present comprehension.

Modern opinions wish to adamantly claim that all biblical records of angelic visitations were exclusively visionary experiences and that there were absolutely no physical materializations at all. The majority of Torah opinions disagree with this view. The prevailing belief is that non-corporeal angels materialize to come down to Earth and then revert to their normal immaterial state. Maybe this is an accurate expression of their travels but this says nothing about their natural state in their natural habitat. Let me explain.

If I wished to travel to another world with an environment absolutely alien to my natural condition, there are two ways I could approach the trip. First, I could prepare a big enough space ship that would carry all my survival needs, including food, water, air, and other necessities for life. I would need a ship of sufficient size for all this and have it powered by a sufficient propulsion system. It would require a lot of work and effort. Yet, there is a second more convenient and efficient method.

Let's say that I could detach my soul, my conscious essence from my physical body and enable it to transport itself through space and time at the speed of thought, a speed that is documented in science to be faster than light. If I were an entity formed exclusively of gaseous material and plasma such a separation might be the easiest of things. I could then project my consciousness to whatever location I choose and then, using the force of mind, combine molecules from that place to build a structure in a form that appears indigenous and is most suited to the local environs. In this way I am fully adapted to the local terrain, and I have no need of a transport ship or for biological support technology. I could fit in locally and even go about unnoticed and I could leave in the same way, with the same ease as I came.

This second method is how the entities which Torah refers to as angels come to Earth. In most cases when these entities appear, as was the case with Avraham, they are referred to as men. They look like human beings and act like human beings; they even partake of a meal, eating human food. Their identities are somehow intuited, but if not for such "spiritual" sensitivity their true identities would go unnoticed, as it was in Sodom.

When messengers from G-d come to Earth from whatever domain, abode or planet they originated, they utilize some process that transports their essence and enables it to materialize in a form compatible for life here on Earth. As such their perceived form would be that of a gaseous or plasmic form or possibly just mere matter-less energy. Yet, while we see them as they are embodied here and while we may perceive them in their gaseous or plasmic "vessel", this in no way confirms that their indigenous form in their domains of origin are anything of the kind.

An angel is a messenger sent for a reason to accomplish a purpose, but what then? Is the angel/messenger no more than a computer program, designed to mindlessly perform a function, only to return to the oblivion from which it came? Are angels/messengers no more than some super advanced form of "alien" software, merely encoded and limited by the boundaries of their programming? If this is so it would explain why some Sages have commented that angels do not possess free will. Yet, we see through biblical example and later Midrashic teachings that angels do rebel against Heaven and challenge the accepted order.

Were the fallen angels spoken of in Genesis 6 designed to fail? Did they not rebel against Heaven, apparently indicating that maybe they came to this conclusion of behavior on their own? In the book of Daniel we read that the angel Gabriel was dispatched from Heaven to deliver a message to Daniel and that he was prevented from carrying out his mission by another angel, the Angel of Persia. Who gave the Angel of Persia the mind and ability to block the angel/messenger of G-d? And then the story relates how Gabriel had to go and get Mikhael and then the two, Mikhael and the Angel of Persia "duked it out" until Mikhael won. Is this how computerized programmed technology is supposed to work? I would think that G-d the great Programmer would have a better operating system!

There is obviously more to these matters than meets the eye and much more than we mortal human beings presently entrapped here on our planet can possibly understand about the true nature and workings of the greater universe. RaMBaM, the Zohar and other sources enumerate an entire spectrum of different angelic races. Many are familiar with the more popular names of *Cherubim*, *Seraphim*, and *Ofanim* but they are at least seven others enumerated in most sources. We are told that there are infinite numbers of such messengers. How many divisions and races of them exist, we have no idea. Are some "smarter" than others? Are some merely artificial intelligences programmed for a mission that when complete ceases their existence? Are some intelligent and somewhat independent entities capable of rebellion and challenge?

Our knowledge of these beings who we have religiously come to call angels and messengers from G-d is severely limited and the true nature of their existence, while not contested is certainly still a great mystery. One thing is for certain, these beings are real, they do interact with us and they are as extraterrestrial as that word can be stretched. Many of us have had close encounters of the third and fourth kind and we are totally unaware of it. What we are dealing with, we are totally unaware of. But dealing with something not of this Earth, we certainly are!

So, what conclusions can we draw? Not many! We know that we are not alone. We know that we are being watched! We know that they are all around us, even now! Just who they are, we do not know! What they are, we do not know. Why they are here, this we do know! They are G-d's messengers and their purpose is simple; they are here to carry out their respective missions and to perform the Will of G-d. This much is certain.

Maybe our entire Earth, our entire universe and even all existence is nothing more than one grand programmed function of the Divine Mind. Imagine all existence is nothing more than the individual operations in the greatest of all computers. If this is true, I wonder, what is the purpose of the Grand Program? I wonder if we will ever know?

Chapter 9

Secrets of Hevron, Eden, Inner Earth & the Real Conspiracy of Silience

There is a great mystery concealed in the Torah narrative of Avraham's burial of his wife Sarah. This mystery is not just another boring mystical mumbo-jumbo philosophical religious lesson that makes us want to yawn. No, this mystery is about a geographical and geological reality, spoken about for centuries in Torah literature and echoed in the literature of numerous cultures from around the world. What I am speaking about is the Garden of Eden being a real physical place and the secret of its actual location.

So, where is the Garden you may ask? And who is living there now? In order to answer these questions, let us delve into Torah, to the time of Sarah's death and to the place of her burial, the "double" Cave of Makhpelah in Hevron.

The Torah story is well known; Sarah, Avraham's beloved wife, mother of Yitzhak passes away at the ripe old age of 127. Avraham, wealthy as he is, still does not own any property in his newly adopted homeland then called Canaan (modern day Israel). In those days, there were no cemeteries. The dead were usually placed in caves which were sealed and protected as family tombs. Avraham sought to purchase such a cave for a familial inheritance, where in later he would be buried alongside his sons and grandsons. Indeed, this we know is what happened and the Cave of the Patriarchs in Hevron is still a venerated place to this very day.

Now, of all the caves in the area, why did Avraham choose this specific one, which we know as Makhpelah? While the written Torah text does not delve into the issue (written Torah seldom delves into any issues), the Oral Tradition dating back to those days brings to us tremendous details, without which much of the written Torah will never be understood. The Oral Torah relates a story retold in many Torah commentaries. It goes something like this.

According to the Midrashic legend, which may or may not be historical, Avraham was out tending sheep one day when one of them ran off. He followed it through the hills and into a cave. Upon entering the cave Avraham was overwhelmed by the sweet fragrances coming out from deep within it. He enters deeper and to his surprise he founds that there is a second cave inside the first one and inside this second cave lay buried a man and a woman whose bodies have not decomposed. Amazed at this sight, Avraham prays to G-d for answers, asking what this place is and who is buried here. The male body then sits up and speaks, saying to Avraham that he is Adam and that this cave is the entrance way to Garden of Eden. This cave was the cave of Makhpelah and this episode was why Avraham specifically wanted it to for his own tomb and for his loved ones to follow. So goes the story.

Now, let us put legend aside and ask the necessary questions. If there is any legitimacy to Makhpelah being an entrance way to Eden, how is this physically possible? Gardens are placed where trees grow and flora flourishes. But these require the light of the sun in order for them to grow. It is known that caves are holes in the Earth, some rather deep, some going for miles and miles, and yet what they all share is that they are underground without any exposure to sunlight. One cannot have a lush garden growing in a cave. How then is the cave of Makhpelah the entranceway to the Garden of Eden? Where on Earth is the Garden, or maybe better to ask where off the surface of the Earth is the Garden.

Torah Sages have forever acknowledged that the Garden of Eden is a physical location somewhere here on Earth. Since the earliest times, the Makhpelah Cave has been associated with the Garden and is acknowledged to be its entrance way. Again, if there is more than legend to any of this, where is the Garden? To answer this we must delve into one of the greatest secrets guarded by the Sages of Torah. There is no better way to reveal it other than by being direct and outright.

There is an Inner Earth and the Garden of Eden is at the center of the Earth thousands of miles down, directly underneath the Cave of Makhpelah. This astounding proclamation is stated clearly in the Zohar and in other ancient sources.

The existence of Inner Earth should come as a surprise to no one. This knowledge has long been known in ancient cultures for thousands of years, even extending across the oceans. The ancient Native American Hopis know of these places. Even in the realm of science there have been some famous names who embrace what has become known as the Hollow Earth theory. Such scientists include Sir Edmund Haley, famous for the comet named after his discovery Haley's comet.

The existence of Inner or Hollow Earth is much more than a mere theological statement made by the Torah Sages. There have been numerous encounters between surface dwelling human beings and the many other inhabitants of the inner realms. Not all such encounters with these entities have been benign.

Our Sages have outlined that Inner Earth is actually divided up in seven sections which in Hebrew are called the Sheva Artzot. These are enumerated in detail in the Zohar (Hashmetut 1, 254a; *Hesed L'Avraham* 2, 4 and Emek HaMelekh, Sha'ar 21). While some modern "Rabbis" want to describe the Sheva Artzot as the land masses here on the surface of the Earth, those propagating this hypothesis are doing so untruthfully. They are either ignorant of what our Sages have taught or they are lying about what our Sages have taught.

From a scholarly point of view we cannot tolerate or condone those who either misunderstand or lie about Torah source material. It disqualifies their legitimacy in the Rabbinate or from holding any teaching position in the Torah world.

With regards to Torah teachings, when there is a disagreement amongst the classical sources about an issue then one may choose which side to embrace based upon one's personal opinion (with the exception of issues of Halakha). When, however, there is no such disagreement, but only a proclamation about the reality of life, the universe, and similar things, one who denies the teachings of the Sages is tantamount to denying the teachings of Torah and Judaism.

By doing so, such so-called teachers place themselves outside the bounds of acceptability, regardless of whether they are members of the liberal or even most Haredi camps. Illegitimacy exists on the extremes of both right and left.

The Garden of Eden is said to be only one of the many locations in Inner Earth. The Zohar teaches that it was there that Adam materialized on Earth; it was from the center-most domain (Eden) in Inner Earth that he was cast out; it was in other domains in Inner Earth that he lived and that Cain and Abel were born. It is even stated that Adam left numerous other progeny throughout Inner Earth over the centuries of his life.

The Zohar states that many who escaped the destruction of the Tower of Babel did so by relocating to Inner Earth. Inner Earth has long been said to be the domain of the fallen angels and the Nefilim mentioned in Genesis 6.

Inner Earth is said to also be the domain of many animals which we have long considered to be mythological, such as the unicorn, the phoenix, the minotaur, centaur and dragon (ref. *Hesed L'Avraham* 2:4).

Inner Earth inhabitants are said to come in many different shapes and sizes, from what we would call giants, to the likes of what we would call hobbits; indeed, there is even said to be a race of two-headed humanoid beings. All these things are proclaimed by our Sages to be physically real.

The Zohar states that the Garden of Eden is a real physical place existing in Inner Earth. In the "Garden" there are said to be numerous "palaces". This indicates that the Garden is no mere botanical location. It seems to imply that the Garden might not be a botanical domain at all, but rather a built-up domain similar to a modern city.

One of the "palaces" in the Garden is said to be the Palace of Mashiah. The Zohar teaches that Mashiah resides here and from here receives "powers and abilities far beyond those of mortal men". It is from here in the Garden that Mashiah sets out to Outer Earth to fight the wars of HaShem and to conquer the surface for Him. As is clear from Zechariah 14, Mashiah comes from out of the sky with an army of angels. Yet, if Mashiah is coming from Inner Earth, from where come the angels with whom he meets and takes their lead? Do they also ascend with him from Inner Earth? If so, when then, is their means of transport?

Questions abound. Answers are plenty throughout the many works of our Torah Sages. One point that our Sages make is certain. We are not alone on our Earth.

There are many races of indigenous intelligent sentient entities living in Inner Earth. Many of these species know about us and many of them have interacted with us for a very long time. Some of these races are benign or even benevolent. Others on the other hand are nothing but trouble.

One of these troublesome races are referred to as the Nishaya, after the name of their domain. They are one of the "Shedim" (demons) spoken of by our Sages throughout the centuries. The Zohar and other literature describes their appearance as being frail, short, with a grayish skin-tone, no noses, just slits to breath. Allegedly they have no females of their species and thus seek our human females with which to procreate.

Many might recognize the similarities between the Nishaya and modern day so-called extraterrestrials and so-called alien abductions. While these experiences are definitely real, still, they are not what people think they are. There is far more material to discuss about this topic than can be related here. Maybe, we can pick up the discussion in future writings, then again maybe not. Maybe it is best for people not to know.

The Garden of Eden is thus accepted by our Sages as a physical domain deep inside Inner Earth. Yet, just as the Garden is located there so are there other domains, even the physical location of Gehenna (Hell). These are not places of myth or the repose of the souls in the afterlife. They are accepted as being physical inhabited domains, whose inhabitants interact with us on a regular basis. They know all about us. It is we who live in ignorance of them. If there really is some sort of conspiracy of silence "out there" somewhere, then it is this that "they" are trying to keep secret. Maybe, they have very good reason.

Chapter 10

Seeing Voices, Telepathic Torah

We are all familiar with the story of the giving of the Ten Commandments, at least we think so. Scripture says that Elohim/G-d spoke the Ten Commandments at Mount Sinai. Yet, Scripture defines for us what exactly the Divine Voice actually was. Indeed, Scripture says that the people SAW the Voice. That which is normally audible in nature was at this time visual. How do mechanical sound waves transform into electromagnetic light waves? Is this indeed what happened, or is there something missing in our understanding?

"And all the people SAW the Voices, and the flames, the Voice of the Shofar, and the mountain of smoke, and the nation saw and trembled and stood at a distance" (Ex 20:5).

What kind of Voice did the people SEE? Did it sound like a human voice? Did it speak Hebrew? If there was actual audible speech, how then was it SEEN? However we may imagine that the Divine Voice must have sounded like, all our guesses most likely will come nowhere close to the actual historical truth of the moment. The Sages of old have chimed in with their insights, and we might find them very revealing and enlightening.

Many of the classical Torah commentaries state that at Mount Sinai G-d's Voice was indeed SEEN, but this Voice was unlike any other audible set of sound waves. Our Sages draw a very important distinction, one that is clear in the original Hebrew, but might not always be understood in translation. G-d's Voice was indeed heard, but not necessarily G-d's Words. The distinction is that there is a big difference between Voice (Kol) and Word (Dibbur).

According to our Sages, when G-d's Voice spoke the Ten Commandments, the nation, while hearing G-d's Voice, did not hear G-d's Words. In other words, the Voice of G-d went forth as a single monotone sound. Referred to in the verse above as the "Voice of the Shofar," it is understood this Divine Voice was not parsed into lingual syllables. In other words, a Voice was heard, but not words. The Voice was SEEN, without Words being spoken, and it was only then understood within the minds and souls of the receivers.

The Voice of G-d that spoke the Ten Commandments at Mount Sinai was seen in a vision. In other words, the nature of the experience of G-d at Sinai was prophetic. The sheer awesomeness of the moment created a national, mass prophetic trance, similar to what is later portrayed in 1 Samuel 19:19-24, with reference to the servants of King Saul, and Saul himself.

The Voice of G-d spoke prophetically, through visualizations, directly into the unconscious minds of the people. The Voice of the Shofar was audibly heard by all. Yet, within that audible Voice, was yet another visual Voice, the Voice of the Living, Speaking G-d.

The Ten Commandments were thus imparted with mind-to-mind communication. This direct mind communication is called telepathy. This also explains an ancient legend that not everyone at Sinai heard the Divine broadcast. Telepathy requires harmonization between like-minds. Those whose minds were not tuned in to the broadcasting frequency of YHWH would not be able to hear His Voice.

As it was then, so it is today. While prophecy, as both an art and science, has ceased today, nevertheless the methods of prophetic communications have never been lost, nor have they ever ceased. To this day, there are those who practice these ancient techniques in proper privacy, and are thus tuned-in with modern day Voices that emanate from "Heaven". While we have no prophecy today, we can still hear the echo of the Divine Voice. This is called in Hebrew, a Bat Kol, (daughter Voice). It is not audible, it is visual. It is telepathic.

To put it bluntly, YHWH still speaks today to those who can hear His Voice. Although metaphorically the nature of today's Voice is broadcast at a lower frequency than was Sinai, still, those who silence themselves to listen, can and will hear the Voice say, *"Oye Laham LaBriyut M'Elbonah Shel HaTorah,"* (*Avot* 6:2), "woe to them, the public, because of the disgrace shown the Torah".

This Voice is not audible, it is telepathic. It can be heard only by those who know how to listen. What they heard, and how they heard it, was not in the form of words, but rather in the form of an impression deep within the mind. This was the way it was with the First Voice originally spoken at Sinai, and why the daily Voice (Bat Kol) also comes forth from Sinai.

I do not see how anyone could ever call the giving of the Torah at Sinai a natural event, within the context of our present understanding of nature. By our present understanding, the sheer nature of the event must, by every stretch of the imagination, be called both supernatural and metaphysical. But here now is a revelation.

Everything supernatural is essentially natural, and thus, everything metaphysical is essentially physical. If this is the case, then the giving of the Torah on Sinai was indeed a natural event. We then have to greatly expand our definitions and understandings of both what is to be called natural and what are the parameters to that which we call physical. As science progresses into the realms of parallel universes, and the existence of both dark matter and dark energy in this universe, we are beginning to discover new levels of reality still far beyond our present understandings.

Nevertheless, some "Thing" from another reality penetrated our reality at Mount Sinai, and delivered the Torah to us. Torah is thus from another reality and it presently resides in this reality. As such, Torah exists in a dual reality and is thus dual in nature. In order for us to understand something about this dual nature of the

Torah, we must first understand a little bit about the dual nature of human beings, the recipients of the Torah.

We believe that the Torah is clearly something extraterrestrial; it is not of this world. We do not believe that the Torah is just a book of words, written by mortal men. It is rather something far beyond even what our present imaginations are able to conceive. Torah is the Word of G-d. We human beings are created in the Image of G-d. Therefore the Word of G-d, from Above, speaks to the Image of G-d, below. This idea has to be understood within our human context.

Scientific research has shown that the organ of the brain is split into two hemispheres, the right and the left. Essentially, we have two brains in our heads with the two hemispheres communicating with one another through the corpus callosum. Nevertheless each hemisphere operates independently and radically different from the other.

The right and left brains within each of us thinks and perceives reality differently. These are medical facts. The Word of G-d was given to human beings, who are created in the Image of G-d. Part of this creation is this dual-hemisphere split-brain within man. Human beings are thus split in the brain, as well as in the mind, in accordance to Divine design.

We know that the mind is divided between what is called the conscious and the unconscious. Psychological studies have shown that there are still powers within the brain that we presently cannot fathom, or even harness. We know that the left brain connects our conscious selves to the outside world surrounding us. Yet, scientific studies have clearly shown that there exists within the brain that which they call "the sixth sense".

This sixth sense might actually be many other senses rolled up into one. These are called telepathy, clairvoyance, ESP and other names. What is important to realize is that these functions of the mind/brain have been shown to exist scientifically. They are not make-believe. They are part and parcel of the Image of G-d in which we were created. As such, this means that a reflection of the

G-d who created us, and equally a part of the Word that He spoke to us, the Torah at Sinai.

Essentially then, the Torah was received by the children of Israel, with our full brains, both right and left hemispheres, each perceiving and understanding the Torah in accordance to the perceptions appropriate for each cerebral hemisphere. This is why the classical Sages refer to both the Voice of G-d (Kol) and the Word (Dibbur) of G-d. The Voice of G-d was heard within the mind, and spoke directly to the right hemisphere of the brain, instilling within it an experience and an exposure to the Divine. The right brain SAW the Voice. The Word of G-d was heard in the ears and left-brain understandings of the nation. Essentially, as the Scripture says, the right brain saw the flashes of fire, and the left brain heard the Word. The right brain heard/saw the Voice, and the left brain understood the Word.

Torah, in order to be received completely, has to be received, learned, studied, and observed with both cerebral hemispheres. Left brain Torah is not complete by itself, and neither is right brain Torah. Torah speaks to both the inner world of the mind, and to the outside world of the human being. Torah cannot be complete one without the other.

This concept indeed, is a sound psychological and political fact. One does not have a stable and sound society, unless the people who make up that society are themselves, for the most part, stable and sound individuals. Societies are made by human beings. These societies will always reflect the minds of their maker.

Those who have the ability to think telepathically, and thus see reality through their right brains will hear a nagging echo emanating out of the back of their minds. That echo is the Bat Kol/Voice from Sinai bemoaning the sorrowful state of the imbalance of human consciousness, the lack of proper, full understanding of the Torah and the terrible societies that have been built by human beings in their half-brained perceptions of reality.

The two domains of Torah have been known to us ever since there has been written commentaries and books. These two domains are today referred to as pshat (left brain Torah) and Sod (right brain Torah). Pshat deals with the realities of the outer world around us. Sod deals with the realities of inner space, the hidden domains of the unconscious, and through them, the higher dimensions which we call, the spiritual. These two paths of Torah study are symbiotic. They are two halves of the same whole. They are the two hemispheres of the brain of the Torah itself.

Torah study that is either all pshat or all sod is thoroughly imbalanced. Indeed one of the great Sages, Rabbi Eliyahu, the famous Gaon of Vilna stated this (Sefer Even Sheleimah 8:21). These are his words.

Whatever one innovates according to pshat, needs to be correlated to the sod. When the secrets of Torah are revealed to a scholar, then he understands that what he innovated in his youth according to pshat is also properly true. For anytime that the sod is not understood, even the pshat will not be clear in his hands.

The Gaon, a master of the rationalist school was equally a master of the mystical school. He knew from experience how the two domains need to be in proper balance for the sake of the greater whole.

When we are commanded to observe the Torah, we are commanded to love/serve G-d with our "all," all of our hearts, all of our souls and all of our wealth" (Deut 6:5). This "all" include all our brain(s). Therefore, one who is not using their right brain, and not studying right brain Torah, is not fulfilling the commandment to "love G-d... with all of our souls". The Gaon of Vilna understood this requirement as did many Sages both before and after him.

Chapter 11

Mind-to-Mind Connections & Remote Viewing

In ancient lore, it is said, that G-d, His Word (Torah) and His people are all connected. It is said that all of G-d's people are likewise connected. The original Hebrew word used to describe this connection is "aruvin," and actually means intertwined. The secret underlying any connection is the unseen and unfelt intertwining that unites us. Although we see ourselves as separate entities and each of us distinct from the world around us, this is merely the appearance of things. This appearance is more of an illusion than a reality.

In the true way of things, any particular is always in a state of connection with the whole. Some connections are stronger, while other connections are weaker. All things emanated from a Single Source, and are still connected to that Single Source, like branches to the root of a tree. This state of connection to the Source creates the reality of what is today being called "quantum entanglement".

Distance in space and time matter not. Things connected stay connected, regardless of distance, or the nature of their differences. The vast majority of human beings have no conscious awareness of what they share in quantum entanglement. Yet, even this lack of conscious recognition does nothing to lessen the reality of higher connections. Although the conscious mind may be oblivious to what it connects to, the unconscious mind, unfettered as it is by consciousness, has no such handicap. At one level, deeply buried within the mind, there is contact and union, which very much unknown to consciousness, guides us. It speaks to us, most often through subtle impressions, feelings, and extra sensory perceptions.

The state of attachment between things is actually the attachment and communication between the sentient consciousnesses within them. This quantum entanglement of minds occurs regardless of distances in space and time. This is specifically because consciousness, the means of communication, is its own dimension unto itself, existing both inside and outside of space and time.

Sentient consciousness should never be confused with human conscious intellectual thought. It is a mental process involving merely the recognition of, and interaction with, the outer world, and has nothing to do with actual sentient consciousness. For this reason, intellectual thought can never expand into extra-sensory perceptions. This is because the intellect alone deals only with the sensory and not the extra-sensory. There are other parts of the mind that deal with the extra-sensory, and through these each individual can communicate with their counterparts in any other individual, be that individual human or not.

Communication between sentients is natural and normal. We are "hard-wired" for this connection to be so. Quantum entanglement is a natural law. Although modern science may not be able to understand it thoroughly, what difference does that make? How many of us are fully knowledgeable in the workings of the combustion engine and auto mechanics? Yet, even without this knowledge we manage to drive our cars and have transformed our world based upon a technology that few understand but many can master.

Psychic communication between sentients works in this same way. All that we have to do is learn how to do it, like learning how to drive a car. And yes, learning to communicate is far more natural than learning to drive. If we can learn how to handle an external automobile, we can learn how to handle our own inner minds.

One begins every path from the beginning, with the very first step. Let us remember this rule, step one along a certain path is, by definition, a step away from the previously walked path. When we walk towards the new, we by definition must be walking away from the old. Apply this rule to the way that we have been trained (brainwashed?) to think.

We are told that we must be rational and logical, and that everything must make sense. This is, in and of itself, true. However, it is also herein that we have a problem. That which is rational, logical, and makes sense differs depending upon one's point of view and one's level of education and awareness. Does college mathematics make sense to a child in kindergarten? Of course not! Then what should be the threshold of rationality, logic and what makes sense? The best science of 100 years ago was painfully primitive in comparison to what we have today. Can you imagine how primitive our present day science will look in another hundred years?

To measure rationality, logic, and what makes sense based on current observations and knowledge of the external world, is limiting humanity to understanding the universe at the level of a kindergarten child. Not much will be accomplished anytime soon.

However, let us shift mental gears here and look towards the child who appreciates the arts. This child, however young, can be inspired by nature, or even art in a museum, and can show promising talent and creativity that inspires them to develop talents that produce great creations. Such a creative child is not limited by rationality, logic, and what makes sense. On the contrary, this child soars on the wings of imagination and dreams. These relaxed inhibitions enable the child to fly into the mental spheres that no rational, logically mind person can follow.

Learn from children what is natural. Reacquire the child-like innocence and imagination that we each had as children, before it was pushed out of our minds by the constant drumming of being told to be rational, logical, and to make sense.

Granted, everything in the universe is rational, logical, and does make sense but we have not yet developed to the point where our human minds can expand to encompass this grandiose, unified knowledge. At present we are walking away from the picture, instead of looking towards it. We move forward in understanding natural law, by looking at it naturally. The natural way for humans to "look" is with the eyes of child-like imagination and dreams.

We are forever in a state of quantum entanglement with the entire universe around us. It influences us, changes us, and directs us, without even our slightest rational awareness. Yet, although we are not rationally aware, the inner suppressed imagination senses these connections and endeavors to communicate them to the conscious mind. But the conscious mind dismisses these premonitions as figments of the imagination, considering them to be unproven and unreal. Thus it is the conscious mind that of itself acts as our greatest impediment to connecting with the deeper felt and known truths.

Walking the new path means retraining the way we think. This retraining is not as hard as we may think. The hardest step is always the first step. It is hardest because it requires of us a turn and movement in the opposite direction from where we were going.

With regards to the external world of work, family, and responsibilities, we must remain rational, logical, and down to Earth. But with regards to our loftier psychological, spiritual, and psychic pursuits, we must not remain down to Earth, but instead we must soar to Heaven. We have to fly with eagle's wings, and severe the chains that keep our minds entrapped.

We are in a constant state of quantum entanglement with our higher, unconscious selves. When we release the tethers of consciousness, the unconscious can take control and begin again to guide us through the new territory, down (or up) into the forgotten country.

Essentially, we really will not be learning anything new. Rather, we will get this feeling that all the new experiences and knowledge that come our way are things that we already have known, that we have always known. We will not feel like we're going into a dream, but rather like we are waking up from one.

One must allow oneself to fall back into imagination. One must allow oneself to reach out with one's feeling, and never doubt. One can begin like this. One can imagine seeing someone close, one with whom there is a distinct emotional bond. One should imagine being in the same room with that person and watching them, as if hidden behind a veil. Watch what they are doing. Are they reading, sleeping, eating, or dancing? Imagine that you can see what kind, and color of clothing they are wearing. And then imagine how they are feeling or what they are thinking at that moment. Let your imagination run wild. Do not hold back. Let your unconscious pour its content into your conscious mind without filters or blocks.

After you have had your mental encounter, make note of all that you experienced. Then, when you next meet this person with whom you have an emotional attachment, tell him/her, "You know, the other day, I was thinking about you. I saw you doing this and wearing that, and thinking about this or that thing". Watch for the reaction you receive. Sometimes the other person may think you're nuts, but then there are those other times, when they will look at you with wonder and awe, and say something like, "Wow, that is really weird. I kind of felt you that other day", or "Yeah! I was thinking about that or doing this and wearing that".

In other words, you have just taken the first step of reaching out with your mind to touch another with whom you are quantum entangled. This is the first step in what many call remote viewing.

Practice makes perfect! Keep trying. Keep letting go of your self-doubts. Let go of your inhibitions. Let your mind run free and unhindered, like a good artist or musician. Think freely by not trying to think. Travel in your mind, without fear or limits. This is how hypnosis works; only here, you are in charge and not subject to the influences and suggestions of an outside other.

Remember this; passion is the key to connection. You will not be able to touch with your mind that which you are not passionate about in your heart. Essentially, you need the emotional component, like gasoline, to operate the engine. Although the inner mind can see, it needs the emotional component in order to quantum entangle, refine the vision, and to remember clearly what is being seen. This is why this type of remote viewing is an experience of altered consciousness that does not place one in an unconscious state.

The Sages of old were able to practice this type of mind travel. Remote viewing is a natural ability of the mind just like lifting a weight is the natural ability of the arms. We go to the gym to exercise the arms to make them strong, to enable them to lift more weight. We exercise the mind in similar manner, to strengthen it, to enable it to see farther and farther away, regardless of distances in both space and time.

Everything begins and ends with connection. We are all connected. We are all part of the collective super-soul. Like individual synapses of a single brain, we are all connected, and therefore, we can remotely view, anytime we wish. All that we have to do is do it right. We know how to lift weights. We know how to drive a car. We do not know how to lift our thoughts, and drive our minds. But we can learn! And learn, we must.

Chapter 12

Humanity Before Adam:
A Review of thePre-Adamic Civilizations
in Torah Literature

Most students of the Bible and religion are unaware that Torah literature is full of references to an intelligent and civilized pre-Adamic humanity.

While this notion may seem to contradict a literal reading of the Bible, the Sages over the centuries have assured the faithful that indeed, this is not the case. Even a literal reading of Scripture is understood to indicate that there is more to history that what Scripture records, and how it is understood on its surface.

Genesis, the first book of the Bible, begins with the famous words, *"In the beginning G-d created the Heavens and the Earth"* (Gen 1:1). Immediately, the following verse states, *"And the Earth was without form and empty"* (Gen 1:2). The Sages have noticed that Isaiah 45:18 states that "the Earth was not created empty". Genesis says that in the beginning the Earth was empty, yet Isaiah say that it was not created that way. How then, was the Earth "not created empty" according to Isaiah, and then become empty by verse two (2) in Genesis? These two verses are not contradictory, but there does seem to be something significant missing between verses 1 and 2 of Genesis 1.

This mystery was addressed long ago by the Sages. Using their traditional metaphoric method of parable, called Midrash, the Sages have revealed to us many interesting teachings. In the Midrash Rabbah (Gen. Rab. 3:7) a question is asked, "What was G-d occupied with prior to His creation of our world?" The Midrash answers and reveals that prior to creating our world; G-d was busy building and destroying other worlds.

Essentially the first creations filled the universe, thus it was not empty. Then, G-d tore down what he had built and began to rebuild, using the same "parts" that He had used before. Therefore, while the Heavens and the Earth were indeed created empty, by the time it came to creating our world, the emptiness had already been filled many a time. Knowing this would indeed resolve the apparent contradiction between Genesis and Isaiah. Yet, this Midrash alone only speaks of creation, destruction and re-creation. It does not refer to pre-Adamic humanity. While this Midrash does not speak of the Pre-Adamites, other *midrashim* do.

In Leviticus it is written that, *"for six years you shall plow your fields, but the seventh year shall be holy to G-d, in that year you shall do no work"*. Based upon a midrashic interpretation of this verse, the Sages (b. Sanh. 98b) stated that, "six thousand years shall the world last, and then for one thousand years shall it remain desolate". Our Sages have learned from an ancient, secret tradition, based on this verse in Leviticus, that the days of our world, our present human civilization, will be measured in the same way, as is the biblical Sabbatical year. Six years shall we labor, and in the seventh year shall we rest. So, our civilization will grow for six thousand years, and then for a thousand years shall it "remain desolate" which means to be left alone to rest. After this time, it is said that G-d will renew (again) His creation.

The Bible proceeds to speak about the Jubilee year. We are instructed to count seven times seven years and then to proclaim a Jubilee, a year of complete release. The Sages have revealed that just as our civilization will last for the Sabbatical period of six thousand years, and one thousand years of desolation, so will there be seven cycles similar to this, corresponding to a cosmic cycle of Sabbaticals and Jubilee. Therefore, according to this calculation, human civilization will rise and fall seven times, each for a period of six thousand years, with a rest period of a thousand years between.

Based upon this understanding, a question arose among the Sages, if we are indeed in the middle of this Sabbatical cycle of seven, in which of the seven are we?

Many Sages look back to the verse in Genesis and conclude that we are certainly not in the first Sabbatical. Most thus conclude that we are in the second. The Sabbaticals are said to reflect the influences of the lower seven sefirot, with each one influencing an epoch of humanity. Previous humanity was in the epoch of the first sefirah Hesed, mercy. The Sages explain that this is why there are so many cross-cultural references to a lost prehistoric advanced civilization of some sort, usually referred to as Atlantis or Mu (Lemuria).

The Talmud, (b. Hag. 13b), employs the midrashic method to extrapolate from Scripture that there were 974 generations of humanity prior to Adam. One of the early Kabbalistic classics, the *Ma'arekhet Elokut*, states specifically that the Talmud is making clear reference to the generations of humanity from the prior Sabbatical.

For some reason, as advanced as they became, the final generation of these 974 pre-Adamic generations somehow corrupted themselves and were destroyed by a combination of Divine design, and their own destructive choices. Our Adam and his biblical story came in the aftermath of their destruction. Indeed, later Kabbalistic literature refers to Adam as coming to Earth, from another domain or dimension with the specific intent to serve as a "Mashiah" (redeemer) to those who came before him. They interpret Genesis 2:15 which states that G-d put Adam in Eden to work and safeguard the Garden as a reference to the redemptive nature of his original mission.

We are thus considered to be in the second Sabbatical, the sefirah of Gevurah, severity. This is said to explain why human civilization, in this period of recorded history, is full of violence and bloodshed, corresponding to the influence of the sefirah over the epoch.

Aside from the ancient legends from the Torah Sages, other more modern Sages have seen references to these pre-Adamic times in the discoveries of modern science. In the 19th century, a famous European Sage, Rabbi Israel Lifshitz, the author of the Tiferet Yisrael commentary to the Mishna, addressed the topic of pre-Adamic life in his introduction to the eleventh chapter of tractate Sanhedrin.

Drawing upon what were the scientific discoveries of his day, and the Darwinian conflict on creationism and evolution, Rabbi Lifshitz pointed out that the Torah does acknowledge the existence of dinosaurs. These, he said, were the creations of the prior Sabbatical. Not only this, but Rabbi Lifshitz goes further to say that Adam was not really the first human being, but that there were countless people before him. He called them pre-Adamites.

The views expressed by Rabbi Lifshitz were unfortunately too radical for many of the fundamentalists of his day. In spite of the centuries old teachings of the Sages, many of the fundamentalists still insisted on a literal reading of Genesis, in spite of the overwhelming evidence of the Sages that contradict such a baseless, fundamentalist stance. A number of years ago Rabbi Lifshitz's essay on this topic was translated into English and published by Rabbi Aryeh Kaplan in his book, Immortality, Resurrection and the Age of the Universe.

Another famous source that culls together many different sources about the cosmic Sabbaticals is the book, *Yalkhut Reuveni*, written by Rabbi Avraham Reuven HaKohen Sofer. The Rabbi's work is a compendium of views and teachings culled from numerous sources. He richly includes many of the teachings about the cosmic Sabbaticals and is one of those rare sources where one can turn to find a treasure of information, often ignored (and even boycotted) by the religious fundamentalists.

There are a great number of both earlier and later generation Rabbis, Hasidic masters and Kabbalists who have spoken quite openly about the doctrine of the cosmic Sabbaticals. With regards to them, Rabbi Shmuel Lifshitz opens his discussion of the matter in his Anafim Shatul Mayim commentary to *Sefer HaIkkarim* by saying *"[I] open my mouth like a talebearer to reveal hidden secrets".*

Throughout centuries of Torah literature, Sages of all kinds alike have written about the cosmic Sabbaticals. Perhaps the largest source material for the teachings about the cosmic Sabbatical comes from the writings of the Kabbalists. Many famous Sages have referenced the cosmic Sabbaticals in their biblical commentaries to Leviticus or elsewhere.

A list of some of the famous books that mention it include the *Sefer HaTemunah, Sefer HaKana, Ma'arekhet Elokut, Shatul Mayim on Sefer HaIkkarim, Sefer Livnat HaSapir , Sefer Shoshan Sodot.* Even the *Tikunei Zohar* makes reference to it in *Tikun 36.*

Among the famous Sages who reference it include the RaMBaN, Rabbeynu Bahya, Rabbi Yitzhak D'Min Acco, Recanati on the Torah, *Tziyuni* on the Torah, and the Radbaz, the Kabbalistic teacher of the *Ari'zal*, and many others of later generations.

Not everyone, however, accepted the doctrine of the cosmic Sabbaticals. Rabbi Haim Vital, the redactor of the Kabbalah teachings of the Ari, in his *Sha'ar Ma'amrei Rashbi 44a*, bluntly claims that the doctrine of the cosmic Sabbaticals is not correct, according to his rendition of the earlier creations (Akudim, Nikudim, Berudim).Rabbi Vital's view of the pre-Adamic worlds is that they were all spiritual in nature, and never manifested physically. This understanding of his is easy to debate and even contradict. Nevertheless, many later Kabbalists follow Rabbi Vital's position on this subject, and accept his views to be the authoritative views of the Ari himself. Yet, not everyone is in agreement with this position.

What is important to note is that Kabbalistic opinions, even those as authoritative as the Ari, should never be considered binding, or obligatory. As Rabbi Aryeh Kaplan so eloquently stated, *"Since this is not a matter of law, there is no binding opinion. Although the Ari may have been the greatest of Kabbalists, his opinion on this matter is by no means absolutely binding. Since there were many important Kabbalists who upheld the concept of the*

Sabbatical cycles, it is a valid, acceptable opinion". (*Immortality* pages 6-7)

Following in the footsteps of the Ari/Vital school was the 20th century Kabbalist, Rabbi Yehuda Fatiyah of Jerusalem. In his commentary *Beit Lekhem Yehuda* (2, 66a), on Haim Vital's major work on the Torah of the Ari, the *Etz Haim*, Rabbi Fatiyah addressed the issue of the cosmic Sabbatical from the point of view of the Ari.

Rabbi Fatiyah, in his other book, *Minhat Yehuda* (pg. 222), expounds on a section of the Zohar that speaks of the pre-Adamic parents of Adam. He even states that Adam's parents copulated on the spiritual plane, that his mother conceived and gave birth to Adam's body, which, the Rabbi emphasizes was completely non-physical. Where Adam's parents came from, Rabbi Fatiyah does not say. However, he makes it quite clear that they are individual beings and not simply an appellation for G-d.

In spite of the Ari's apparent objection to the concept of the Sabbaticals, not all Kabbalists following the Ari interpreted Rabbi Vital's teachings in this way. Interesting to note is the *Sha'at Ratzon* commentary on the *Tikunei Zohar* (36). The author Rabbi Shlomo Kohen is one of the greatest, later-generation Kabbalists of the Ari/Vital/Rashash school. He is also the author of the authoritative commentary to Rabbi Vital's *Etz Haim* entitled *Yafeh Sha'ah*.

In his commentary to the *Tikunei Zohar* 36 Rabbi Kohen comments on the clear reference made there to the cosmic Sabbaticals, and then mentions Rabbi Vital's objections to this view. Rabbi Kohen then elucidates a brilliant compromise how the view of the ancients and the view of Rabbi Vital can be synthesized. Thus, no present day student of Kabbalah should be so quick to dismiss the doctrine of the cosmic Sabbaticals out of hand based on the comments of Rabbi Haim Vital, for as we see, they are open to various interpretations.

Many Kabbalists in the generations after the Ari maintained their embrace of the cosmic Sabbaticals, even while at the same time, they would warmly embrace the teachings of the Ari. A short list of these include the author of the book, *Tekhelet Mordechai*, Rabbi Lifshitz in his *Tiferet Yisrael*, Rabbi Tzvi Hirsch Eichenstein of Zidatchov in his *Ateret Tzvi* commentary on the *Zohar HaRakia*, and even maybe the most famous of later generation Kabbalists, Rabbi Eliyahu, the Gaon of Vilna. All of these religious leaders, plus many more all understood how Genesis was to be understood, and how that Adam was not the first man of the human race.

Rabbi Tzvi Hirsch Eichenstein, in his commentary *Ateret Tzvi* (126b) on the book *Zohar HaRakia*, states that even though the Ari himself was silent on this matter, he definitely ascribed to the doctrine of the cosmic Sabbaticals, and that *"G-d forbid anyone would disagree with the holy Sages of Israel".*

What we learn from all this is that the Sages have always known to read and understand the creation story in Genesis as a metaphor, not to be taken literally.

We can also safely conclude now that the early Sages were not ignorant fundamentalists, who ignored or denied the realities of G-d's creation discovered through science.

The Sages of old knew well the secret of pre-Adamic man and the civilizations that they built. The Sages of old even knew of ancient man's extraterrestrial connections, but this is a topic that I have discussed elsewhere.

In light of this prior review of the subject, we should look towards the past with added interest and curiosity. We should ask: what secrets are hidden, buried out there, and possibly ignored or denied by modern archaeologists who may have fallen into the same fundamentalist mindset trap as have their religious peers?

As it is said, the truth is out there, not just for those who want to believe, but also for those who want to explore and discover. So, happy hunting!

Final Note: What makes this topic so interesting, and maybe even relevant, is the other topics that are related to it, specifically the beliefs about Inner Earth, extraterrestrials, angels, demons, the fallen ones, (the Nefilim), and the coming of Mashiah.

In the ancient literature and especially in modern "conspiracy" literature, all these issues overlap. If this were just an invention of modern times, I would dismiss it outright as fabricated entertainment. However, due to the fact that these intertwined topics are found in the most ancient literature and cross-culturally around the world, I am not so quick to dismiss them.

Indeed, being that the Sages of Torah also validate these beliefs, as a student of Torah, I am morally compelled to embrace them. As a student of life, along the path of discovery, my own curiosity has led me to my own encounters and experiences, of which I have documented in much of my literature.

These topics are indeed relevant today, very relevant indeed! And I believe that it is just a matter of time before everyone finds out just how relevant and shocking they really are!

Chapter 13

Pre-Adamic Civilizations, Secrets of the Kabbalistic Shemitot

(This essay is an older version of the previous one. It covers pretty much the same material as the previous essay, and is included here to ensure that this collection of essays is complete).

"For six years you shall plow your fields, but the seventh year shall be holy to HaShem, in that year you shall do no work"
(Lev 25:3-4).

One of the most controversial teachings among Kabbalists is the doctrine of the Shemitot, the cosmic Sabbatical epochs of pre-Adamic times. According to many of the great Rabbis, Adam was not the first human to have walked the Earth. These Rabbis teach that there were full pre-Adamic human civilizations that had arisen and were eventually destroyed.

Among the earlier generations of Kabbalists, prior to the *Ari'zal*, the doctrine of the Shemita was written about by nearly all Kabbalists, including the *Ari'zal*'s Kabbalistic teacher, Rabbi David ibn Zimra. These Kabbalists taught that not only is the source for doctrine of the Shemita to be found in the Oral tradition, they went directly into the simple and plain words of the Torah text to show that the history of time is not fully told in the Bible.

In the very beginning it is written, *"In the beginning G-d created the Heavens and the Earth"* (Gen 1:1). Immediately, the following verse states, "And the Earth was without form and empty" (Gen 1:2). The Kabbalists have noticed that the prophet Isaiah has written (45:18) that "the Earth was not created empty," revealing an apparent contradiction between Genesis and Isaiah. Yet, as it is known to every true scholar of Torah, there is no contradiction between what Genesis says and what Isaiah says. Something, however, is definitely missing; for when G-d created the Earth it was not empty upon its creation, as per Isaiah. How then did the Earth become empty as related in Genesis 1:2? This leads us to the inevitable conclusion that something is missing; not that part of the text is missing (G-d forbid), but rather something has been intentionally left out of the narrative. This is glaringly obvious to any student of the Bible.

I have even spoken to one Christian minister who, upon learning about this anomaly, had mentioned that he had heard of this before from reading Christian biblical commentaries. Therefore, it seems that we have a mystery, the secret solution of which, of course, is known to the Rabbis and Kabbalists. In the Midrash (Gen. Rab. 3:7) a question is posed of what was G-d occupied with, prior to His creation of our world. The Midrash relates that G-d was busy building and destroying other worlds. The Kabbalists have always had profound insight and understanding into the nature of these pre-Adamic worlds. Much of Kabbalistic literature discusses these worlds in detail.

Nevertheless, one will not be able to just open a book and read about them. Before I proceed, I find it necessary to provide you with the following introduction into the methodology of Kabbalistic study. Without this understanding, Kabbalistic teachings will never be fully comprehended.

Kabbalistic language found in the literature is highly cryptic and coded. One cannot just pick up a Kabbalistic text, read it, and receive the correct understanding of what is read. Only one knowledgeable in the literature can guide another through it. This is why this material is called Kabbalah, which means, "to receive". Only one who has directly received from one who has himself received from a qualified giver can be called a real Kabbalist. Even in religious Jewish circles, the majority of the students of Kabbalah are not learning from such Sages.

As for those outside of religious Jewish circles, whatever Kabbalah they think they are learning; they are sadly mistaken if they believe that what they are learning is legitimate and authentic. Unfortunately, teachers who are not properly qualified to be teaching Kabbalistic material are often misleading many secular students of Kabbalah. One can only be a true Kabbalist when one is trained, and is an expert in all areas of its subjects, and practices, and has received the Kabbalistic tradition from a known and bona fide Kabbalistic rabbi. Unless all these criteria are met, no such person has any business teaching Kabbalah.

Regardless of how many books one may study, this does not qualify a person to teach Kabbalah. The reason is that the would-be teacher has never been given the true keys to understanding the inner system. As for those who think that somehow they have gone around the system and received the inner understandings other than in the accepted way, such teachers may indeed have deep and profound insights. But at the same time, because they lack certain training, many of these teachers will be missing certain vital principles, which are necessary to know, and practice, before one can become a proper instructor to others.

The *Ari'zal*, the Ba'al Shem Tov and others have repeatedly taught that Kabbalistic understanding does not come about as Talmudic understanding does, meaning through rational, analytical learning. Rather, Kabbalistic understanding comes because of the unique introverted lifestyle that a Kabbalist chooses to lead, over and above that of his peers.

The observance of the Torah commandments, and an introverted lifestyle are two elements (among others) that enables a Kabbalist to receive that which in Hebrew is called Ruah HaKodesh, guidance by Divine inspiration. The job of the true Kabbalist teacher is to make sure his students are not only learning the right things, but that they are learning them in the right way. Only learning right things in the right way leads one to the right place. The opposite is, of course, true. If the right thing is learned in the wrong way, then the wrong way will make the right thing work in the wrong way.

Since the days of the *Ari'zal* (1570's), Kabbalah has been allowed to be made public to those who meet the ethical and moral criteria required to study it. The schools of the Kabbalah have, therefore, grown dramatically for there are a good number of worthy students out there. Yet, just because Kabbalah is now allowed to be made public does not mean that all of the Kabbalistic teachings are passed to every student, nor does it mean that all the secrets are revealed.

I assure you that among Kabbalists the vast majority of true knowledge still remains hidden in small private circles, each of which is guarded like the inner circle of the best intelligence agencies in the world. These Kabbalistic inner circles have been around since Talmudic times (and before). They are the ones who truly know what is going on in the world. They are the ones chosen by G-d to have the power to influence the course of human events. Through these secret groups of Kabbalists is fulfilled the verse, *"For the L-rd G-d does nothing unless He has revealed His secret to His servants, the prophets"* (Amos 3:7).

Now to return to the topic of the Shemita. It is written in the book of Leviticus that, "for six years you shall plow your fields, but the seventh year shall be holy to HaShem, in that year you shall do no work". It is also taught by our Sages in the holy Talmud (b. Sanh. 98a), *"six thousand years shall the world last, then for one thousand years shall it remain desolate".* Our Sages have learned from the secret meaning of the verse in Leviticus that the days of our world, i.e. our civilization, will be measured in the same way, as is the biblical Sabbatical year. Six years shall we labor, and in the seventh shall we rest. So, our civilization will grow for six thousand years, and then for a thousand years shall it "remain desolate" which means to be left alone to rest. After this time, it is said that G-d renews his creation.

The Bible proceeds to speak about the Jubilee year. We are instructed to count seven times seven years and then to proclaim a

Jubilee, a year of complete release. The Kabbalists have revealed that just as our civilization will last for the Sabbatical period of six thousand years and one thousand years of desolation will there be seven cycles similar to this, corresponding to a cosmic cycle of Sabbaticals and Jubilee. Therefore, according to this calculation, human civilization will rise and fall seven times, each for a period of six thousand years, with a rest period of a thousand years between.

Now arises the question, which Sabbatical are we in today? Many Kabbalists look back to the verse in Genesis and notice the discrepancy. They answer the problem of the emptiness of the land (Gen 1:2), when this was not the way it was created (Isa 45:18), by saying that we are not in the first Shemita. The Earth was indeed created full. It only became empty as a result of the previous civilization. They are the ones who left the land *"empty and desolate".* According to many of the Kabbalists, therefore, we are in the second Shemita.

Although they hold we are in the second Shemita, the Kabbalists do not exclude the possibility that we are in the third, fourth or fifth, but rather conclude that we are definitely not in the first. They say we are in the second, meaning we are in at least the second.

Rabbi Israel Lifshitz, the author of the authoritative commentary to the Mishna, *Tiferet Yisrael,* addresses the topic of pre-Adamic life in the introduction to the eleventh chapter of tractate Sanhedrin Drawing upon what were the scientific discoveries of his day, and the Darwinian conflict on creationism and evolution, Lifshitz points out that the Torah does acknowledge the existence of dinosaurs. These were the creations of the prior Shemita, he says.

Not only this, but Rabbi Lifshitz goes further to say that Adam was not really the first human being, but that there were countless people before him, which he calls pre-Adamites. This controversial view of Rabbi Lifshitz has placed his commentary and other written works on the taboo list in certain Jewish circles. They considered his revelations not in accordance with the spirit of Judaism. However, nothing could be further from the truth.

There are some Kabbalists such as Rabbi Yehuda Fatiyah who, in his *Beit Lekhem Yehuda* (2, 66a), wrote questioning certain aspects of the doctrine of the Shemita. Yet, even Rabbi Fatiyah, in *Minhat Yehuda* (pg. 222), expounds on a section of the Zohar that speaks of the pre-Adamic parents of Adam. He even states that Adam's parents copulated on the spiritual plane; that his mother conceived and gave birth to Adam's body, which, as I referenced earlier, was completely non-physical. Where Adam's parents came from, Rabbi Fatiyah does not say. However, he makes it quite clear that they are individual beings and not simply an appellation for G-d.

The Talmud in Hagigah 13b speaks of 974 pre-Adamic generations. One of the early Kabbalistic classics, the *Ma'arekhet Elokut*, states specifically that these generations refer to the pre-Adamic Shemita cycles. There are a great number of both earlier and later generation Rabbis, Hasidic masters and Kabbalists who have spoken quite openly about the doctrine of the Shemita. With regards to the Shemitot, Rabbi Shmuel Lifshitz opens his discussion of the matter in his *Anafim Shatul Mayim* commentary to *Sefer HaIkkarim* by saying *"[I] open my mouth like a talebearer to reveal hidden secrets".*

Not everyone, however, accepted the doctrine of the Shemitot. Rabbi Haim Vital in his *Sha'ar Ma'amrei Rashbi* 44a says outright that the doctrine of the Shemitot is Kabbalistically incorrect. Many later Kabbalists follow Rabbi Haim's position on this. Nonetheless, many more do not.

Rabbi Aryeh Kaplan has written on this topic of the Shemitot and pointed out correctly that Kabbalistic learning does not follow *Halakhic* learning. Whereas in Halakha there is need of an authoritative conclusion to decide proper practice, this is not the case with Kabbalah. Therefore, although Rabbi Haim Vital himself did not accept the teachings of the Kabbalistic Shemitot this in no way makes his words the final authority, even more so seeing that almost every other master Kabbalistic, before him and after him, disagreed with him on this matter.

Interesting to note is the *Sha'at Ratzon* commentary on the Tikunei Zohar (36). The author Rabbi Shlomo Kohen is one of the great later generation Kabbalists of the Rabbi Haim Vital/Rashash school. He is also the author of the authoritative commentary to Rabbi Vital's Etz Haim entitled *Yafeh Sha'ah.*

In his commentary to the Tikunei Zohar 36, Rabbi Kohen comments on the clear reference made there to the Shemitot and then mentions Rabbi Vital's objections to this view. Rabbi Kohen then elucidates a brilliant compromise how the view of the ancients and the view of Rabbi Vital can be synthesized.

Thus, no present day student of Kabbalah should be so quick to dismiss the doctrine of the Shemitot out of hand based on the comments of Rabbi Haim Vital, for as we see, they are open to various interpretations. Indeed, even the Gaon of Vilna in his commentary to the *Tikunei Zohar* 36 clearly states that the text is speaking about the pre-Adamic Shemitot.

Though my readers who are not Orthodox Jews will not recognize the following names, they are still important for me to document for the sake of my Orthodox Jewish readers. This is only a partial list of those Rabbis and Kabbalists, and works from the earlier and later generations, which held that the doctrine of the Shemita is correct and true:

- *Sefer HaTemunah*
- *Sefer IlaKana*
- *RaMBaN*
- *Rabbeynu Bahya*
- *Rabbi Yitzhak D'Min Acco*
- *Recanati on the Torah*
- *Tikunei Zohar*
- Tziyuni *on the Torah*
- *Ma'arekhet Elokut*
- *Shatul Mayim on Sefer HaIkkarim*

- *Sefer Livnat HaSapir of Rabbi David ben Yehuda HaHasid (Sefardi)*
- *Sefer Shoshan Sodot*
- *Radbaz, Rabbi David Zimra (the Kabbalistic teacher of the Ari'zal)*
- *Tekhelet Mordechai*
- *Rabbi Lifshitz's Tiferet Yisrael*
- *Rabbi Tzvi Hirsch Eichenstein of Zidatchov in his Ateret Tzvi commentary on the Zohar HaRakia*
- *Rabbi Eliyahu, the Gaon of Vilna.*

My orthodox Jewish readers will recognize that these names are giants in the world of Jewish learning; they are the pillars upon which our holy traditions rest. To say that all these giants of Torah are incorrect is to both dishonor these Rabbis and the Torah itself. The legitimacy of the pre-Adamic worlds has never been questioned in authoritative Torah literature.

Rabbi Tzvi Hirsch Eichenstein, in his commentary *Ateret Tzvi* (126b) on the book *Zohar HaRakia*, states that even though the *Ari'zal* himself was silent on this matter, he definitely ascribed to the doctrine of the Shemita and that *"G-d forbid anyone would disagree with the holy Sages of Israel".*

Chapter 14

Extraterrestrial Man, Israel & Torah

Introduction: *Every year at Shavuot, I perform traditional "yeridah" (descent) meditations. My travels, and the guides that I experience within them, never cease to enlighten me. What I see, and what I hear, I often keep private. Yet, this time, what I saw also came with the deep impression that I am supposed to be revelatory, but not necessarily to press dissemination with any real efforts. I got the impression that the following information is meant for those for whom it is meant.*

There is Torah. There is Man. There is Israel. There is Torah, Man and Israel here on Earth, and there are multiple (and possibly an infinite number of) manifestations of Torah, Man and Israel spread throughout the universe, and in parallel dimensions.

Torah, Man and Israel are all expressions of what is called in the later Kabbalah, the "Small Face of G-d," Zeir Anpin. The Zeir Anpin (ZA) is a cosmic reality throughout the entire universe. It exists everywhere. Therefore, we must conclude that no matter where we go in space or in parallel dimensions, there will always be there an expression of Torah, Man and Israel for they are ZA.

Here on our Earth we are all aware of the familiar forms of Torah, Man and Israel. Yet, as we travel to the stars and to dimensions beyond, we will come across other races of intelligent sentient beings. What we must realize is that like our Earth, their planets will also have Torah, Man and Israel, but these three will take forms that are indigenous and proper for those worlds, even as these three take the forms proper for our world.

Here on our Earth, Man has taken the form of the species homo sapien. But that which makes us Man is only wrapped in the garment of the biological form of homo sapien. That which makes us Man is far more than our mere biology. Man is said to be created in the Divine Image of Elohim G-d. We should never be so primitive to think that the Image of G-d is that of the Earth species homo sapien. Elohim G-d is far more grandiose than this, and so too is Man.

Man is created in the Divine Image. That Image, it is taught here on Earth, follows the pattern of the Ten Sefirot of Emanation (whatever that actually means). Our Divine Image is within, not external, and not biological. Therefore, if that which makes us Man can be put into the bodies of homo sapiens here on our Earth, then that which makes us man can also be placed into any other sentient life form, on any other planet, or in any other dimension.

As this is true of Man, so too, is it true of the concept of Israel. Again, Israel is an expression of Zeir Anpin, as such; Israel/ZA can never be conceived as existing in only one form, in one place alone. In order for G-d to be everywhere, so too must Israel.

What makes Israel to be Israel can never be limited to just one planet and one manifestation within one biological life form. Israel is itself a grade, a level within Man. As Man is everywhere, so too then is Israel. Israel is that level within Man that transcends the physical and higher dimensional planes. Israel is the conduit and the bridge between parallel dimensions. Israel is that part of Man that serves to unite the higher and lower domains, be it in the universe at large, or on each specific planet, with each specific manifestation of Man, in whatever form that they may take.

Ancient legend teaches us that in the beginning G-d gazed into the Torah and from it created the universe. Thus the entire universe came forth from out of the Torah. Therefore, everything in the universe has its source in the Torah. Everything in the universe is thus connected to the Torah and operates in accordance to its laws. Essentially, the laws of nature and the Halakhot of the Torah are one and the same. This insight is lost on the blind, but those with sight can see it clearly.

If Torah is the source of the laws of nature, then surely any and all other planets, races, and civilizations, in this universe or in any parallel plane, by exploring natural law are essentially studying Torah. Torah is everywhere in the universe, therefore, our Earth can never be considered its exclusive domain.

As we know from our Earth, Man includes Israel, and Israel received the Torah on Mount Sinai. As the Revelation happened here, so too did it occur on every planet, in every universe, in every parallel dimension, wherever there is a manifestation of Man. Yet, we must never forget that there is still only one Man, one Israel and only one Torah. It is just that this oneness is in essence and not necessarily in their finite, physical forms. There exist many faces but only One Voice that speaks through them all.

Throughout Torah literature there has always been talk of heavenly Jerusalem, the heavenly Temple, the heavenly High Priest, Israel above, and the original Tabernacle vessels, which our Earthly ones are only copies. These are all references to the realities to which I have referenced above. These teachings of our Sages are not just symbolic metaphors, built on Grecian philosophical speculations, and centered on teaching moral concepts. On the contrary, the Sages are teaching us about realities, the likes of which even modern man has a hard time to grasp.

If we ever wish to actually draw closer to G-d, to truly act as beings created in the Divine Image, to fulfill the destiny of Israel/Man on Earth, and to study Torah the way it was meant to be from the beginning, then we really need to redefine some of our fundamental beliefs. For far too long we have believed fairy tales about religion, when in fact the truth has been staring us in the face all along. No one will ever be able to move forward, unless one first unties the bounds that are keeping one back.

Redemption is bought with a price, a price that most are unwilling to pay. Although our world appears to be presently isolated, this will not remain the case for much longer. Revelations are coming, and once they arrive, they will not be denied. Who will be able to stand in the knowledge of the true Light of G-d?

For the record, homo sapien Man is not the first race of Man here on planet Earth. There were others, many other Men, before our present form. The older "men of Earth" have evolved off our planet to their own Olam HaBa (afterlife), from which they serve the Creator as Watchers (Teli) over the younger races of Man. Science fiction? No! Torah secrets, yes!

Chapter 15

Reconciling Religion with its Extraterrestrial/Telepathic Origins

We need to be ruthlessly blunt here. If one is to believe what is written in the Bible, then there are certain uncomfortable conclusions that we are required to accept, and equally uncomfortable questions that we are required to ask. Let's review some of them.

Number One: G-d is presented in the Bible as being all-present (omnipresent) and all-knowing (omniscient). G-d is essentially an alien "life-form," an "Entity" that is not of this Earth. G-d certainly is not human by any standard of definition with which we define what it is to be human. We can even question whether we can refer to G-d as an entity, or life-form at all. Essentially, what we call G-d would be a form of life completely outside the context of any presently known application of those terms.

Number Two: Prayer, we know, is a method of communication through which we communicate with G-d. Yet, prayer cannot simply be a dialogue of verbal communication, similar to that which one would have with a friend. When we pray, we are talking to G-d who certainly is not there physically to be seen in any manner. As such, prayers "ascend to Heaven," whatever that means. Essentially, prayers travel from "Point A," (us), to "Point B," (G-d). That "Point B" is a destination, again, not of this Earth. What is that place? How do prayers travel there? What is their energy source that makes this travel possible? What exactly is making the trip, is it the sound waves of the words of our prayers, or is it the brain waves of the thoughts of our prayers? If G-d is omnipresent, then does the concept of prayers traveling to Heaven really even exist?

Number Three: Torah was given to Moshe on Mount Sinai. Yet, where did it come from? Torah came to Earth from another domain, not of this Earth. The Bible says that at the giving of the Torah, the Heavens opened up. What does this mean? Is this referring to some kind of wormhole that opened into a parallel dimension, or acted as a bridge through space in this dimension? Moshe is said to have gone up to Heaven. Where exactly did he go? How did he get there? The Bible says he was up there for 40 days and nights. Did Moshe experience his time in Heaven as 40 days as those at the foot of Mount Sinai did? We have many legitimate questions, and only homiletic tales for answers. If there is anything actual and real to this story (as religious people believe), then we can no longer ignore the questions that we have raised here.

What really happened at Sinai? Where did Moshe really go, and what is this Torah that he received? According to the Bible, there is this entity which we call G-d. However non-human that It is, It still enables us humans to contact It (prayer), and then It made contact with us (Sinai/prophecy). These seem to be the undeniable biblical claims, three distinct biblical facts for believers in "the Word". There is a G-d, there is His Word, and we communicate with G-d, just like He communicated with us. Yet, we know that G-d's Word, the Torah, came from off-world. G-d Him (It)self exists in a state that by definition is off-world.

Prayer is communication with that which is off-world. We have a modern word, which we can use to sum up all these off-world references, and that word is "extraterrestrial". Now, I know that many "traditional religious" type of folks do not use, and do not like the use of the word "extraterrestrial," with regards to their spiritual and religious beliefs. Nevertheless, I think it is the right time that we dispel with religious myths and begin to embrace religious realities. If there is any reality, whatsoever, to religious/spiritual experiences, then such experiences must rightly be called extraterrestrial. This is simply because, if these things are real, then they certainly, are not of this Earth, and are thus by definition "extraterrestrial".

If one wishes to continue to believe in G-d, to believe in G-d's Word communicated to human beings on planet Earth, and to believe in our human capacity to communicate back with G-d, then in light of modern discoveries and revelations about the true nature of science and reality, we are required to discard old prejudices, and embrace what might be, for some, unpleasant truths, and these are that G-d, Torah, and prayer are all extraterrestrial by definition. Essentially, if the Bible is to be believed, then rather than look into the future for our first human contact with alien life, we had better start to properly understand our past. Let us turn our thoughts for a moment to science, and the laws of nature for some further insights into their matters. The universe is governed by the laws of nature, right? All things in the universe follow the course of the natural, right? All things follow nature, with rigid, unyielding accuracy. Oh really?

Practically speaking, it is true; everything does follow nature, and always will. But, what makes us so arrogantly sure that we understand nature and the natural way? In spite of all our recent discoveries, there is so little about science which we understand, and then there is so much more than we do not. All things may very well be natural, but we are a long way off from discovering the true parameters of nature.

While we observe nature, we expect nature to follow the laws that we see operating in it. Yet, scientific discovery is based upon seeing new things in nature that we did not see before. So, how much that is unseen and unknown today is still nevertheless operational natural law? Essentially, how many unseen, unknown, and undiscovered scientific forces are out there influencing us even right now that our present understandings of science does not yet include or acknowledge? Before one wishes to dismiss the supernatural and the metaphysical, one should recognize that there is more to these domains than meets the present eye.

Today, what is supernatural might tomorrow become everyday science. One will never understand the realities of that which we call the spiritual and the Divine, until we first begin to understand them scientifically, as actual and natural, telepathic, clairvoyant powers inherent within the human mind. Developing our latent mental/spiritual powers is the key to opening up experiences with those domains which today we mythologically call the spiritual. Yet, the spiritual is scientific, actual, and real. We only need to reexamine our relationship with it, to learn how to redefine it, and include it into our growing understanding of science and the universe. Many of these other domains experienced through spiritual practices are not physical in the same sense as matter is understood here on Earth.

Modern science now postulates that there are many alternate dimensions and parallel worlds. These claims have also been made by religionists for millennia. Rather than refer to these domains and the dominions that inhabit them as mythological angels or demons, the proper term to refer to them is extraterrestrial. Whether we refer to angels or entities, we are referring to, and seeking to interact with, life forms that are alien to both our forms of life and our world in general. With this being said, let us understand that real extraterrestrial alien life forms do not necessarily have to resemble any form of life that we can possibly imagine.

Other entities may or may not inhabit physical bodies, as do we, or they may be of an entirely different composite, possibly of substances that our modern sciences have not even yet discovered. Remember that according to modern science, based upon our present measurements of time, our universe is billions of years old. Who knows what forms of life were the First Ones, who have existed and evolved over a period of billions of years (as we measure time today)? Where are these First Ones today, what are they doing? Do they know about us? Are they possibly involved with us, as ancient teachings suggest? Are these First Ones the legendary angels that ancient tradition states were created on Day Two of creation? Are they the Watchers spoken of in the Bible? Are they the holy Dragons who are in the universe, as a king on his throne?

Think about this, if humanity continues forward without destroying itself, what form will it eventually evolve into over the next million years or so? Where will our technology take us a million years into the future? Now, extrapolate on this, and think, if the First Ones have been out there for a billion (or more) years, how much have they evolved? What is their science like? What have they discovered about the Creator? Would we even be able to recognize them as life forms? Would we consider them to be gods?

Our science fiction novels and movies have, for the most part, brought to us images of aliens as hostile physical entities out to take control of our planet. Granted, there may very well be numerous alien races out there, who, if given the chance, would conquer foreign worlds, rape them of their natural resources, and either ignore or exterminate the indigenous population, depending on what was convenient and believed to be correct. We should not be surprised that such hostile alien life exists. After all, we too are just like them.

We would be the hostile alien invaders, if given the chance to attack and conquer a desirable world, inhabited by what we would consider to be an inferior race. We have already done this throughout our history to numerous nations of people right here on our own Earth. We should never entertain the fantasy to think that we would not do this again on a foreign world, if given the chance. Fear of alien invaders is just a modern psychological projection of our own inner fears and hostile intentions. Yet, we should never allow ourselves to believe that actual alien life forms, however different from us they may be in appearance, will be very much different from us spiritually.

Humanity embraces certain spiritual/psychological universal constants, such as the struggle between good and evil. Yet, we should never limit the definitions of good and evil to applications and definitions subject to life here on Earth. In many ways, alien life will be so very, very different from us; then again, there will always be a side through which we will have commonality. And it will be through this commonality that we will be able to communicate. Yet, this commonality will not be through physical verbal speech, but rather through mental/spiritual telepathic communications. It is amazing, how in the greater scheme of things in the universe, we human beings are so insignificantly small. Yet, we aggrandize ourselves as being of central importance to the universe.

Religious teachers have taught about the importance and centrality of humanity to the universe. However, these teachings were never meant to be taken literally, in reference to our present finite, physical state, to create within humanity a sense of a delusional inflated ego. These ideas only endeavor to forward the agenda of humanity being more than just physical homo-sapien animals.

Indeed, from the relative side of our soul existence, we truly are great beings. However, almost no single human being alive, or who has ever lived, has ever tapped into their soul content, to unleash the extraterrestrial part of our humanity, while trapped here in our terrestrial bodies. So, practically speaking, although we have the potential for greatness, that potential is very far from being realized. Essentially, we are very small life forms in a very big (and crowded) universe.

In order for us to unleash our inner soul potential and psychic powers, we must come to an understanding of the way natural law directs the flow of natural energies. For the energies of nature, the energies of the mind, and the energies of life and reproduction all overlap one another in accordance to a very precise natural pattern.

Someone who can access their energy field can gain access to all the others'. This is why the scientific principles of the natural world, mind sciences like meditation, and energy practices having to do with reproduction and sex, all complement one another, and fit together like a hand-in-glove.

Being that these energy fields, of which I speak, are essential parts of the natural world, we can rest assured that the ancient First Ones, and those who have come after them, still, many millions of years before our present incarnation, know these things, and have been working with them, and using them for what for us may be billions of years.

We may religiously refer to the First Ones as archangels, who were created on the second day of creation. They wield the Divine powers of G-d, and are often called *El* or Elohim. But call them what we may, the underlying reality of their existence remains the same. If we wish to truly communicate with higher life forms not of our planet, then we are obligated to learn the form of communication that they use to transmit and receive. Being that energy is the commodity and language of the universe, energy itself is the language of choice. Being that our knowledge of science is so pitifully minimal, whatever we would broadcast in this wavelength certainly would not be strong enough, even to be detected. However, we can cultivate usage of these latent energies that lie unused in the mind and use them to tap into realms of higher consciousness.

We can even augment the mind/soul content by charging it with creative libido sexual energy. In the language of the later Kabbalah, the combination of these two are referred to as the union of the sefirot Tiferet and Malkhut. Essentially, doing this is nothing new; on the contrary, it is something very old. While many readers might conclude that I have delved here deeply into science fiction, I assure you that this is not the case. The difference between science fiction and science fact is a blurry line that is constantly subject to change. One should never be so quick to condemn and dismiss something as science fiction, because it may become tomorrow's science fact. Indeed, who knows what scientific discoveries and secrets presently reside in government laboratories or military bases.

Do not be so quick to judge and condemn based on prejudice and ignorance. Humans have a very long and ancient history of relations with entities from other worlds, be they in this dimension, or another. Biblical records clearly document this interaction and extra-biblical literature only reinforces it. Some will wish to dismiss all of these records out of hand. There is never a shortage of those who wish to proverbially stick their heads in the sand, close their eyes and deny everything. Yet, if we wish to move forward in human history, then the search for discovery, and the desire for uncovering truths, cries out to us to first look backwards into our past.

We have the technology to take us into realms previously inaccessible. What will we find there? Will we find those extraterrestrial races that the Bible and other religions have long referred to as angels and demons? If there is any truth to the Bible and to religion in general, then, in order for humanity as a whole to move forward into our collective future and growth, we must properly understand that which we already know, from our past, in light of that which we are now learning. Imagine the possibilities of discovering the realities of ancient lost truths, and what such knowledge can do for our future. The true religion of the future will be our revitalized understanding of the revelations of the past.

Chapter 16

Angels & Emotions, How to Best Serve G-d

Ask yourself a question. Do you believe that angels act with rational, calm, cool, and collected forethought? Do you believe that angels are like computer programs or the fictional race of logical Vulcans from Star Trek? Do you feel that angels are college professors and philosophers, or more like musicians and artists? Do you believe that angels think more or feel more? Are angels created in our own image, or are they actual and real extraterrestrial entities that exist in a way and follow rules of being foreign, unknown, and possibly unknowable to us?

How angels act is of paramount importance to those of us who believe in the Bible and believe in angels. Daniel 4:14 clearly states, *"The matter is by the decree of the watchers, and the sentence by the word of the holy ones".* If angels direct human fate, how then do they direct us, in accordance to what they think or in accordance to how they feel? If the angels are real and their influence is real, then how they interact with us is really important! Don't you think?

If you do not believe in the existence of the other side of reality, if you do not believe that there are entities out there, next to us, watching us and in many ways guiding and controlling us, then you really do not have to read any further. Some things cannot be seen with the eye, but they can be seen with an inner eye. Some things cannot be made rational and logical, but are nonetheless known to be true somewhere deep inside ourselves. So, if you are the platonic, superficial type, then have a nice day, go off into your blissful ignorance and live your life oblivious to the greater world in which you live. You will be awaken when the times comes. But for now, those of you who wish to be awakened now, please, read on.

For those willing to take the trip, passageway to the other side is both frightening and exhilarating. It both scares the pants off you and at the same time rips the wool off from over your eyes. Once you begin to see with the inner eye, nothing can make you go back to the blindness of mere physical sight. The passage over is not a one-time single act of meditation. On the contrary, once the trip begins, the passage continues. Meditation is not a single period of silence and isolation for a set period each day. Those who meditate like this and this alone are doing nothing other than relaxing. They are not going anywhere and are missing the boat that enables them to travel.

Real (kosher) meditation is for the sake of connection, to expand consciousness, to become aware of and to integrate awareness of the other world that is right alongside of us into our waking consciousness.

Meditation is not about the means; it is about the ends accomplished by using whatever means that one uses. This is why there are so many different paths and techniques. It is not that one is better than another (although this is true), it is rather that one works better for a specific personality type whereas a different technique works best for another personality type.

Long ago, the master Sages of the Passage clarified that teaching people how to pass into the parallel world should be taught best one-on-one and then only to one who already has inner foresight to see within. Those who can learn usually seek out learning. Those who cannot learn usually avoid learning and twist and turn it in every which way to make sure that in the end they truly learn nothing. So it is with blind souls.

Angels are a strange lot. As is clearly documented, there are many different races of foreign beings that interact with us. The term "angel" in English comes from the Hebrew word Malakh, which means "messenger". Yet, not all of the entities who we refer to as angels are actual messengers to us. Many of these races interact with the forces of nature and other life forms here on Earth.

We are taught that even every single blade of grass has its own angel who serves as Heaven's messenger to direct that blade of grass in Heaven's direction. Yes, everything really is under Divine control and direction, even down to the minutest detail. The idea of the Deist that G-d created the universe and then left it alone for us to handle is not true. G-d is very much involved with every aspect of His creation. Then again, it is the Divine edict that we too be involved and exercises our G-d given free will.

Angels direct and guide. That is their job. Yet, some angels, for some reason, take matters into their own hands and take actions disagreeable to Heaven. This situation was the case referenced in Genesis 6, when the sons of G-d (angels) came into our world and took human wives. Needless to say, this really "pissed off" Heaven and led to the desolation of the world with the Flood. When angels mess up their jobs and get involved wrongly with those that they are supposed to be guiding, Heaven acts swiftly and sharply to rectify the situation. As it was in the past, so too will it be at any other time in history, including today.

Now, back to our original question, are angels intellectual or emotional? For that matter, let us ask an even bigger question, is G-d intellectual or emotional? Maybe it is better to ask, does G-d deal with humanity intellectually or emotionally? Do you think you have the answer to this question? If you do, in order to be correct, your answer better be that G-d acts with us emotionally and not so much (if at all) intellectually. This fact is clear throughout every occurrence in the Bible where G-d is mentioned.

G-d can become angry, G-d can be appeased, G-d can be offended, and G-d can be honored. It all sounds rather symbolic and metaphorical, and indeed when the Bible does say that G-d feels this way or that, it is actually symbolic, but ask yourself, why are the symbols of emotion used? The answer is because G-d is a feeling entity, and so are the angels and so are we!

G-d created us in His Image, and this is the source of the human personality and human emotions. While the angels do not share with us the fullness of the Divine Image, they too are nonetheless emotional beings and can be offended or honored. Angels are emotional beings and they interact with us based upon human emotion and not human intellect. This is the reason why angels can be felt, but not seen. Our feelings within can become sensitive to the presence of angels, whereas our intellectual minds can reach out and intellectualize them. This is why psychic phenomena are emotionally based and not an intellectual faculty. It is a sixth sense, but it is empathic.

What we call the spiritual world, the dimension closest to us, is not balanced between intellect and emotion as we are supposed to be (but seldom are). The entities over there are feeling entities. What they feel is what they do. This reality also helps us to recognize their influence in this world, when they appear to influence the minds and actions of human beings. Whenever a human being acts based upon some irresistible emotional urge, with passion and zeal, the chances are that such irrational behavior is being motivated by a "little voice" whispering into one's ear.

"Little voices" of this nature, we can plainly see do not always come from the side of good. They can equally come from the side of evil. Many times, either individuals or even nations commit murder and bloodshed because of some irrational, illogical compulsion that just drives them forward, motivated by hate or whatever. All these murderers know is that they just must shed blood. Regardless of how irrational such actions are, if one pauses to stop and think about them. Those so possessed by this spirit never stop or slow down to think, until their nefarious activity has been accomplished. Then, all of a sudden, it is like a cloud has lifted itself from over their minds and their minds are able to see. Only then do they ask themselves, what did they do? Many murderers have experienced exactly this.

Just like the "little voice" can motivate one for evil, so too can such a voice motivate one for good. The biblical example of this was Phineas (Pinchas) as recorded in Numbers 25. The Bible records the episode that Midian used sexual seduction as a means to attack Israel. The intent of the Midianite women was to seduce the Israelite men into weakness and passivity, thus not to attack their nation. Even one of the leaders of the tribe of Simeon (Shimon) was so seduced. When a man of such a stature can be toppled, it is a bad sign and a terrible role model to the nation.

Phineas, son of the High Priest Eliezer is incensed with this act of flagrant disobedience, endangering the entire nation with its blunt public challenge to Divine authority. Without any authority and without any human direction, Phineas picks up a spear and takes matters, and the law, into his own hands. He pursues the offending leader, executing him and his Midianite paramour in the midst of love play, in the man's private tent.

This action is clearly an act of murder. This was in total violation of the law. Phineas himself should have been arrested, tried and when found guilty, executed for the crime of murder. Yet, this was not to be. For Phineas did not act on his own accord. His was not a premeditated act. Phineas was possessed by a spirit (angel) of righteousness and indignation. His act was one of fiery emotion. But his act was not one of hatred, not at all!

Phineas was possessed by an angel of G-d. Many say, he was possessed by the spirit of the prophet Elijah, who is known to be the angel Sandalphon. G-d knows all things. Thus, G-d spoke and declared that Phineas's actions, while technically murder by human standards, were considered to be proper, right and holy by Divine standards.

Phineas's act of zeal shocked his nation, but impressed Heaven. Heaven is motivated by emotion and is impressed with emotion. Phineas acted emotionally, possessed by a spirit of righteous zeal for his L-rd in Heaven. Knowing this, G-d intervened in the normal course of jurisprudence and informed the Children of Israel that Phineas's great act of sacrifice will be rewarded. Heaven was impressed with his emotional zeal and thus such a man, in the future will be of great value in communicating with Heaven. Phineas is, therefore, ordained to become the next High Priest, after his father retires.

Phineas was not originally designated for this job, and a murderer is disqualified from it, but G-d intervened and showed that the Ways of Heaven are far different than the Ways of Humanity (Isaiah 55:8-9). As it was with this episode in the Bible, so too is it with us today. G-d always looks to our hearts and not to our heads.

This is why G-d commands us to love Him with all our hearts (Deut 6:6) and to place the words that He commands us upon our hearts (Deut 6:7). G-d does not tell us to put these words into our heads, but rather into our hearts. G-d wants us to feel His words, not just think about them. In this way, we become like the spiritual beings that surround us.

Those who can integrate emotional passion into their thinking processes can open themselves up to spiritual realities. Whether or not one will be opening oneself to good or evil will depend upon the nature of the individual, their personal moral character and the righteous choices (or lack of them) one chooses to make.

The other dimension, next to ours, might rightly be called the World of Emotion, or the World of the Heart. The Sages of Wisdom have called it such for centuries. Learning how to feel is not an easy thing. Living by feelings alone is outright dangerous. People who always follow their hearts, not listening as well to their heads, usually follow their hearts into terrible places, with much suffering and personal harm. Today, we are not Phineas. G-d will not intervene prophetically to defend us from our wanton choices.

Our best bet today is to live by G-d's commandments, to take time daily to commune with Him and to keep communing until it becomes our second nature. We must learn to feel again, this is true. But our human feelings must be tempered with our human rational thought. When these two are in proper alignment and balance, we can unleash our latent psychic abilities and know things that are invisible and even foresee the future. This inner psychological balance is the key that unlocks the doors inside the mind that allow us passage to the other side, to enter and to exit in peace and to commune with the angels themselves.

Chapter 17

Secrets of Contacting the Angel Raziel

It is through the power of concentrated thought that one can create and project an image into the greater collective consciousness. While all humanity shares a collective consciousness, so too is humanity's collective consciousness part and parcel of the even greater collective consciousness of the universe. It is these mechanics that enable human souls locked in physical bodies to reach out and communicate with non-physical entities of all levels of intelligence from various dimensions and other places in space and time.

Communication with other races and species is a natural process and it happens all the time. However the modern rationalist approach seeks to deny the reality of these things. Therefore, often all such communications are condemned as being mental illnesses. A person who publicizes one's interactions with non-human, pan-dimensional, and possibly extraterrestrial beings is mocked, possibly imprisoned in a mental hospital or put on drugs that poison and confuse the mind thereby jamming any further communications.

Those who are willing to cast aside the fears, prejudices, and mind control of those seeking to enslave the masses can easily restore their innate abilities to communicate with the Others. Prepping the mind for contact is not hard. Yet, once appropriately primed and ready to communicate, proper communication must then ensue.

Consider it to be similar to communicating over the Internet. First one learns enough computer basics to know how to get on and get connected, then one learns about email, eventually about online chat and maybe even live video conferencing. One's skills develop one step at a time and lead one to greater abilities to be in touch with those far away.

Yet, now that one knows how to "reach out and touch someone" just whom it is they want to reach out to is clearly demarcated. The Internet is full of charlatans and evil people who misrepresent themselves for the sake of harming other souls. Communication in the higher realms is no different. Once one learns the proper skills, one refines their availability and only accepts communion from those of their choosing. However, it is during the process of "learning the ropes" that is the most dangerous of times.

As one reaches out into the great collective, like on the Internet, one draws much attention to oneself that is most unwelcome. To defend oneself against cyber infiltration we have computer firewalls and security protocol software. In the higher realms, we have equivalent spiritual measures, which are as valuable and important for guarding the soul as the programs on the computer are in guarding the machine.

Safeguards for the mind/soul are essential for psychic self-defense. These safeguards, like computer software, serve as precise "software" for the mind/soul (hard-drive). These safeguards are not subjective realities; they are not subject to personal opinion or taste. There is nothing artistic about them. Mind/soul safeguards function as objective realities in the greater collective consciousness. They cannot be invented or made-up. Like software and firewalls, either one has the "real deal" or one will learn the hard way by not having the proper means to work in the right way at the right time.

The mental safeguards have been passed down in the Hebraic oral tradition since they were first given to humanity in the days shortly after Adam and Eve's original descent to Earth. The legend describing this reception is well known in Judaic literary circles to this day. The legend, in highly metaphorical terms, describes the encounter between Adam and G-d's messenger (angel) Raziel, whose name means, "secrets of G-d". The common element in the various different versions of the story is that Raziel transmits to Adam a secret book that reveals to him the working and mechanics of the universe. This sacred manual dealt with all the laws of nature created by G-d and included all that we consider today to be the physical and metaphysical, natural and supernatural.

Mental safeguards are not just psychological beliefs and concepts. They are actual elements incorporated into the mind/soul and most essentially include one's making allegiances with other entities of various levels and races whose job it is to join with us to jointly confront and attack the forces of evil. Not all of these other entities are what we call angels. Their personal involvement is essential, for without it we could never navigate the necessary course through the dimensions that they inhabit.

The later, theoretical mystics have forgotten all about the need for guides and have mistakenly viewed the literature that documents this travel and interpret it in light of their own lack of experience and practice. In these vital areas of precision there is no room for the blind, especially the blind that wish to lead the blind. Those with experience who walk the path in reality, simply ignore the blind and leave them behind, knowing full well that they will never be able to see or understand. Part of the path is being able to recognize these false guides and to avoid their snares.

Passage into the other realms requires precise ritual observances similar to the laws and procedures for developing software or for building hardware. One can have all the good intentions in the world, but if one does not do the right things, in the right way at the right time, then nothing right will result. If one wants to design a computer program, one has to be precise and detailed. Flaws cannot be tolerated, for the damage they cause can be catastrophic. This lesson holds true with the means of communication, the message of communication, and the work that entails once communication has been established and solidified.

Raziel is a "real" entity, so is Sandalphon and so is Metatron. Yet, what most do not know is that these entities themselves are collective beings. Many entities share a single hive-mind, all thinking together as one, although their number is legion. There is only one Raziel, but many entities are part of the collective Raziel. The same is true of all the others in the angelic host. This is what is meant when it says that an angel has so many underlings serving under him. Essentially they are all part of him and are essentially he, himself. This is a reality shared by us human beings, but at present, we are for the most part oblivious to this.

As we tap into the higher forms, our scope of vision increases enabling us greater insight into the universe and into the collective consciousness of humanity. This level of access is called in some modern circles the "Akashic Records". In Torah tradition, this is called the "Primordial Torah" and the "Well of Souls". This is the collective consciousness and the collection of all souls in Adam.

From this point of higher insight, the one so attached can read and see the thoughts, ideas and minds of others, learning from them and influencing them. One can put thoughts into another's mind without person knowing that the thoughts in his head have come from some other, outside source. This is mind/soul manipulation. It can be used for both good and evil.

One who can tap into the collective record realizes that there are no limits placed by time and space. They can mind travel through time and across space to anywhere and to anyone in existence. This travel was well known to the ancient mystics and practiced regularly by them. In this way, one living in this world could make actual contact with someone from another time and place. The procedures for this interaction are known and taught to this day. They were practiced by some of the greatest Sages throughout the history of Israel (modern and ancient). Contact of this nature is actual, conscious and can often take physical appearance, as the entity contacted takes form using the material matter of this dimension.

True leader mind-souls will humble themselves and walk towards the light and towards the others who are there waiting for them. It is often frightening coming to learn and experience new things. But without learning and change, our mind/soul sleeps deep within us and seldom awakens. It is time for the sleeper to awaken.

Chapter 18

Metatron, the Secret Soul
of the Jewish Mashiah

(In this essay that I wrote long ago, I used the politically correct form of the Name Metatron, Mem-Tet, and did not spell out the angelic name Zagnazgael. I no longer care for such useless political correctness, however being that this essay was written in this format, I decided to leave it as written, with just this small introduction as an explanation).

"The staff shall not depart from Yehuda, nor the scepter from between his feet, until Shiloh comes, and the obedience of the people be his"

(Genesis 49: 10).

In the final Torah portion of the book of Genesis, Ya'akov Avinu blesses his sons before his death. With regards to Yehuda, Ya'akov makes reference to "Shiloh". Yet, no explanation is given as to whom Shiloh is. According to Onkelos, Midrash Rabbah, and Rashi, the name Shiloh is a reference to the future Melekh HaMashiah.

Belief in Mashiah and awaiting his coming is one of the Thirteen Principles of the Jewish Faith. It is a core belief of Torah. Yet, study about the coming of Mashiah, how this is to occur, and what this is to mean for mankind is not widespread.

RaMBaM writes about the coming of Mashiah in his Hilkhot Melakhim. Yet, he emphasizes there that what he writes are his own opinions and not necessarily the only way to understand the subject. On the other hand, the mystical literature of the holy

137

Mekubalim (Kabbalists) is rich with material about the topic of Mashiah, who he is, why he is, and what he is to accomplish. This material however is rarely made available to outsiders of the Mekubalim schools, all the more so available in a language other than Hebrew. While this topic rightly deserves to be covered in depth in a book of its own, let it suffice for now just to skim the surface and learn who Mashiah really is and what we can do to help speed his coming.

Concerning the name "Shiloh", the commentator Ba'al HaTurim notes that its gematria (numerical value of the letters) is the same as that of the name Moshe. While the Ba'al HaTurim does not elaborate on this significance the master Mekubal Rabbi Haim Vital does, in his *Sha'ar HaPesukim* (*Vayehi* 20b). There has always been an interesting mystical relationship between Moshe Rabbeynu (Moshe our Teacher) and the Mashiah. Moshe was our first redeemer and the Mashiah will be our last. The question is whether this relationship goes any further. Moshe Rabbeynu and Mashiah; what is their relationship? Rabbi Haim tells us:

It has already been referred to in the Zohar (1,25b), Ra'aya Mehemna (Pinhas 246b), and the Tikunim (21, 52b) that [the name] Shiloh is numerically equal to [the name] Moshe, for it is he who is Mashiah ben David. ... Now, regarding Mashiah ben David, it is written, "Behold, my servant shall be enlightened, he shall be extolled and exalted, and be elevated immensely" (Yishaya 52, 13). [He shall be] "extolled" more than Avraham, "exalted" more than Yitzhak, "elevated" more than Ya'akov and "immensely" more than Moshe. This is the explanation, Mashiah ben David will merit the Neshama of the Neshama [essence of the soul], that which not even Moshe merited receiving. We thus find that the first shepherd, Moshe, he himself will be the final shepherd, even as our Sages have referred to in the Midrash. Therefore "Shiloh", who is the Mashiah and Moshe, add up to an equal numerical value. For they are one, [the only difference] is that the Mashiah is the Neshama of the Neshama of Moshe.

Apparently, Rabbi Haim is telling us that Moshe Rabbeynu himself is to come again and be the Mashiah. While this is true, it is at the same time not exactly true. Rabbi Haim clearly states that

Mashiah will be the Neshama of the Neshama of Moshe Rabbeynu, which is a level of soul that Moshe did not acquire when he lived here on Earth. However, Rabbi Haim fails to mention to us here that this Neshama of the Neshama of Moshe Rabbeynu has already incarnated on Earth and we knew this soul by a name other than Moshe Rabbeynu.

This is an intriguing mystery, the higher soul of Moshe Rabbeynu, who is none other than Mashiah himself already incarnated on Earth. Who? When? In order to understand this question we must first learn more about this Neshama of the Neshama of Moshe Rabbeynu and what relationship Moshe had with this lofty aspect of his own soul. This will require of us to delve into some of the deeper secrets of the Torah.

In Exodus 3:2, it states, *"and the angel of HaShem (G-d) appeared to him in a flame of fire from within the bush"*. This is the famous story of the burning bush, but notice that it specifically is the "angel of HaShem" who appears to Moshe, and not HaShem Himself. The Ben Uziel Targum even identifies this angel by name, and translates the beginning section of this verse as, "and Zag***, (sorry, no angel names allowed in translation) the angel of G-d was revealed to him". The *Perush Yonatan* identifies this angel and calls him Moshe Rabbeynu's teacher (Rabo, i.e. his Rabbi). This angel is also referred to as the Prince of the Torah. What we must do now is to learn more about this angel Zag*** and his relationship to Moshe Rabbeynu and to the Torah.

The Gaon of Vilna reveals a profound secret in his commentary to the Sefer Yetzirah (1:1, ofan 3, 3a) that sheds great insight on the relationship between a man and his Neshama soul.

The Neshama soul is the mind [of a man] that teaches him knowledge. It is a man's mazal (guiding destiny) and his angel (spiritual teacher), as is known. [The Neshama soul] exists in Heaven and [only] sparks [of it] descend to a man to guide him and to enlighten him.

The Gaon is telling us that one's angelic teacher, magid, and guide is none other than one's own higher soul. As for Moshe Rabbeynu, his Neshama soul was actually the Neshama of his

Neshama. Zag***, the angelic teacher who taught Moshe Rabbeynu Torah in Heaven was none other than Moshe's own Neshama of his Neshama. In other words, the angel who taught Moshe Rabbeynu was none other than his higher Self, who is none other than Mashiah.

Apparently, therefore, Melekh HaMashiah is an angel. Yet, what type of man is an angel? Angels by definition are on a lower level than the Neshamot of men. Therefore for this angel to be an "angel" and at the same time be Moshe Rabbeynu's Neshama of Neshama, he must be a very special lofty being. Indeed, this Zag***, Prince of Torah, is none other than the Sar HaPanim (the angel of G-d's Presence), Hanokh-MemTet himself. Enoch, as is well known, ascended to Heaven alive (Gen 5:24) and was transformed into the angel MemTet. He is the chief archangel whose name is the same as his Master's and like HaShem also has seventy names, one of which is Zag***

Rabbi Haim Vital confirms this for us in his Likutei Torah (Vilna 19a) where he clearly states that:

Enoch was on a higher level than Moshe for he was his teacher. He was the angel Zag*** for he achieved the Hayah (the Hokhma soul) and Moshe the Neshama (the Binah soul), but Mashiah will achieved the Yehida (the Keter soul).

Zag*** was Moshe Rabbeynu's teacher in Heaven; thus, Moshe's teacher was none other than Enoch-MemTet. He is related to the Neshama of the Neshama of Moshe Rabbeynu in that he is one step higher on the ladder of souls. Yet, Mashiah is still one step higher. Moshe Rabbeynu, Hanokh, and Mashiah thus share a unique bond. These three individuals all share the same soul, each at his own level. This is not a unique occurrence, for Avraham, Yitzhak, and Ya'akov also shared the same soul, each at his own level.

One must understand something here about the relationships of souls. All souls of Israel are interconnected and in a sense form one great super-soul. This was the nature of the soul of Adam before the Fall. According to a secret teaching recording in *Sefer Emek HaMelekh*, certain souls left Adam before the Fall and thus did not descend with the others. These were the souls that emanated from the three supernal sefirot Binah, Hokhma, and Keter. Collectively these souls became known as MemTet. The three sefirot of Binah, Hokhma, and Keter are forever joined. Therefore, Moshe Rabbeynu, Hanokh, and Mashiah are all the same soul. Each of them together therefore is Zag***, MemTet, and Melekh HaMashiah. Yet, the highest of the three, the soul of Mashiah, is the Keter (crown). He is called the source soul of Adam and of Israel. I confess in my brevity that I have revealed an inch and concealed a mile. This is necessary for now.

MemTet rules over G-d's entire universe, not just here on planet Earth. Thus when Melekh HaMashiah comes, he will be MemTet incarnate. As such, he will serve as G-d's regent over the entire universe and not just king here on Earth. Mashiah will be to HaShem what Yosef was to Pharaoh in Egypt. Thus, we see that the role and authority of Mashiah is not merely limited to this world. Much more is revealed in the mystical writings about Mashiah and his mission; yet, I must be brief for lack of time, and space.

There is a practical lesson to be learned from knowing the true identity of the Mashiah. Understanding that he is the source soul of all Israel, each one of us must realize that we have a spark of Mashiah within us. The Ba'al Shem Tov, (S.B.S.T. Nitzavim 8) writes:

Every one of Israel needs to rectify and prepare that part of the stature of the Mashiah that is related to his soul. As it is known [the three letters that spell the name] Adam (A'D'M) stand for Adam, David, Mashiah. The original stature of Adam [before the Fall] was from one end of the world to the other (Hagigah 12a). The souls of all Israel were included [and united] within Adam. After the sin, his stature was lessened. Thus, Mashiah will become the "complete stature" of all the souls of Israel... as Adam was before the Fall. Therefore every one of Israel needs to prepare that part of the stature of the Mashiah that is related to his soul, until the entire image is rectified and complete.

When we ask when Mashiah will come and what we can do to shorten his way, we must first look within before we look without. By reading RaMBaM, we might draw the conclusion that to bring

Mashiah, we must wage war. While this is true, we must remember that the first war we need to wage and win is the war against the blemishes within our souls. We must bring Mashiah to ourselves psychologically before we can expect to bring him politically.

The coming of Mashiah is no mere political event. When Mashiah comes, it will change the course of human events and evolution forever. The incarnation of archangels among us is no small matter. Mashiah is no mere man, nor mere angel. Although he will be born a normal human being of a flesh and blood father and mother, (as were Enoch and Moshe Rabbeynu), the soul of Mashiah will include within it all of ours. He will be a real "superman" as were Enoch and Moshe Rabbeynu before him. Yet, each of us has a spark of this "superman/woman" within us. When we observe Torah and mitzvot, we are strengthening the aspect of Mashiah within ourselves and within collective Israel. Mashiah is the "father soul" of Israel. As such he can and will transform the world using the power he has received from us.

At this time, we must renew our efforts to strengthen ourselves, to refine our souls for the sake of collective Israel (which is all humanity, far beyond the confines of physical Israel). We must make ourselves ready for Mashiah. Only then will Mashiah be ready for us.

Chapter 19

What to Expect When Mashiah Comes

The nature of Mashiah is often misunderstood. Granted, Mashiah is supposed to come as a savior, to step into the middle of a very nasty war between Israel and its enemies and to destroy those enemies with an overwhelming show of force. Then, once Israel is safe and its enemies no more, we are all supposed to live happily ever after. Everyone is supposed to love one another; we expect all to live carefree lives, and life will be blissful and utopian. This is what the majority expect the Mashiah is to accomplish. There is however one simple problem with all this: this utopian fantasy is not what the biblical prophets prophesied.

The same prophets of the Bible who informed us that there would be a future intervention of superior force to overwhelm and destroy the enemies of Israel also tells us that what follows is no "kumbaya" love fest, similar to a gathering of 60's-style hippies. On the contrary, Mashiah is expected to overwhelm and destroy a lot more than the military enemies of Israel, he is prophesied to also destroy entire segments of human civilization that have not lived up to certain expectations.

Mashiah comes to rule as a king and dictator. Nowhere in any biblical or later Torah literature does it state, suggest or even insinuate that Mashiah will rule by force of love. The hippies aren't going to make it; neither will the "kumbaya" crowd. Mashiah is not going to be very open to variables or questions to his rule, authority and power. The future King will rule with a rod of iron, not one of rosebuds. Symbolically our Sages referred to this when they said that in present times Torah Law follows the lenient views of House Hillel and when Mashiah comes Torah Law will follow the strict views of House Shamai. Of course this is a metaphor, not to be understood literally, nonetheless, the intent is clear. When Mashiah comes, there will be "no more Mr. Nice Guy".

King Mashiah will not be known for his sweetness, but rather for his swift and quick judgment, which the prophecy states, he will execute by literally smelling the litigants. No trials, no testimony, no deliberations. One sniff and he'll know whether you're guilty or innocent. Mashiah will know all hidden truths and judge telepathically. Some today might not consider this to be the proper liberal way. Then again, where throughout all of biblical literature is Mashiah ever referred to as a liberal?

Biblical prophecy and later Torah literature all describe the coming of Mashiah as an event of global if not galactic proportion. The consequences of his intervention in human history will certainly not be limited to the nation of Israel. It is prophesied that Mashiah comes with an army of angels from out of the sky. In other words, they literally come from out of this world. And this signifies that not only will Mashiah's invention be global but its influence and affect will reach far beyond the reaches of our planet, and possibly beyond the confines of our presently known universe. After all, where did this "angelic" army really come from? The term Heaven is mythical. It obviously refers to some real place; yet where this place is, in our universe or in another is not clearly understood.

The prophet Zechariah clearly states that Mashiah marches on Earth backed by an army of angels. It amazes me how so many are oblivious as to what this prophecy seems to suggest, especially in light of modern technological knowledge. Angels are clearly described in the Bible, some are humanoid entities that seem to glow with some kind of energy; others are clearly described as having multiple faces, animal-like features and other traits that we can only describe as un-earthly. So, when Mashiah appears in the skies over Jerusalem with an army of these entities, I do not believe that such an advent will be recognized in the religious context. I do not believe that those witnessing this event either live or on worldwide television, will be saying, "look, up in the sky, Mashiah has come!" I think they will use words very different from "angel" or "angelic" to describe the invading Messianic army.

Rather than call out "Hooray! Here comes Mashiah," I believe those witnessing this event will rather call out "Aaahh! Invasion from Outer Space!" Yes, you guessed it, the world will call the coming of Mashiah as an invasion from outer space. In light of today's loss of biblical religiosity and the embrace of secular science as the new world religion, the world will interpret the fulfillment of biblical prophecy in light of modern myths. Therefore, Mashiah's coming will indeed be interpreted as an invasion from outer space. And who amongst us can say what is science and what is spirituality, and what exactly is the difference between the two?

Judging from how prophecy describes the way Mashiah and his army is supposed to act, extraterrestrial invasion might be the proper way to understand the coming event. After all, Mashiah's army will display a superiority over all the world's technology and weapons. With the greatest of ease, the Messianic army will completely demolish the forces opposing it, just like what we would expect from an invasion from outer space.

Just like in our worst-case scenario science fiction movies, where the evil aliens come, smash the Earth and take over, so in reality, according to biblical prophecy, Mashiah comes, wipes out a massive army of resistance and then takes over the world. Once he does this, he is not transformed into a loving sweet grandfatherly-type of guy. Nowhere is Mashiah prophesied to go around singing, dancing and hugging everyone in the streets.

Mashiah is not going to be personally accessible to the general public any more than any other present political leader today. No one is going to be able to travel to his seat of government, walk in on him and just say hello. If today one were to attempt to approach a President, Prime Minister or King without permission and clearance such an endeavor would be prevented by a wall of security. Why on Earth would anyone expect access to King

Mashiah to be any more lenient? Such a wish or hope is beyond wishful thinking, it is delusional and unrealistic in the highest sense. Even G-d is unapproachable to the angels, so much more so Mashiah will be to the everyday common person.

The prophecies clearly state that during Messianic times much will be expected of the nations of the world and any failure (or rebellion) on their part will be met with terrible consequences. True, all Messianic prophecies speak of a world finally in an utopian state, but arriving at this state and maintaining it is never described as being a simple, free and easy process.

While enlightenment is supposed to be enjoyed by a good portion of the world population, not everyone is to be so blessed. True, they will reap the benefits of the Messianic utopian state but they will still have the ability if not the will to rebel. Mashiah will thus maintain order for a very long time with stern vigor. True, they will beat their swords into plow shears and their spears into pruning hooks and nations will no longer wage war, but where does it say that these events are going to transpire willingly? Just because prophecy states that they are destined to happen, nowhere does prophecy state that they will be desired to happen.

One thing is clear about the Messianic age; religion will become a thing of the past. All the world's religions, and these include Judaism, will cease to exist in their present forms. The entire human race will be exposed to a grander reality about the universe, our own human past and our collective human future in the greater universe.

Kabbalistic Messianic prophecies state that during messianic times the human race will advance to such a point that the very wall that divides the physical/spiritual divide will finally be broken down. We will be able to interact with what today we call the spiritual on a regular basis in a very regular way. Spirits will be recognized as another form of real actual life, living in a parallel dimension of sorts. No longer will spirituality be a subject of religion, but rather of science, and not science fiction, but actual science fact. This reality alone is what will shatter everything that is old and usher in upon us all a truly new age for all humanity. But don't think for a minute its revelations will be warmly welcomed and easily embraced.

Even the coming Third Temple is not going to be the religious edifice and return to the past that many today think it will be. The oldest tradition in Torah, recorded in the Talmud itself, speaks of the Third Temple descending down from Heaven fully built, and that it will "land" on the top of an earthquake-adjusted, now very high peak that was once Moriah, the Temple Mount. When this grandiose edifice is witnessed descending from Heaven; what will the witnesses call it, a building, or something else? Possibly in the UFO/invasion mindset that will be so prevalent at the moment, many will interpret such an event as the landing of the "mother-ship," something akin to recent Hollywood films.

I pray that I have shown here that the long awaited coming of Mashiah is not going to be what the vast majority in religious circles think it will be. The dawn of the Messianic era will bring with it tremendous iconoclastic upheavals. Almost everything that we all know and believe will be altered, changed or gone. It will indeed be a whole new world and a fresh page in a new chapter for the continuing saga of humanity.

Chapter 20

Different Kinds of Angels & the Master Plan

Angels are among us, but what are they really up to? While we say that they work for G-d, what really is their master plan?

If we are all surrounded by guardian angels, then why do so many bad things happen to good (angelically guarded) people? Are the angels not doing their job? Or, is there more to their job than what we believe?

If angels are working for G-d, and they are faithfully executing the Divine Will, and still, bad things are happening to good people, then we are left with a troubling question, what exactly is it that is G-d's Will? What does He want, and what, if anything, do we have to say about it?

If we cannot get direct answers from G-d, then maybe we can receive some answers (however direct or indirect) from G-d's messengers, the angels. Yet, contacting angels, while not impossible, is still not an easy task. After all, there are angels, and then there are angels.

There are angels that appear like human beings, there are angels who appear like dragons, and then there are angels who appear like things that defy description. Of all angelic appearances recorded in the Bible, never is there recorded an encounter with an entity that is anything other than a wonder.

The Bible is clear that there are many different types of angels. Although some are described by name and appearance, nevertheless, the full list of angel species, their descriptions, and their functions is nowhere biblically documented. Later Torah literature provides much more information than does the Bible alone. Yet, even with all the information that we do have, we can rest assured that there is so much more that we do not know.

When angels interact with human beings here on Earth, they always take on the forms of fellow human beings. As is recorded with regards to Avraham in his tent, Lot in Sodom, and Joshua overlooking Jericho, the angels here are all described as human beings, indistinguishable from other human beings. Even later, with regards to the angelic announcement of the birth of Sampson, a very human-like angel appears. His secret identity is not ascertained until the entity turns into a puff of smoke and ascends with the smoke of the sacrificial offering.

We have other recorded instances where the angels are described as somewhat human, in that they are humanoid. However, these humanoid beings have a glow about them. Their skin color is clearly not human, and there are other elements about them, which we might interpret to be supernatural. While they are humanoid, they are certainly not human.

Then there are those angels, the likes of which are described by Isaiah and Ezekiel. These classes of angels, referred to by names such as Ofanim, Hayot/Cherubim, and Seraphim are clearly not human, possibly not even humanoid, and very clearly extraterrestrial in every way. While these entities certainly have their duties and responsibilities, they do not seem to be the same messengers that are appearing to, and interacting with, human beings. Thus we see that there are angels, and then there are angels.

Throughout Torah literature, there has always existed ways and techniques as to how to contact the various species of angels. It must first be realized that there are angels whose essential existence is similar to a computer program. They come into existence to perform a purpose or task, and once said task is complete, so are they. These messengers can be compared to a programmed operation on a computer. They might have differing levels of artificial intelligence to enable them to fulfill their mission, but that is about it. These types of artificial life forms have no soul. They have no past, nor any future. There is nothing to talk to them about and therefore no means of dialogue.

While one may become aware of their presence, and with training, even possibly change their programming, (however much this may upset Heaven). This reality underlies a teachings of our Sages how Heaven can issue a decree and the righteous can nullify it. Needless to say, for a righteous person to be able to nullify a Heavenly decree, he has to know what he is doing, and cannot rely on delusional self-deceiving wishful thinking, and hollow religious proclamations.

Those angels who appear to us from time to time as fellow human beings seem to be under strict instructions never to reveal their true identity, and to never allow our human wishes and desires to get in the way of them fulfilling their missions. While this type of angel has a soul and can very much think, its thoughts, nevertheless, are on its mission, and nothing else.

While every now and then one may be recognized, and if engaged in conversation may, from time to time, drop some interesting hints, or secrets about this or that, still, these angels very much maintain control of the relationship. They cannot be pushed, bargained with, or pleaded with. Indeed, those who try such endeavors will usually find a friendly face quickly turn unfriendly, often with unpleasant consequences. Essentially, when it comes to this kind of angel, they (if they chose) contact us. We do not contact them.

The next variety of angel is the type that we can absolutely reach out and touch. These angels are not physical, but they are nevertheless, always with us. They are what have become popularly known as our Guardian Angels. In Hebrew, these entities are called *Magidim*, Guides, and their purpose is to be our teachers, and even our protectors, if and when we deserve such protection.

Magidim are our personal conduits to the other dimensional planes and to those that dwell in them. If and when we were to astral travel in our body of light (*halukha d'rabbanan*), our Magid actually serves as our chariot (merkava) of transportation. Essentially, we begin to experience our Magid as an external entity, and as a being separate from the self. Yet, as the relationship develops over time, and with training, we merge consciousness with the Magid, and essentially join minds with him/her.

When there is a communication of any sorts from within this state of merged consciousness, we have channeled telepathic communication. Some call this Divine inspiration, or the Ruah HaKodesh. It may very well indeed be such, or then again, it may be something entirely different. Not every channeled work that comes from a higher source necessarily comes from G-d; even if and when it comes from a being that we may call (for lack of a better word) an angel.

Magid work is very common. Indeed, over the centuries, many a great Torah sage had his individual, respective Magid, who was responsible for channeling to him many profound secrets. Yet, being that the Magid was an individual's Guardian Angel, the Magid was limited in teaching the individual within the context of that person's learning and mental context. All Magid revelations are subjective in nature. This is what is referred to in prophetic meditation literature as the *"Espekloria Sh'ayna Me'ira"* (the indistinct mirror). Rather than receiving a clear and pure reflection of absolute, universal reality, a Magid only reveals that which is unique to each individual. This is why numerous works of Magid literature do not all calibrate with one another. Each one reflects the reality of its author.

Once one has achieved the level of Magid absorption, he can indeed penetrate further into the higher realms, and seek contact with actual Cherubim, and maybe even Seraphim. However, contacts of this nature, which include actual revelations from the Sandalphon and Metatron collectives, are most often very dangerous.

Entities of this collective are ancient, conscious, sentient beings, each with a life and purpose of its own. To be drawn into conversation with a flesh and blood human here on Earth is considered a terrible inconvenience, an almost painful experience for these entities. They do not like to be drawn here, unless it is absolutely necessary and directed by above.

If and when a human being is successful to call upon one of these entities, and contact is made, usually in the *halukha d'rabbanan* (astral) world, the first thing any one of these very fiery entities asks is why has a mere mortal of flesh and blood drawn them away from what they were doing in order to talk to him? If one does not have a very, very good answer and reason, he might find himself quickly succumbing to a heart attack, or some other form of quick death.

These entities are not to be trifled with. While ways of contacting them are known, nevertheless, such methods are closely guarded secrets of those "in the know". To release these secrets could be compared to putting a loaded gun in the hands of an infant. The resulting damage could be lethal.

What we must learn from all this information is that we live in a very complex and crowded universe. We must learn that reality is far from what we think it is. We must learn that others are watching our every thought, our every desire, and certainly our every word and deed.

Essentially, human beings here on Earth are like toddler children in school. While we think that we are here to play, there is an entire school administration in place to make sure that we are educated. We may be totally oblivious to the school administration, and the school curriculum, but regardless of our ignorance, these things are nevertheless there, and indeed, they are strictly enforced.

What we think is real, is a fool's dream. Our entire reality is like a single bubble among infinite realities. All the bubbles bump into one another, and push each other around. Some even pop others. Our individual bubbles are our individual subjective perceptions of reality. However, we are so convinced (and wrongly so) that each perception is the ultimate true objective reality. And we wonder why others are so stupid and dumb that they cannot see the things that are so clear to us. Often, the reason for this fact is that one's person's reality is not the others. This is true in this world, and most certainly in the higher worlds.

Quantum reality is as much a reality in human consciousness, as it is with the sub-atomic particles that form the vessels for our consciousness.

Yes, angels are among us. Yet, they live in a quantum state of flux, which makes their reality very much relative and subjective. They know this, and know of no other way. We are the ones who do not know the bigger picture. And so, it is the job of the messengers (angels), from higher domains, to teach us, and direct us so that eventually we will get to the point where our education can take hold, and the purpose for us being in school is accomplished. This is why THEY are here, and this is THEIR plan.

It might not as nice and pretty as we would wish, but this is the underlying truth beneath all our individual relative, subjective realities. They are all expressions of Din and Gevurah. Rigidity is called Din (judgment). Rigidity is Gevurah (severity). As long as we are narrow-minded in a singular point of view, we will forever be under the powers of the subjective (Din/Gevurah) nature of this reality, which we ourselves create and maintain.

The master plan exists in a quantum state of flux, and until we can elevate human consciousness to such a quantum state (Hesed/mercy), we will have to remain in school until such time that our lessons are complete. This is THEIR plan, and THE PLAN. This is why THEY are called the WATCHERS. THEIR job is to watch us, and help us grow.

Chapter 21

Angelic Dominions & Human Influence

Learn from the Sages the ways of the Messenger/Watchers, the angels sent from Above to observe and to intervene here below.

Sefer Tziyuni

"And the Canaanite was then in the land" (Genesis 12:6). The Kabbalists have written that one is not settled in a place until one's guardian angel first comes and establishes his presence there. This is why the verse says, "And the Canaanite was then in the land". Afterwards, it is written, "And the Canaanite dwelt then in the land". Also with the Covenant Between the Pieces (brit bayn habatarim), immediately the angels of Israel descended into Egypt and remained there until the exodus. This is the meaning of "at the end of 430 years all the forces of G-d came forth," meaning, even the angels...

Rabbi Avraham revealed another secret: The truth is that no nation falls below on Earth until its guardian angel is first toppled in Heaven, as it says, "G-d attends to the Hosts of Heaven, in Heaven". The wonder of this is that we do not find the exile of Israel in Egypt to be properly measured at 430 years, unless we begin the time from the Covenant Between the Pieces, for that is when the angel of Israel descended from his heights and was made subordinate beneath the angel of Egypt. This is when the actual slavery began.

Sodei Razaya

Angels have bodies that are very
thin [ethereal], like the wind (spirit)
that is fine and not seen, for their bodies
are from air and fire.

Angels whose names end with "el" are the guardians of the
nations, and they fight with one another like bucking rams.

Angels are judged on what they
could have thought, but did not.

Angels are different from one another so that they will
recognize who is who. This is true of the Princes and souls,
not one of them knows what the thoughts of another are.

The angel who guards over a person
has the image of that person.

Imarot Tehorot

G-d send angels to each individual in accordance to the
individual's thoughts. Angels are dispatched to the righteous, and to
the wicked, each in accordance to their thoughts. A good angel will
guide the righteous in the ways of righteousness and truth. An evil
angel will guide the wicked along the path of deception. An average
person will be guided only in an average way.

Let us draw some conclusions based upon these revelations. It is taught that not only does every individual have their own personal guardian angel; nations as a whole also have their national guardian angels. Just like one's personal behavior directs how his angel interacts with him, so too does the behavior of a nation dictate how its angel interacts with it. While our nations are under angelic dominions, we, as the citizens of our individual nations, have the power to influence those dominions. This is why social and political involvements are so important. While we may not be able to single-handedly change the course of national events, each of us individually can contribute greatly towards influencing the spiritual dominions that guide us. One should never underestimate the power of one, even when opposed by the many.

Angels, by no means, should be understood to be benevolent entities, like they are popularly portrayed today. Scripture, and later Torah tradition, makes it very clear that the angels are messengers for higher powers not of this Earth. Like G-d, their thoughts are not like our thoughts, and their ways are not like our ways. Call them what you will, but angels are the very definition of what we call extraterrestrial. They are not like us, even though they are very much interconnected with us. While they faithfully obey that which is dictated to them, nevertheless, they have a will of their own, and the power to execute it as they will.

Those who think that all angels are nothing more than some form of glorified spiritual computer program, that only act in accordance to their programming, without any sense of consciousness or will, are not thinking in accordance to the Sages. Those of the rationalist/philosophical schools within religious thought can only speculate about the reality of angels based upon what they read in books; know next to nothing about the real nature of these actual extraterrestrials entities, whom we have come to call angels of G-d.

It is clear from Torah sources that the angelic dominions fight and struggle with each other on a regular basis. It is because that these entities struggle with each other for dominion and power that their conflicts are experienced in the unconsciousness of the members of their respective nations, causing there to be conflicts and wars among men here on Earth.

Little do we understand the psychological connection we have with these clearly extraterrestrial entities. Little do we understand how they regularly influence us, at the personal and national levels.

Little do we understand that these influences can be a two-way street; as they influence us, so too do we have the power to influence them. It all depends upon our actions and behavior.

Chapter 22

The Angelic Watchers
& Our Human "Big Brother"

The sentence is by the decree of the watchers, and the demand by the word of the holy ones; to the intent that the living may know that the Most High rules in the kingdom of men, and gives it to whomever he will, and sets up over it the lowest of men.

(Dan 4:14).

The materialization of a [Heavenly] edict into actuality, [in other words] enacting and enforcing the edict is by [intervention of] the Irin (watcher/angels). And they received the matter from the words of the Kodashim (holy ones/archangels). These are the higher angels who asked of this matter from those above them [who in turn ask it] from the One above them who is the Holy Blessed One. And the reason for such edicts is so that all life will recognize that the Kingdom of Heaven rules over humanity.

Malbim Commentary to Daniel 4:14

Torah is clear on this point. All matters of unfolding world events be they great or small, are decided by higher non-human authorities.

This may sound like the plot of a science fiction novel or the subject of the latest conspiracy theory about a coming "new world order". Yet, there is nothing new about this concept. This agenda is not fiction and there is nothing conspiratorial about it at all. This is Heavenly revealed truth directly out of the Bible itself.

We live in very special times. As a planet and as a race we are about to experience great changes from the ways things always used to be. We are at the dawn of a new age and a "new world order". Yet, as with every new day, it is always darkest before the dawn. Night must conclude before the sun begins to shine. Dawn is upon us, but it is not yet sunrise. Before one eats the fruit, its peel and husk must be removed. While we are in the process of its removal, we have reached it thickest, most hard to remove section. With just a little bit more effort we will soon be able to enjoy the succulent fruit.

Torah is clear; we need no conspiracy theory to warn us; there definitely are secret hidden powers that are molding and shaping everything that is happening in the world today from behind closed doors. Whatever crises that may arise, whatever threats of war or devastation; they are behind it all. They are its authors. Their motto is simple; "out of chaos comes order". Create and control the chaos and one can then impose and maintain order. It may sound ominous and threatening, but ultimately, it is G-d who is running the show. All forces here on Earth, under it or from outside it who may have a hand in world affairs are still but mere pawns in the Greater Hand of Heaven.

Yes, a new world order is being molded all around us. It will encompass everything; all areas of life will be integrated into the great new global system. No part of human life or interests will escape it or be exempt from its influence. A global world culture of secularism is already taking root. It is succeeding in breaking down the attachments billions have had with their former religions. While the forms of religion are maintained the essence of true religion is being gutted. Soon there will be a push to organize a new one-world religion and new social order will follow. Almost everyone will embrace the new with great expectations and hope. They will embrace the new world order and all the promise it holds.

As for those remaining few who stubbornly refuse to go with the flow and who ignorantly wish to cling to the old antiquated ways of the dead past, they will be viewed as dinosaurs with no future other than extinction. Those who want to live in the past can die with the past; this will be the attitude of the new world order and its population of happy to follow, willing to obey citizens. The old-timers, regardless of age or background will become outcasts; unable to live or interact with the new world in any size, shape or form.

The old guard will be stripped of property and possession, dignity and rights. They will effectively become non-persons, homeless, and jobless, without any way to make a living or to fend for themselves. Many will be rounded up for efficient disposal. Others will flee to wherever the long arm of the new Big Brother will not reach.

As treacherous and overwhelming as this new world order may appear it is still nothing more than the latest manifestation that Heaven allows here on Earth to test the will and souls of individual human beings. Big Brother or no Big Brother; it is the Big Father that we have to fear. Big Brother is merely one of his many sons and totally under Big Father's complete control. Torah has taught us, it is not humanity that decides human fate, but rather it is the Higher Hand of Heaven. Whatever is destined to come upon us, each of us will face our individual destinies in accordance to the Heavenly decree.

Many people are preparing for an apocalypse. Many are preparing for the collapse of western civilization and an ensuing period of anarchy and social, civil war. Many are preparing for the big Israeli/Arab war. Many are preparing for a nuclear World War III that who knows who will start but is expected to last only twelve minutes, during which time one-third of the world is expected to be destroyed. We have no end of apocalyptic, end-times scenarios. No one knows which if any will play out, but one thing is for certain, change is coming. What forms it will take and when it will occur only time will tell.

We must understand a lesson about predicting the future. The future is not exactly written in stone. Biblical prophecies that are objective and unchangeable still have a number of different ways in which they can be fulfilled. Although we know what the end may be and even though we know things that must happen before the end may come, still no one knows exactly the order of events, the intensity of their occurrence and the exact form in which they will manifest.

Prophecy is a rather quantum form of communication. Prophecy is fulfilled dependent upon how it is viewed and how we approach it. Our human choices can make the fulfillment of prophecy either benign and painless or severely harsh. It is all up to us. Prophecy tells us what will definitely happen, but it does not tell us how it will come to pass. There are numerous divergent roads we as a race can choose to walk.

Regardless of whatever form prophecy is fulfilled; regardless of whatever powers the coming new world order acquires; no matter what happens, everything is still under the watchful Eye and Hand of the Almighty above. When I am asked what people should do to prepare for the times to come, I tell them that the only preparations needed are spiritual and psychic. One must cultivate their inner spiritual power. This alone will enable one to see the moving Hand of G-d through all the coming turmoil and deception. Only with this spiritual insight will one be able to dance and move across the stage of life, to be in the right place and the right time for the right things to happen in the right way.

There is no plan that one can learn; there are no other preparations that one can make. For today one must learn to live the Way of Torah and allow this Way to transcend and transform every fiber of one's being. One who surrenders to Torah becomes a living, walking, and breathing Torah. The Torah will always live forever. The secret of eternal life, therefore, is to become living Torah.

Living Torah marches to its own beat, to the rhythm of the *ta'amim* (cantillations). They move high and they move low, then they move in between; always in movement, always in flux, ever changing, ever moving, like the beat of a living heart. This is the secret of survival. The one who uncovers this secret will unleash tremendous spiritual powers. Those who know have the knowledge and more so, they are the knowledge, for they bond with it. The knowledge, the knower, and the known, merge together and become one. As it is above, so is it below. This is the secret unity of G-d, Torah, and Greater Israel (Knesset Yisrael, referred to in the Zohar). This is something no Big Brother can control.

Prophecy states that the coming redemption will mirror the ancient redemption. The coming of Mashiah will mirror the coming of Moshe. Just as we see the veils of the darkness of exile about to close in around us again, let us keep the faith that this too shall pass. As in the past, so will it be in the not too distant future, the light of dawn and true freedom shall reign supreme. The Big Brother and all his cohorts will fall and this time they will be finally destroyed. This is prophecy and its fulfillment is inevitable.

The Watchers are watching all. Like master chess players, they are the ones moving all the pieces. In this game of life, we are all the pawns, even the great secret powers that are moving things behind the scenes. They give their orders in secret and make things move and shake on a global scale. Yet, they themselves know that they too are only following the orders dictated to them from higher, more concealed powers. The influence follows up the chain to the very top, to the Head Commander, who is none other than the Holy One, blessed be He.

Let the nations maneuver and plot. He who is in Heaven laughs at them with a mocking roar (Psalms 2). Let them send forth their hand against us. If it is Heaven's Will for us to succumb to their schemes, then we will succumb. After all, if Heaven wishes to test us or harm us, G-d does not need a Big Brother to carry out a grand conspiracy. We could easily slip on a banana peel or choke on a chicken bone. Just as easily as G-d keeps us safe from that banana peel or from that chicken bone, so too can He keep us safe from Big Brother. This is our faith and our life. We are in Higher Hands. We just have to keep this mindset and not allow ourselves to be lulled into slumber and thus lose focus.

The Watchers are watching us. Their role is to teach us to watch Heaven and to watch for the Hand of G-d to move us. When we live Torah, Torah lives inside of us. In this way we will hear its voice speaking within our hearts and our conscience. We will know what to do, when to do it, and in what way; all at the right time. One does not need a ticket to board a flight before being ready to embark. When the time comes, those with vision will see that they already have everything that they need. As for the rest of us, the present time is our gift to get ready by learning how to see with the eyes of the inner Torah.

As the great Sage of old said, *"The day is short, the workers are lazy, the reward is great and the Master is urgent".* He also said, "It is not incumbent upon you to finish the job, but neither are you free to avoid your share". The Watchers are watching and waiting. What are you doing?

As the Torah never really ends or begins, so our relationship with HaShem is continual. We pass through many cycles in our relationship with our Creator, at times feeling close and at times feeling distant. Yet our relationship with our Creator resembles the cyclical nature of the Torah or the steady march of the Earth around the Sun. Like clockwork we pass through times of enlightenment that are bright as a summer day and we pass through sad times where we feel lost as in the dark wintery night. Yet, cycles always flow, there is always movement. So it is with our souls before G-d. We are always in a process of movement towards our own self-perfection, guided as we are by the invisible Hand of G-d.

Chapter 23

Be Mindful of the Watchers! But, Fear Not Their Coming Agenda!

Imagine a combination of the most sinister conspiracy theories, coupled with the scariest of science fiction thrillers. This may closely describe the way things really are "behind the scenes" today. The situation today is utterly different than it appears at first glance. Efforts to begin exposing the truth will only be immediately dismissed, and denounced, as insanity and paranoia.

The general unrest in the world is indeed so bad today that to try to expose its underlying causes, or even anything close to it, may prove to be a dangerous undertaking. Yes, the world today is really that bad! And worst of all, as chaotic as everything seems to be, it is all, in reality, under a very tight and strict control.

Yes, everything is proceeding exactly according to plan. And there is nothing that anyone is able to do about it. Every detail is thoroughly under tight, secure control. In spite of any appearances to the opposite, the only amount of free choice left to us, is that which was planned from the outset. Things are the way they are, and maybe the scariest revelation of all is that this is exactly the way G-d wants it to be!

According to ancient "ascent" literature, both biblical and post-biblical, the earliest of which dates from the days of the Babylonian exile in the 5th century BCE, humanity is under the constant eye, and control of a group of extraterrestrial entities, referred to in the Bible as the "Watchers". This arrangement is apparently ordained by G-d, and it is through the system executed by these messengers from On High, that real governance of our planet and our race is maintained.

Generically, in English we call these extraterrestrial entities, angels. However, by applying this term to them, we inevitably fall into mythological fantasy, and project onto these otherworldly entities human-like notions of goodness, kindness, and love. We ascribe to them everything good and pure the way we imagine it to be. We fail to comprehend, and often refuse to accept, the contrary. We have been programmed to believe the deceptions and lies, most likely projected into collective human thought by THEM, to conceal their true identities, and their true agenda.

In truth, people love to be lied to, and they love to believe lies. Most people do not want to awaken from the lies and fantasies that they embrace. I suppose that if the agenda of the Watchers was to keep humanity in a state of perpetual mental sleep then it would not matter much at all what we did, or did not, dream. But the Watchers' agenda is not to perpetuate humanity's permanent sleep. On the contrary, their plan is to awaken us, and our awakening requires that we stop dreaming, stop believing fantasies and lies, and begin awakening to the frightening reality that we have been oblivious to for far too long.

The sleepers must awaken, and this is not an enjoyable or rapturous experience. On the contrary, it is like awakening from a nightmare. The last thing in the world it will be is easy. On the contrary, the nightmare always gets the most frightening just before we awaken, and this is where world history, and collective human destiny, is now heading. So, what secret reality is humanity being prepared to awaken to? This, of course, is the big question!

Whatever be the answer, in religion, the answer has always been referred to as the Messianic Age. Yet, even the usage of this term, "Messianic Age," creates within our thoughts mythological images that have been imprinted within our minds by thousands of years of religious interpretations of ancient prophecies and texts. They may indeed contain secrets and mysteries that have not been discovered even to this day.

Essentially, something big is coming for human history. This event, and the transition that it will introduce, have been planned from the very beginning of human history, and apparently, all of human history has been orchestrated to bring us towards its predestined end. So where we are today in history is simply on one of the ever-turning pages in the great book of the never-ending story of man.

One fact that we must always keep in mind is that no matter how bad and out of control events appear to be, everything is still, nevertheless, under the constant scrutiny of the Watchers, and ultimately under the guiding Hand of G-d, the Creator. Everything that is transpiring now behind closed doors, under the tightest security, on or inside this planet, everywhere else in this universe or in others, is all transpiring following the Higher directives issued from the Source of All, in Heaven. Humanity's history is G-d's game. Heaven has designed us, and has never ceased directing all of the action. Just because we do not see the production crew behind the scenes does not mean that they are not there.

The Watchers are indeed there, they are indeed very much in charge, and it is they who are pulling all the strings behind everything that is occurring now on Earth. Just remember, as they pull our strings, so too are their strings being pulled on High. Puppets controlled by puppets, controlled by puppets, controlled by puppets, controlled by G-d, this about sums it up.

Remember, this planet is not ours, it belongs to G-d. The human race is not ours, it too belongs to G-d. All the aliens races, out there and in here, also, all belong to G-d. G-d will do with His creation as He wishes. And the Divine plan, we must understand, deals with the fate and destiny of many more races of beings than our own.

Life is indeed a long road. Human history is indeed a mystery. Our future, is not blessed or bleak, rather it will be what it will be, all based upon the Word and Will of G-d. Humanity, and this planet, has a schedule to keep, and Heaven will indeed make sure that the Watchers keep things proceeding according to the Divine plan.

As for us, for the most part, we should sit back, let go, and watch the play unravel about us. We too are each being watched. We are being observed to see whether or not we have learned the lesson to act humanly, and humanely. Crises only come to test us, to see if indeed we have learned the lesson(s) which we came initially to Earth to learn. If we learn our lessons, then we get to move on to bigger and better places and things (Heaven, Gan Eden). If we panic and fall back in fear, acting like little frightened animals instead of like rational humans, then this too will decide where we end up next (Hell, Gehinom).

Remember, the choice is always ours. The Watchers are watching; G-d is judging. The world is heading towards its destiny and we will have to choose whether or not to let go of that which must pass, or to continue to embrace it, and go down with it when it finally sinks.

Attitude is everything! We either witness a world heading towards its very destruction and doom, or we witness a world in crises heading towards adjustment, rectification, and rebirth.

Attitude is everything! Do you see just the darkness of the tunnel, through which we walk, or do you see the light at the end of the tunnel, and thus pay no mind to the darkness presently surrounding us?

Please, accept this warning. Do not let curiosity drive you to try to contact the Watchers. They are not what you expect. For good reasons they keep their identity and true nature concealed from all but a very few souls.

Although there is literature out there that identifies both them and ways to contact them, nevertheless, such paths are extremely dangerous. The Watchers do not value human life the same way we do. Do not fear them, but be mindful of them, and keep your distance. The Watchers are not here to be benevolent or malevolent. They are here simply to do their jobs, and that is just what they do! So, fear them not, and fear not their program and plan for humanity's future. Stand by the side, be like the Watchers themselves, and keep your focus on Heaven, serve G-d, fear not, fear nothing!

Live today, and let tomorrow be taken care of by G-d. What is happening behind the scenes hidden from our eyes would terrify and frightened even the most stone-cold heart. So, let it be! This is G-d's world, G-d's plan, and G-d's Watchers! G-d is even in control of those little gray guys, with the buggy night vision eyes, in their gravity-free ships. Big deal!

In time, those proven to be true human beings, because of their humane behavior, will get to know and not fear all the other creatures in the Universe that G-d has made. Like us human beings, not all of them are good guys, but nevertheless, they are still G-d's creations. Our job, now and forever, is to serve Heaven, and to act humanely, even to nonhuman entities, and so we shall!

As for the rest, let it go, and let it be! G-d is with you, now it is time for you to be with Him. In conclusion, what the Watchers appreciate most are good and decent humane human beings. They are obligated by Heavenly law to respect them and to make sure safeguards are in place for their wellbeing. All we have to do is to follow suit, and take care.

Chapter 24

You're Being Watched? So What!

You're being watched, you do know this, don't you? Now, don't get paranoid and think that Big Brother and the New World Order conspiracy is behind all this surveillance. Even if they are real and indeed monitoring and influencing everything that we do, nonetheless they too have to be taking their orders from somewhere, and someone. Conspiracy theories abound on just who THEY may be.

One of the fundamental concepts of Torah is the reality of absolute "Singularity". This is what we call the unity of G-d, as embodied in the Shema Yisrael prayer, quoting Deuteronomy 6:4, "YHWH our G-d, YHWH is One". The concept of the Singularity essentially states that everything in existence came forth from a single Primordial Existence and it is still essentially connected to that Primordial Existence. This Primordial Existence is responsible for everything that is, has been, and will be. It controls each and every aspect of reality, great and small; similar to how a programmer writes each and every detail of a computer program. Ultimately, however complex and diverse existence may appear, nonetheless the entirety of creation is still essentially and functionally under the control and operation of the master program, which is none other than the Singularity; the Primordial Existence.

So when we look out upon our world and see all types of ominous happenings, when we read about so many strange things and find our minds assaulted with conspiracy theories and paranoid fears, in the end we must recognize the ultimate Singularity and understand that everything happening, however intricate and varied it may seem, is still just part of the great program written by the master programmer. Every bit and detail is part of the greater whole.

Therefore, if there are secret powers that are controlling our human destiny and guiding all humanity towards an ominous future, rest assured that these secret powers are taking their orders from yet even higher authorities. Know for certain that even those higher authorities take their marching orders from yet even higher authorities following up the chain of command until eventually we arrive back to the ultimate source, the Singularity, Primordial Existence, the Great Programmer itself. So, ultimately, however diverse and complex as things may appear everything is still running within the normal operational parameters as designed by the Primordial Programmer.

So, what then is there to worry about? What then is one's great concern? We might think that because everything is under control, then nothing really matters and that we might as well just live life as easily as possible and just float along for the ride? This flippant attitude is responsible for so many of the troubles that we presently face. Our attitude needs a serious adjustment!

Think about this; what is existence all about? Yes, I know, it is a really big question, but its practicality and personal relevance cannot be denied. Ask the great question in this way: why am I here; what is my life all about? Am I here on Earth to do nothing more than I am already doing? Does my life have any meaning or purpose? Am I lost; am I found, am I in the right place or am I out of place and out of touch? Ultimately, does any of this matter? Shouldn't I just live my life the best I can and be done with it? After all, who knows what, if anything, awaits us on the other side. Is that interest really worth any concern here and now?

Let me be blunt. We are each here for a specific purpose. Each of us has a destiny. We each have a job to do while we are alive here in this lifetime. More than this, we have assistance to accomplish our individual goals and destinies. This assistance is nothing nebulous or generic; it is very real and specific. We might call it angelic, or we might ascribe to it another, more modern name. Names are irrelevant, so I choose not to us them. Allow me to basically state that we are not alone; not in our universe and not on our own Earth.

We are being watched. Yes, right here and right now THEY are watching us. THEY record everything that we do, say and even think. THEIR existence is not like ours. THEIR agenda is not like ours. THEIR essence is not like ours. IF we were ever able to see one of THEM their appearance would "freak us out big time". This at least was the experience of the biblical prophets, Isaiah and Ezekiel who did indeed see them. The biblical book of Daniel talks much about THEM. Daniel called them the WATCHERS.

THEY are the ones watching us and it is THEY who are spiritually giving the marching orders to the political, social and economic world leaders. If there really is any kind of world-wide conspiracy for a New World Order out there, then we can rest assured that whoever may be in charge of it, are themselves being directed under the influence of our Heavenly Father, and His angelic court.

Many of you might be laughing now in disbelief. But so what? Your disbelief or mocking attitude will change nothing; it will not alter reality in the least bit. You can deny the truth of anything all you want; it does not make that truth go away or become any less relevant and real.

The WATCHERS are doing their job as they were sent here to do. THEY are in control of governments and world events. THEY do this through the influence they exert over the minds of human beings. Through our dreams and unconscious THEY communicate with us and essentially program us, just as if we were individual programs in the great computer. Although we still have free will and the ability to choose whether or not we follow the program, still THEIR presence surrounds us and THEY manipulate our individual environments to curtail our possibilities making it almost certain that we choose to do one thing over another. This explains why when we may desire or choose a course in life we find that either there are many doors open to assist us or many doors closed that inhibit us. It is THEY that are creating the open and closed doors. There is no coincidence or anything random about life at all.

Life is full of distractions. Anything that keeps our minds from recognizing the Great Singularity is a distraction. The Watchers are here to help keep us focused. If we seek to discover Truth, then they prepare the way for us so that we will ultimately succeed. However, if we choose another path, one that entails our embrace of distractions and worthless pursuits, THEY stand there in the inner recesses of our unconscious minds gnawing at us, making us feel shame and loss.

Sometimes, when we are so distracted and removed even from our own inner thoughts, the presence of the Watchers produces within us feelings of depression and lack of strength or will. The Watchers are there to remind us that we allow ourselves to get lost. It is their job, as designed by Heaven to watch over us; to guide us back home when we are ready and to constantly nudge us all the while that we are not.

We live in a universe that is much more complex than anyone today can possibly imagine. We human beings are subject to forces and powers that we cannot even presently imagine to exist. Our lack of insight does not make these universal natural forces any less real or influential. Today, we understand scientific concepts that only a century ago would have been laughed at and mocked. Think about what we will know in another one hundred years that we mock and laugh at today.

There is an old saying; where there is smoke, there is fire. What this saying means is that if we suspect something and there tends to be some evidence of validation, then we should conduct a thorough investigation to explore and discover what is really out there. Rest assured that modern talk about extraterrestrial life and related topics have their foundations in fact. Rest assured that the powers that be know more than what the public is told. Rest assured that this is nothing to fear. The Singularity that we call G-d is well in charge of all things and what we know and do not know is still very much under the control of His greater hand.

During the special days of Rosh HaShana and Yom Kippur we perform many different religious rituals. Many perform these services by rote, without much depth of thought or sincerity of heart. These individuals are often diverted by many distractions that they have no room inside themselves for a sincere approach to Heaven. The Watchers see this lack of focus and THEY know! Their job is to do something about this. They are thus directed to use the coming year to influence and direct the individual towards their ordained destiny.

We will not escape their influence, we cannot. The Watchers are with us. THEY are all around us. There are no secrets from THEM. THEY watch our behavior and THEY read our thoughts. Everything that THEY record and pass on to their higher ups, who pass this up all the way to an administration which we call the Heavenly Court. There, our individual destinies are discussed, decided, and ordained. Their edicts are then passed down into the hands of the Watchers who then do their job.

Do not consider this procedure to be simply a myth and allegory to inspire our religious repentance. While what I describe here might sound like a child's fairy tale, in light of modern revelations we might want to reevaluate our disbelief and reconsider matters in a more realistic, more extraterrestrial way. The Watchers are not cute little baby-faced angels with pretty wings and harps. Like I said above, their actual appearance is very frightening and very "out of this world". They are real; their presence is real and their function and influence are equally real.

The Watchers definitely have a control and influence over us. Yet, we too can exert our own influence. This is what we call Teshuva. When we divest ourselves of our wasteful distractions and seek the will of Heaven with sincerity, THEY take note. The New Year then brings with it the opportunity to accomplish our desire to return to G-d and bond with Heaven. This is our return to walking the natural path, the one ordained by Heaven for each of us, individually. This repentance is our individual human destiny. This is the directive of the Singularity to each part of its complex program that we call creation.

When we do what is right, Heaven matches us and supports our endeavors. When, however, we choose to walk a different path, then Heaven responds accordingly and informs the Watchers to influence and direct us towards what our souls require. We might then find their influence and direction most intrusive and anything but pleasant. This is why so many people are having such difficult times. The Watchers have been instructed to direct us and we often resist their subtle nudges. THEY are then obligated to push however hard they need to in order to get our attention. What happens then depends upon how we respond.

Do not come on the High Holidays and expect to impress Heaven with your petty shows of piety and religiosity. Heaven looks towards our hearts and judges us based upon the truths concealed within them. Heaven seeks our sincerity and our return; a return to the natural path, a return to our individual inner truths, and our return to unity with Heaven and with G-d. The path is clear; we call it Torah and mitzvot. There is nothing more natural and normal than this.

We each have a lot of work ahead of us. I suggest that each of us, must indeed, take it seriously. The Watchers are watching. What will we show THEM; what will THEY see? What we show THEM and what THEY will be instructed to do is all in our hands. Each of us had better get to work, right now, or THEY will be instructed to get to work on each of us in short order.

Chapter 25

Conspiracy Theories

Tell me what you think; is there ever any legitimate reason to keep certain information secret? Is there or should there ever be a group of individuals who are "in the know" and chose to keep specific information out of the public eye and/or who seek to mold public opinion or to clandestinely direct social evolution?

We are all entertained with the numerous conjectures of conspiracy theories that exist on almost every topic. Most individuals, if asked, would acknowledge awareness of many of these claims and beliefs, yet, most would equally claim to disavow them and not to believe in them at all.

Yet, in spite of what people do or do not believe about conspiracy theories in general, do their beliefs have any influence upon the reality of whether or not a conspiracy theory is either true or false? In other words, it really does not matter what we believe, truth is going on all around us regardless.

While we may not see such truth that does not mean that they are not there. There is an old joke told about the paranoid individual, "just because one is paranoid does not mean that they are not really after you".

In our modern world we are inundated, literally bombarded, with all types of information. Claims are made and supposed evidence abounds for validation. Yet, then an opposite claim will be made, contradicting and totally disproving the first. It too will be back up with abundant evidence. On and on this goes, both sides burying the other and itself under piles and piles of contradictory information. Who can tell anymore what is true, what is false, what is purely made-up, and what is a cover-up?

The problem today is not that we do not have enough information; the problem is that we have too much information that we do not know what to do with it all. We quickly arrive at the point of mental overload and instead of trying to discern through the burdensome, we seek rather to dump the whole load. Most just want to sit back, live their lives, and be happy that "ignorance is bliss".

Yet, there are those who are not happy with the bliss of ignorance. There are those who want to know the truth. There are those willing to take the chance of being afflicted with mental confusion. Some feel compelled to find the truth that is "out there". Others chose instead not to go "out there" but to stay safely inside their little programmed minds, accepting everything that they have been taught and not ever bothering to learn or to practice thinking for oneself.

The close-minded will never discover truth. The close-minded would not recognize truth regardless of how it is revealed. For the close-minded, truth is what one wants to believe or accept what is expressed by the authority figures that dominate one's personal life.

So, what should one believe? Should one believe what he is told, or should one question what is told and fact-check for oneself? However simple this question may appear, how simple is it really to seek out and discover accurate information?

With the increased propagation of "fake news" and "alternative facts", how can one verify if what one has discovered is indeed true? After all, what is the definition of truth? Is it subjective or objective? These questions are enough to confuse anyone! For although we may discover information, even secretive information, who is to say that what we have discovered is true in the first place and more so, even if what we find is absolutely true, who is going to believe us and accept what we discovered anyway?

People generally do not like to think too hard. People generally do not like to make any extra efforts if they can be avoided. This tendency is especially true when it comes to moving mental muscles. While many might have mighty muscles, nevertheless, the "muscles" of the brain for most remains weak and atrophied. With such a mental handicap it is no wonder then that people are simply inclined to believe what they are told and go along with the flow. After all, to stand up against "what everyone else knows to be true" requires tremendous stamina, an effort most are unwilling and/or unable to make.

How did the masses become so docile and unconcerned about whether or not what they hold dear is actually true or a lie? The answer is the public media. Yes, the now worldwide information superhighway, it did not begin with the Internet, it began with newspapers, magazines, radio and then advanced to television. For as long as we have had the "six-o'clock news," we have been spoon-feed, directed, educated, and molded to accept a certain way of viewing things. Subtle nuances of persuasion are weaved into the script of every news report, be it in the newspaper, or on radio or TV. The same way of relating facts, elevating some, while belittling others is the way that we have been "brainwashed" to come to regard certain things as natural, normal, proper, and good, when in truth these certain things are subtle forms of evil, like the proverbial wolf in sheep's clothing.

In the modern world of overwhelming amounts of public information, the best place to hide an absolute secret is out in the open, buried alongside piles and piles of other bits of information. The best way to hide the truth is to broadcast the truth, but of course, it is never broadcast as truth, but rather as fiction. For once fiction has hit the public, everyone will accept it as a given that such and such a story is made-up, make-believe, and completely fictitious. Once accepted as fiction, any claims of there being any truth to such a matter are met with laughter and scorn. In this way the biggest of secrets remains secret with the public convinced, through the media, that such a secret is nonsense and fiction, not worthy of any serious consideration. Even these words and my mention of this idea and concept, I am sure, will be resisted by many, and subject me to ridicule by no small number. It goes to show just how well this process of hiding something in clear sight works so successfully.

Under the circumstances of people believing that they know the truth, the real truth has next to no chance of being believed. And on top of the truth and to disguise it more and more, ever more ridiculous lies are told. They are presented with such copious amounts of so-called proofs, and being presented ever so subtly as the real concealed truth, now being exposed with ample evidence to back it up. This is how conspiracy theories always work. But in truth, what is happening here is a good, old-fashioned "bait and switch" game.

Rather than have one look at the real culprit, the real culprit points a finger at its enemy accusing it of doing exactly what the culprit itself is doing and then the culprit makes sure that there is no lack of so-called evidence to validate the guilt of its enemy. In this way, the public eye turns away from the real culprit and turns on the culprit's enemy, thus doing the work of the culprit for him.

In this way, the innocent get blamed while the culprit gets away with murder. Whenever we see one group making loud and emphatic noise, accusing another of being responsible for this or that problem, one should pause, stop listening to the one(s) making all the noise and accusation, and start paying closer attention to those making the accusation.

Pay no attention to what they are saying; rather pay attention to what they are not saying! Rather than turn away from them to look at what they want you to see, look and pay closer attention to them! You may not like what you see! Then again, they will like even less what you see and will turn against you, to prevent you from seeing the truth that they seek so hard to cover up. Granted, this is a dangerous course for one to follow. Nevertheless, no one ever said that discovering the truth would be either easy or safe.

Specific examples of what I am talking about are irrelevant, indeed, they might even be counter-productive. For once I would claim that such and such a conspiracy theory is either true or false, immediately opposition would arise claiming that I was covering up the truth or further perpetuating lies. Going public to confront positions, claims, and information that cannot be proven or disproven is a waste of time and effort. All such attempts are merely entertainment.

Once a person is convinced of their position, however flawed, foolish or ridiculous it may be, they are not open to hearing anything that will budge them from what they have come to accept and believe. Indeed, any attempt to budge them will be interpreted in their minds as the "bad guys" coming after them to lie to them, confuse them and make them give up what they, in their own eyes, know to be the truth. Ultimately, in the end, there are those people who cannot be reached, simply because they do not want to be reached.

So then, how does one expose truth in a world full of lies? The answer is that one doesn't! The system is way too fixed in favor of the opposition. Our entire information system, newspapers, magazines, radio, TV and now the Internet, are merely tools. What matters is who is wielding those tools. It is not enough to just present information, what convinces people is not what they are exposed to, but rather how they are exposed to something.

Portray the greatest idea and the most worthy hero in a bad light and all of a sudden, the great idea becomes a lousy one and our worthy hero is transformed into a person of scorn. On the other hand, publicly present garbage as valuable and "low-lives" as role models, and all of a sudden, garbage has become the new valuable, and "low-lives" are now the new celebrities. We see this happening around us every day. This has been going on for a long time now such that a reversal of values has almost completely overwhelmed our society.

Again, we can point a finger at the public media, and claim that those who run the media are corrupting us and lying to us. So, blame those who control the media. But stop and think for a moment. Who taught us to blame the media bosses, if not those self-same media bosses themselves!

Who is being presented as controlling the media? Who is being presented as being the guilty party here? There, you have it! Just like I said above! Bait and switch in action! If the media is to blame and those who control the media are to blame, then look at all the overwhelming evidence there to verify without doubt who the guilty parties are. Rest assured that such a finger pointing and such a blame game is the old "bait and switch" tactic. The public is being fed a story by the real culprit to provoke hatred and reprisal against the culprit's true enemy. Again, do not pay attention to where the finger of accusation is pointing; rather look towards the one pointing the finger and making the accusations.

So, in the end, we are in no better place than where we began. Are there secrets out there? You bet there are! Governments keep secrets, businesses keep secrets, organizations keep secrets, and so do ordinary everyday folks, like us, keep our share of secrets. Some of these secrets may cover up "Earth-shattering" truths, such as the evidence of extraterrestrial contact. Some of these secrets may be covering up nefarious plans to manipulate the world public to turn against the innocent, after the world is wrongly convinced that they are guilty.

Yes, secrets, big secrets abound. Real conspiracies, controlled by secret organizations are really out there. We are subject to their subtle influences without even realizing it. Their nefarious plans are hatched behind closed doors and are carried out right under our noses, without the public even being aware of their existence.

Like I have long said, Big Brother is watching us, all of us, even now as I write these words and as you are reading them. My response? I quote to you the character of Alfred E. Neuman, of Mad magazine, who says: "What, me worry?" Why should I worry about Big Brother? If I am on his target list, so what? And how can I be so brazen not to fear Big Brother? Again, "What, me worry?" Granted, B.B. is there watching. But little does B.B. (Big Brother) suspect, but B.A. is watching B.B. Yes, our Heavenly Father, "Big Abba" (B.A.) is watching over all. All the present deceit, lies, and manipulations are all measured, watched, and monitored. Big, bad B.B. cannot lift a finger, or even think a thought that did not first come forth from B.A.

Yes, G-d in Heaven is and has always been in charge of the whole show. All the lies and deceptions are known to G-d. He allows the minds of poisoned people to become poisoned, just like G-d allowed the heart of Pharaoh in Egypt to become hardened. G-d is watching and G-d is judging.

Not for naught does the Scripture command us that, "these words which I command you this day shall be upon your hearts" (Deut 6:6). For G-d does not judge us based upon what is in our heads. G-d knows that our thoughts are "full of mush". G-d knows that our fundamental thinking faculties have been blemished by the "eating from the forbidden fruit of the Tree of Knowledge, Good and Evil". Therefore, G-d does not judge the mistakes of our intellect. G-d knows how much we have been lied to and how many of those lies we all believe, simply because we have no way to know better. G-d instead watches our hearts. He watches us and sees whether or not we will allow into our hearts any corrupting poison that will contaminate our souls.

Our hearts are connected to our souls, and our souls are connected to Heaven. We each have inner access to the Higher Truths. These cannot be blocked out. They cannot become confused because of all the external noise, and lies presented in the public media. Here then is our solution. Silence the outside noise, turn within, and listen for the still, silent Voice that arises from within your soul and tells you how to follow G-d. Read your Bible and allow the inner voice to echo through the words and pages of Scripture.

B.B. may indeed want to do everything in his power to turn you away from B.A. Your test is not to let him. When you can tune out the noise of B.B., you will come to hear with ever-growing clarity the inner voice of your soul, echoing to you the Voice of B.A. So, forget about the conspiracies and forget about the world. Focus instead on what is truly important, your immortal soul! G-d is with you, right now! Don't ever allow B.B. to blur that reality in your mind or heart.

Chapter 26

THEM & THEIR Plan

Flesh to light, light to spirit. There is a plan. It is secret and concealed, and it is being directed by real clandestine powers. Flesh to light, light to spirit.

The plan has been in operation for a very long time. It is multi-generational.

Regardless of whatever happens, everything that transpires globally is part of the plan.

Regardless of appearances, everything is under control, under the control of the real THEM. It is THEY who control everything, just like THEY always have.

There is a real conspiracy. Some governments know about it, and others do not. Some governments are heavily involved with it, and others are equally heavily involved fighting it.

It does not take too much imagination to know which side will win. THEY always win. It's just that those fighting THEM do not know this, and do not want to acknowledge this.

Those who fight today are losing the fight, and they know it. Those who fight today cannot defeat THEM, because THEY are far too entrenched, and THEY have been so for a very long time.

THEY tolerate the fight, because for THEM, the fight is part of THEIR plan.

Likewise Solomon of old said, "vanity of vanities, all is just vanity".

Who are THEY? Time will tell! But this much I can tell you, with absolute certainty!

THEY are not Masons. THEY are not the Illuminati. THEY are not the Knights Templar. THEY are not even the Catholic Church. And certainly, THEY are not Jews.

THEY can hide behind the name of any group with which people label them.

It is definitely THEM who promote world anti-Semitism, but not because THEY hate Jews, but rather because THEY know that the Jews are chosen by G-d to serve as G-d's people, G-d's tool, G-d's scapegoat. THEY know that part of the plan is to use the Jews to test humanity, to see if humanity can, and will, act humanely, or whether they will act depraved. Many today are Jews, and do not know it, their identities lost over generations.

When humanity acts depraved, THEY act to correct humanity's course. We are presently in the middle of such a course correction The Jews again will be held up, like a lightning rod, to see where lightning will strike, and where the clap of thunder will be heard. Being chosen is not the glory that many believe.

This is all part of the plan.

Must there be war? No! This part of the plan can be rewritten, as so many other parts of it have been over many centuries. Indeed, it is part of the plan to instruct the nations to overcome the temptations of war, and to resolve conflicts in wise and peaceful manners.

It is only when greed and foolishness reign supreme that THEY allow wars to happen, with the intent to teach those who fight such wars of their ultimate futility. The reason why THEY have allowed weapons of mass destruction to be developed is to "up the ante," to make war that much more devastating and destructive.

THEY do not want war, but they do allow it.

THEY want order, and THEY are patient to wait for it.

THEY do not want conflicts, but tolerate them. THEY want peace.

There cannot be peace and order without control.

Therefore, THEY seek control to ensure that order is maintained. Order serves THEIR purpose.

What is THEIR ultimate plan? The answer to this should be obvious. They seek control, to establish a united Earth, under control of a singular body.

Who are THEY? Time will tell! But this much I can tell you, with absolute certainty!

THEY have been here for a very long time.

THEY have been in control for as long as it can be remembered.

THEY are ancient, and even spoken about in the Bible.

THEY should never be trifled with.

THEY understand, but THEY do not forgive, nor forget.

Who are THEY? You should be able to figure it out by now.

If you have, then you understand why THEY maintain their anonymity.

If you have, then you know why THEY cannot be successfully challenged.

If you have, then you see why the future must unfold according to an ancient, but certain pattern.

THEY are who THEY are. THEIR plan is THEIR plan.

Just know this, that whomever THEY are, like us, THEY too take their "marching orders" from "higher-ups," who still take their orders from yet even "higher, higher-ups," and so up the ladder we go. Flesh to light, light to spirit. At the top, there is only ONE.

And the ONE is the only ONE who is truly in charge, at all levels.

PART TWO

A DEEPER LOOK

The Ministers of the Zodiac that reside in the air, these are the Princes of the Teli (Dragons)... The reason that they are called the Princes of the Teli is because to these Princes (of the Teli) belongs the leadership over all the hosts above. By their mouths all the spheres of heaven go forth, and by their mouths, [all the spheres of heaven] stay still. In the language of our Sages this is called the Nahash Briah (fleeing serpent) and the Aklaton (winding) [Ouroboros]. The astrologers call it the tail of the dragon, head of the dragon, meaning good and evil, for all born of the head are good, and of the tail, evil. These Princes are the souls of the spheres for each sphere vibrates, each has a separate intelligence that guides it in accordance to the secret of the emanation of the Name that radiates upon it. The Princes of the Teli themselves are influenced from the angels above, these are the four Princes above, the angels of the Merkava.

Rabbi Menahem Tziyuni,
Sefer Tziyuni on the Torah, Parshat Aharei

Chapter 1

Non-Extraterrestrial Alien Origins: Angels & Demons

While the possibility does exist that we are being visited by actual physical beings from other planets, there are other possibilities. In order to ascertain just who these "alien" visitors are, we must consider these possibilities as well.

The Sages of Israel have always known that we are not alone. Abba Benjamin is quoted in Talmud Berakhot 6a as saying if the eye could see, a person would not be able to function normally due to the abundance of spirits surrounding one at all times. Who is it then that is with us? Who are our invisible neighbors? What are these spirits? From where do they come?

From biblical and Talmudic times, our Sages have identified our invisible neighbors as being the different races of the angels, and another race called demons. Unlike the Christians who believe that all demons are fallen angels, Torah has always known demons to be a separate race different from any of the angelic races, and that they were created as such. Before I proceed to discuss the nature of demons, I must first discuss the nature of angels.

Chapter 2

Angels

The great twelfth century law codifier Maimonides, in his Laws of the Foundations of Torah (Y.T. 2:3) speaks of angels as being "creations which have form, but no matter at all ... they ... do not possess bodies or corporeal being, but rather are forms which are separate from each other".

Regarding their corporeal appearances in the Bible, Maimonides clearly states that these are "metaphoric", and not to be taken literally. Maimonides explains (Y.T. 2:5-6) the nature of angels as follows:

Since they possess no body, what separates the form [of the angels] from each other? Their existence is not alike; rather each one is below the level of the other and exists by virtue of its influence, [in a progression of levels,] one above the other. Everything exists by virtue of the influence of the Holy One, blessed be He, and His goodness. Solomon alluded to this [concept] in his wisdom saying (Ecclesiastes 5:7): "Because above the one who is high there is a watcher [and there are others higher than them]". The expression "below the level of the other" does not refer to height in a spatial sense as [one might say], he is sitting higher than his colleague [but rather, in regard to spiritual level]. For example, when speaking about two sages, one of whom is greater than the other, we say, "one is above the level of the other". Similarly, a cause is referred to as "above" the effect [it produces].

Maimonides (Y.T. 2:7) proceeds to enumerate the ten species of angels:

1. The holy *Hayot*, who are above all others;
2. The *Ofanim*, the wheel angels;
3. The *Er'elim*, the great, exalted ones;
4. The *Chashmalim*, "the fiery beings which communicate" (Ez 1:27);
5. The *Seraphim*, the burning ones, the reptilians;
6. The *Malakhim*, the messengers;
7. The *Elohim*, the judges of the lower realms;
8. The *Benei Elohim*, the workers for the *Elohim* angels;
9. The *Keruvim*, the childlike angels;
10. The *Ishim*, the humanlike angels who appear to mankind as human beings.

This is not the time or place to become involved in detailed angelology. Therefore, I will only continue to discuss those aspects of those specific groups of angels that are applicable to our present topic. Maimonides, and the other Rabbis and Kabbalists, are quite clear that there is a direct connection between angels, and the planets.

Maimonides writes in his Laws of the Foundations of Torah (3:9) that "All stars and planets possess a soul, knowledge, and intellect. They are alive... The knowledge of the planets is [however] less than the knowledge of the angels." The famous Bible commentator Nachmanides reveals even more information. He states in his commentary to Deuteronomy 18:9-12, that there are certain stars that are guided by archangels, and that these archangels are the souls of those planets. They are called the "Princes of the Teli (Dragon)".

This Sage is saying something here that is quite profound: the planets are the bodies of the angels. Therefore, the relationship of an angel to a planet is like that of a human body to the soul within it. Both are one. We thus see that there is some aspect of physical manifestations for the angels. This relationship of the archangel to the planets is accepted by numerous Sages and Kabbalists.

Another question to ask is regarding the angelic hosts. Each of the archangels is known to have camps of supporters, lesser angels, who serve the archangels in carrying out the service of G-d. Are these lesser angels inhabitants on these planets? Considering these planets are in fact the bodies of these archangels, these lesser angels most definitely have a connection to these planets. Are these angels being perceived today as extraterrestrial aliens? No definite answer can be offered to this question.

One thing is apparently clear; there are some physical forms that certain angels appear in. Nowhere is this made clearer than in the Bible itself. In Scripture we have a number of angelic visitations. Yet, with very rare exceptions, all biblical angelic appearances are rather underwhelming experiences. There is no sound and light show accompanying their manifestations.

In Genesis 18, three angels come to Avraham, and they appear as normal men. They even sit down, and eat with him. Two of them leave him and proceed to Sodom and Gomorrah to destroy it. Upon arriving in Sodom they are met by Avraham's nephew Lot who recognizes them as special, but their appearance is still quite human.

Later, in Genesis 32, there is the famous story of Ya'akov wrestling with an angel. But the Bible doesn't say that the entity is an angel. The word used to describe this being is an "Ish," a man.

Again in Joshua 5, Joshua sees an Ish, a man with a sword drawn in his hand. He is prepared to do battle with him until this man identifies himself as leader of G-d's armies (Josh 5:14).

In Judges 13, Manoah's wife sees an Ish Elohim, a man of G-d, whose appearance was awe inspiring like an angel. Manoah himself later sees this man, and innocently invites him to supper. Only upon offering a sacrifice to G-d, and seeing this man ascend to Heaven in the smoke from the altar, does Manoah understand that he was speaking with no mere mortal man.

All of these instances make angelic-human interaction a very human affair. Only in the singular event of the angel's ascent in front of Manoah do we find anything about his behavior to be in the least bit out of the ordinary. Maimonides has already addressed this issue.

The type of angel being seen is called Ishim, which Maimonides enumerates as the tenth, and lowest form of angelic manifestation. But if angels, including Ishim, have no set form or corporeal being, how then can they appear as human? Again Maimonides has answered this question. The angels' appearances are metaphor; the angels take on the necessary human form so as to accomplish their task at hand. Once they ascend again from the Earth, they remove their physical appearance in the same way we would take off our clothing before retiring to sleep.

Who are these mysterious Ishim angels who come and go in whatever disguises they so choose? Are they corporeal extraterrestrial aliens from another planet? According to the Sages of Israel, they are no such things. Rather they are far above the corporeal world all together. According to Maimonides, they are non-corporeal beings that have their unique existence in another dimension, one that is very close to our own.

The Master Kabbalist, Rabbi Haim Vital in his Kabbalistic classic Etz Haim (150, 8) writes that the form of these Ishim is a physical one, but far more pure and refined than that of the human body. Their bodies do not consist of the four elements of water, fire, air, and Earth, but only of the element of fire. This type of body is called the Halukha D'Rabbanan, today referred to as the astral body.

In his commentary to the holy Zohar (within Ohr HaHamah, Terumah, 184a), he writes that these Ishim angels exist in the form of men, and that their place is a dimension beneath the ten levels of Heaven. This realm of the Ishim angels is said to be called the Teli, the place of the Dragon.

Rabbi Vital quotes as the source of his information the ancient book of Enoch which he said was in Gentile hands and that he re-translated it into Hebrew. This is significant, for he is the only classical Jewish source to overtly quote the book today called I Enoch.

Chapter 3

Guardian Angels – The Watchers

The book of Enoch has many wondrous and mysterious events described therein about a group of angels called the Arta'layin, the Watchers. First introduced in the biblical book of Daniel, Chapter 3, as the Ir V'Kadosh, these Watchers are said to be the loyal servants and agents of G-d who carry out His instructions here upon the Earth. We might call them a Heavenly civil service.

The Ishim-Watchers have the responsibility of making sure that things on Earth go along as intended. Regarding them the Sages have said, *"There is not even a single herb which has not a guardian angel in heaven that stands over it, and makes it grow"* (Gen. Rab. 10:6). With all the power and ability given these Ishim-Watchers, no reference is ever made that they are from another (corporeal) planet or use any means of a machine-oriented technology. But there is more to be told about these dwellers in the Teli.

The first and only source for knowledge of the Teli is the ancient Sefer Yetzirah. In Chapter Six of this sacred text it is written that the Teli rule space like a king upon his throne. Many Rabbis and Kabbalists understand the Teli to be a code name for the Milky Way galaxy. If the Ishim Watchers are the dwellers and masters of the Teli, does this mean that they are the guardians of the Milky Way galaxy and thus, by definition, corporeal inhabitants of another planet? No, not necessarily. The Ishim, like the higher angels, may be non-corporeal entities existing above our time-space continuum. Then again, maybe not!

Is it possible that these Ishim-Watchers are revealing themselves to mankind, and is it they who pilot the UFOs? This scenario does not seem to be the case. As all the literature about the Ishim-Watchers suggests, these servants are very busy performing their G-d given tasks. Ishim angels have no business dealing frivolously with mortal human beings as UFO encounter scenarios suggest.

If the Ishim were to contact people in such a frivolous manner, their act would be a violation of the angelic laws that direct angelic-human contact. Any angel violating the law would be immediately removed from its post. Considering these angels are holy, they do not violate the spiritual laws of illegal angelic-human contact. When an angel legally communicates with a human, he is doing so as G-d's agent and will always announce that he has come in G-d's Name.

Based upon the visitation accounts that are publicly available, none of the so-called extraterrestrials come in the Name of G-d nor do they have any knowledge of, or respect for, G-d's Word. This, in and of itself, is most revealing.

Chapter 4

Demons

As mentioned earlier, Abba Benjamin said in the Talmud that if the eye could see we would go insane due to the numerous spirits among us. I must now be more precise and confess that Abba Benjamin was not talking about benign spirits. He was talking about malevolent ones, the mazikin, responsible for causing harm to mankind. They are the ones whom we call demons. Like angelology, Judaism has extensive knowledge of demonology. Many texts have been written detailing whom the demons are, what their hierarchy is, and most importantly how to recognize them.

Jewish tradition has always differentiated between two different types of malevolent spirits. There are the demons that were created by G-d to be what they are, and then there is a second, more diabolical category. In Genesis we read that the Benei Elohim, a race of angel known as the sons of G-d, descended to Earth, and corrupted themselves. These entities are the group that has become known as the fallen angels. Before I proceed to discuss the fallen angels, I must first discuss the topic of the original demons.

In the Talmud, Avot 5:6, it is stated that the demons are one of the things that G-d created on the eve of the primordial first Sabbath. Legend says that because the Sabbath had come, and G-d ceased from His works, these demons were left only partially created. Our Sages report that these demons were left without bodies. This teaching introduces to us a problem. For the Sages to say that these demons have no body, we would understand this to mean that they are non-corporeal entities of a similar nature to the angels. But this is far from the truth; our Sages have also taught something else most interesting about the nature of these demons.

In Avot D'Rabbi Natan 37:3, it states that there are six known things about demons, three of which make them similar to angels and three of which make them similar to humans. It is said that demons can fly about, have access to knowledge of the future, and travel around the world. It is also said taught that they can take on any appearance they so choose. They can see all, but are not seen. In all these ways demons are similar to angels. Demons are similar to humans in that they eat and drink like humans, they sexually procreate like humans, and they die like humans. Now this poses a problem to what is mentioned above. How can non-corporeal entities without physical bodies, eat and drink, have sex, and die? After all, death means separation of the soul from the body. When the Sages said that the demons were left not completely created, they had a very profound teaching in mind that they hinted to us by saying that the demons have no bodies.

During their process of creation the demons, similar to humans, started in embryonic form, soul and rudimentary body together. When the primordial Sabbath came, which was not so much a physical time as much as a level of evolutionary development when the work of creation was considered complete, these demons were left with bodies which were not completely formed by human standards. Of course they had some type of physical form. How else could they eat, drink, have sex, and die? It is just that their physical form is less complete than the physical form of mankind. This inferiority is something that angers them considerably. They have never forgiven G-d for this perceived injustice.

To this day these demons are jealous of mankind, and hate us. They have continuously caused us all kinds of harm on an individual and collective basis. This is why our Sages call them Mazikin (those who cause harm). Like angels, these demons appear and disappear; they can know the future and get around. Yet they have appetites for food and for sex, and they can die. Their major activities are directed against their mortal enemy, mankind, whom they continue to deceive in innumerable manners.

Rabbi Yehuda Fatiyah of Jerusalem, one of the great Kabbalists of the 20th century (died 1942), has written one of the most revelatory works of how these demons act today and deceive people in the most malicious ways. In his work Minhat Yehuda, Rabbi Fatiyah enumerates a number of personal experiences which he witnessed how demons appeared to people in dreams, and while awake in all kinds of forms with the intent of deceiving them for some unknown devious purpose.

Rabbi Fatiyah was an expert in exposing these demons, and casting them out. He has recorded the procedures for doing these things in his work. One other additional point should be mentioned. The Sages have taught in the Talmud and Midrash that the place where these mazikin demons reside is in the subterranean depths under the Earth. More on this subject will be discussed later.

Unfortunately, these mazikin demons are not the only invisible enemies of mankind that inhabit the Earth along with us. There are two other and more devastating forces. The first of these forces I have already mentioned above. These are the fallen angels.

Chapter 5

Fallen Angels

In Genesis 6:2 we read that the Benei Elohim (the sons of G-d) saw the daughters of men, for they were good, and they took for themselves wives from any that they would choose. This is a most strange event! These Benei Elohim are supposed to be non-corporeal angelic entities. Why would they want to become physical, with all the limitations of consciousness and angelic abilities that come with it? Most of all, what on Earth would attract them to human women? In many ways these angels are far above the human on the physical evolutionary scale. For them to desire a human female is the equivalent of a human wanting to marry a gorilla! What on Earth happened?

Who are these Benei Elohim? According to some Rabbis the Benei Elohim is merely a reference to the sons of Seth, and the daughters of men refer to the daughters of Cain. But not all the Rabbis accepted this opinion. The Kabbalists understood this text very differently. The Zohar, Ba'al HaTurim, Rabbi Yitzhak D'min Acco and others teach that the Benei Elohim is a reference to the fallen angels, led by Shamhazi and Azael. The Zohar (Z.H. Ruth 92a) teaches that the Benei Elohim are the angels who rule the night. Elsewhere in the Zohar, ancient Midrashic sources quoted by the historian Josephus and others, as well as in works unearthed in the Dead Sea Scrolls (ref. Encyclopedia Judaica 5, 1526), these Benei

Elohim angels are none other than the Watchers mentioned in Daniel, of whom we have spoken above.

Jewish tradition teaches us much about these angels and why they fell. It must be understood that the creation of the Adamic race was not met with overwhelming support from the Heavenly angels. Living above time and space they knew that Adam was destined to fall from his high stature, and that G-d would forgive him. To put it bluntly, this eventuality angered many of the angels. One of them went so far as to cause the fall of Adam and Eve. This was his attempt to prove to G-d that He was mistaken in creating man. Many of the angels approached the heavenly throne and boldly, if not foolishly proclaimed, *"L-rd what is man that You know him, the son of man that You think of him"* (Ps 144:3). The Holy One, blessed be He, responded to those angels saying that if they were to descend into the physical realm upon Earth they would sin even more grievously than man.

Shamhazi, Azael, and other angels wanted to prove that G-d was wrong. They left their home in the spiritual abode. They abandoned their posts as watchers of the night. They secretly descended to Earth to prove a point. The only problem was that they were dreadfully mistaken. G-d was, of course, right. The first thing that happened to these angels was that they experienced human lust. Unable to overcome it, they cohabited with human women who bore superhuman children whom the Bible (Genesis 6) calls the Nefilim, the fallen ones. It is these bastard children who caused the destruction of old Earth by the waters of the flood. Jewish tradition (Yafeh Eynayim, Gen 105) teaches that Shamhazi recognized his wrong decision and repented, even though G-d has still not forgiven him. Azael on the other hand, along with the other fallen watchers, joined the forces of the mazikin demons, and together continue to plague mankind. The Nefilim, as the Bible teaches, survived the flood, and lasted until the days of Moshe (Number 13:33). Physically they were giants; the smallest were over ten feet tall. Goliath, who fought with young David, was of the last of this fallen race.

Chapter 6

Adam in the Garden

An interesting side note, throughout Kabbalistic literature (ref. Ben Ish Hai, Bereshit, S.R. in the name of the Ari'zal) it has been taught that originally, in the Garden of Eden, Adam was not a physical being as we know physical at all. He existed in a body of light, what today is referred to as the astral body. As a result of having eaten the fruit of the forbidden tree did he descend, and become encased in the crude physical matter of this world. This is the secret meaning of the verse in Genesis where it says that G-d gave them (i.e., Adam and Eve) skins and clothed them. These skins were bodies of flesh and blood. However, the Sages continue and say that Adam's original body of flesh and blood after the fall was still not like that of ours. Our physical stature is a result of the atmospheric changes that came about due to the flood. Prior to this time, when people lived for almost a thousand years, their physical statures were much larger. Jewish tradition teaches that Adam was a being of over one hundred feet tall, as was Cain and his descendants.

There is one more category of evil spirits to be covered before we can move on to our next discussion of the subterranean worlds. We must speak about the Nahash, the serpent in the Garden of Eden. Yet, prior to discussing the evil serpent, I must discuss the origins of evil itself.

Chapter 7

The Creation of Evil

One of the most controversial teachings among the Kabbalists is understanding what G-d was doing before He created this world of ours. In the Genesis Rabbah 3:7 we are taught that prior to creating this world of ours the Holy One, blessed be He, created other worlds and then destroyed them.

The Kabbalists teach that there were seven such creations prior to our own. These seven worlds are referred to as the realms of chaos (*olam hatohu*). The secret lessons regarding these seven worlds are hidden in the Torah within the enumerations of the genealogy of the family of Esau in Genesis 36 It speaks there of the "kings who reigned in the land of Edom, before there was a King in Israel". These Edomite kings are a secret reference to those primordial worlds.

It is said that these earlier creations did not properly receive the influx of G-d's Divine light. Each world is said to have been a vessel that needed to be filled with G-d's light in order to live. The seven worlds/vessels were not strong enough to receive G-d's light. Therefore, when the light did shine into them, the vessels being too weak shattered and were thus destroyed. It is from the broken pieces of these fallen vessels that came forth one of G-d's most mysterious creations: the creation of evil.

The Bible (Isa 45:7) is quite clear that it is G-d Himself who created evil. Our Sages have revealed to us profound insight as to why G-d has done this. In the Zohar it is asked, what good is a torch during the daytime? What value has righteousness if there is no possibility of wickedness? Where can there be room for reward and punishment if there is no opportunity to earn either one? How can mankind be said to have free will if he cannot willingly choose to receive G-d's blessing or reject it? The purpose for G-d's creation of evil is clear. Something cannot exist outside of the context of its opposite. We would not know what good is unless we could compare it to bad. We would not know love, if there were no hate. We would not know day, if there were no night. G-d's wisdom is truly profound. Evil had to exist so that good could exist in contrast to it. Yet in the beginning, the place of evil was outside of the soul of man. And this brings us to the Garden of Eden.

Chapter 8

The Serpent in the Garden

The story of the Garden of Eden on the surface conceals more than it reveals. As with the entire Torah, each word and letter is a code revealing more information than can be provided by a simple translation. For this reason, the whole truth of what really happened in the Garden of Eden is known only by those who have mastered the Kabbalistic teachings.

In Genesis 2, we read that Adam was created in the image of G-d and then placed in the Garden of Eden so as to "work it and watch over it" (v. 15). Adam, however, is alone. G-d chooses to make a helpmate for him. The result was the creation of Eve.

But not so fast! We are missing a very important point. In Genesis 2:18, G-d says He will create a helpmate for Adam. We should expect then that verse 19 would immediately proceed to speak about the creation of Eve. But it doesn't. Before creating Eve, G-d brings before Adam all the animals for him to give them names. This task itself was a test of Adam's wisdom, for each animal already had a name. It was Adam's test to be able to physically look into each and every creation, discern its true essence and then call it that, thus manifesting its name. Adam passed his test. Yet verse 20 reveals something that most people overlook. Verse 20 states, "But Adam did not find a helpmate who was compatible to him". It is clear that the purpose of bringing the animals before Adam was for him to choose from them a helpmate.

While he did not find his true soul-mate, our Sages teach us that Adam did however find one of the animals, which was the highest created being next to man, to be his assistant. This was the Nahash, the serpent. This is why, in Genesis 3:1, he is to be found in the Garden alongside of Adam and Eve. As is known in Jewish tradition, and best summed up in Rabbi Yehuda Fatiyah's commentary to the Bible, *Minhat Yehuda*, the serpent, before his sin, was vastly different than what a serpent appears like today.

The serpent before the fall was humanoid. He stood erect, had two arms and two legs, and was considered the most beautiful of the creatures, next to Adam himself. The Bible is also clear about two other points. Genesis 3:1 states that the serpent was very wise and, that like Adam, he was a cut above the rest of the animals in that he too could talk. Due to the serpent's wise nature and his beautiful human-like appearance Adam and Eve did not consider him a threat.

The serpent was Adam's "trusted" assistant. Jewish tradition teaches us that it was the serpent that helped Adam with all the work in the Garden. But then, along came Eve. It is interesting to note that the serpent did not originally attempt to deceive Adam. It is also very interesting to note exactly what the serpent said to Eve to get her to eat of the forbidden fruit. Before I comment on this topic, I wish to divert for just a moment to note an interesting observation.

Chapter 9

Reptilians

The serpent, even though he was of humanoid appearance and beautiful at that, was nonetheless still reptilian. He was a reptilian humanoid. Many extraterrestrials are described in somewhat the same fashion, as being reptilian humanoids. This description has become so well known that it has become a part of popular culture when portraying enemy aliens invading Earth from outer space.

I also remember watching once a public television series on the dinosaurs. Dinosaurs, according to Rabbi Israel Lifshitz's Mishnaic commentary *Tiferet Yisrael*, were creatures in one of the seven primordial worlds prior to our own. In this PBS special was a most peculiar segment. The question was asked: if the dinosaurs would had survived, what would they have looked like today? The show then presented a model of a reptilian humanoid saying that this is what these beings would look like today. I found that to be a most curious segment. Why would someone ask such a question in the first place? How did they come to the conclusions that they did? I cannot say that PBS was suggesting anything. I just saw more into their investigation than most others would have.

Is it possible that some of these creatures from the fallen worlds of the seven kings did survive in corporeal form? Is it possible that there are advanced, highly intelligent reptilian beings? The answer to this second question is a definite, yes! There are spiritually highly advanced reptilian creatures, the race of angels called the Seraphim, as mentioned by Maimonides.

Though the name Seraph connotes fire and burning, the name clearly also refers to the Hebrew word for reptile, which is seraph. Can we postulate, and say then that these Seraphim angels are really evolved dinosaurs? I would not be so fast to jump to that conclusion. G-d still has a number of secrets hidden in His treasure chests of Torah. Maybe there were holy remnants from the primordial worlds of the Edomite kings. Who knows? We still do not know everything.

All that can be said is that Jewish tradition teaches us that the dismembered head of Esau was buried in the cave of Makhpelah in Hevron, which is the burial cave of Adam and Eve, Avraham and Sarah, Yitzhak and Rivkah, Ya'akov and Leah. This special cave is said to be the interdimensional vortex that leads back to the Garden of Eden. The Zohar (1, 128b) teaches that more than Jerusalem, Hevron is the center of the world.

The importance of Hevron does not seem to be known only to the Rabbis and Kabbalists. Robert K.G. Temple, in his book The Sirius Mystery (Destiny Books, VT. 1976), also asks some interesting questions regarding its importance to the ancient Northern Semitic Hititte tribes who were in Hevron in the days of the biblical patriarch Avraham.

Using historical and archaeological data, Temple shows that the Hititte people were not indigenous to the Hevron area. He ascertains that they had come to Hevron on a "divine mission," to safeguard it, because it was known as a powerful oracle center. Unlike the Zohar, Temple however claims the spirits of the oracle are really extraterrestrials.

Another interesting point that Temple mentions is that the Hititte oracles involved the use of severed human heads, and the "magical" element that they claimed was to be found within them. He also references the Rabbinic story regarding Esau's head being buried there. What, you might ask, does this have to do with dinosaurs and angels? The answer to this lies in Judaism's understanding of the significance of having Esau's head buried alongside the body of his father Yitzhak.

According to the Kabbalistic teachings, not all of what was created in the worlds prior to our own was evil, and thus destroyed. There was a remnant; the best was spared. The best is always referred to as the "head". Esau (Edom), Ya'akov's evil twin brother, is always the symbolic name given to the primordial worlds of evil prior to there being the world of good ("a king in Israel" as the Bible puts it).

The "head of Esau resting in the bosom of Yitzhak" means that there were survivors from the ancient worlds, and that they too are holy. Were the survivors of the pre-Adamic civilizations (the kingdoms of Edom) transformed into the Seraphim angels? I have no source that I can quote to validate such a statement, therefore I cannot confirm or deny this speculation. Whether Esau's head is physically buried in Hevron or whether it is just a symbolic legend also cannot be factually ascertained.

What I can say is this: it is known throughout the Bible, Talmud and Zohar that evil always attempts to imitate good, and masquerade as it. In this way evil deceives people; by making them believe what they are doing is good. This fraud is what happened to Eve and what still happens today with people being taken in by deceptive cults.

Chapter 10

The Holy Dragon

The serpent in the Garden of Eden, from its origins, was evil. The serpent was possessed by the spirit of the accuser angel, Samael. He was (and is) very wise. He disguised himself in a form of holiness so as to deceive Adam and Eve. Originally, the image of the reptile was something holy; the Dragon is the quintessential holy animal. To this day the Teli, the holy Dragon, is the abode of the holy Ishim angels. With this insight the passage quoted above will begin to make sense. Here it is again:

The Ministers of the Zodiac that reside in the air, these are the Princes of the Teli (Dragons)... The reason that they are called the Princes of the Teli is because to these Princes (of the Teli) belongs the leadership over all the hosts above. By their mouths all the spheres of heaven go forth, and by their mouths, [all the spheres of heaven] stay still. In the language of our Sages this is called the Nahash Briah (fleeing serpent) and the Aklaton (winding) [Ouroboros]. The astrologers call it the tail of the dragon, head of the dragon, meaning good and evil, for all born of the head are good, and of the tail, evil. These Princes are the souls of the spheres for each sphere vibrates, each has a separate intelligence that guides it in accordance to the secret of the emanation of the Name that that radiates upon it. The Princes of the Teli themselves are influenced from the angels above, these are the four Princes above, the angels of the Merkava.

Rabbi Menahem Tziyuni,
Sefer Tziyuni on the Torah, Parshat Aharei

Samael used the holy image of the dragon and disguised himself as the serpent. Not fearing the holy image, and not knowing evil, Adam and Eve were deceived. To this very day, in most cultures worldwide (with the exception of the Chinese and the Kabbalists), the dragon is still viewed as a symbol of evil. Even the Talmud (A.Z. 42b) states that the image of the dragon is idolatrous. Its original form in holiness has been forgotten due to the deception done by using its visage.

<u>Chapter 11</u>

The Fall of Man

The manner of how the serpent caused Eve, and then Adam to sin is most interesting to note. The serpent confused Eve, not by lying to her, but rather by telling her the truth. Indeed, her eyes would be open to know good and evil if she ate of the forbidden fruit.

The serpent said to Eve, "G-d knows that on the day you eat from it, your eyes will be opened, and you will be like G-d, knowing good and evil" (Gen 3:5). After Adam and Eve ate of the forbidden fruit, G-d says, "Man has now become like one of us in knowing good and evil" (Gen 3:22). In this respect the serpent did not lie. The sin of Adam and Eve was not so much that they ate "fruit" from a tree. The sin was that they disobeyed a direct order from G-d.

G-d has ordained law and order in His universe. Everything progresses and moves according to its preordained patterns. Adam and Eve were also under these same laws. Eventually they would have been able to eat of the Tree of Knowledge, Good and Evil, but only when they would have been ready. Their sin was that they "jumped the gun".

The great Kabbalist, the Ari'zal, explains that Adam's sin was that he attempted to spiritually evolve prior to being mature enough to do so. After all, why did Adam and Eve eat of the fruit of the tree? They wanted to be more like G-d. In other words, they wanted to get closer to Him. But one cannot get closer to G-d by disobeying Him. One can only get closer to G-d by doing what He says. This enables us to spiritually mature and thus become more like G-d. The serpent deceived Eve, and then Adam by making them think that this command was not true. We still are suffering from the results.

Why did the serpent seek to destroy Adam and Eve? Did he not have it good enough? Our Sages say that the serpent's plan was that Eve should eat of the "Fruit of the Tree" and then give it to Adam. G-d only commanded Adam directly not to eat of the fruit. Only Adam was warned of the punishment for violating G-d's law. Maybe Eve would be left alive. If so, the serpent thought, then he would marry her, and he would then inherit his master's house, not having to serve Adam anymore. And if Eve were also to be punished, then at least he alone, the serpent, would have inherited the Garden of Eden and taken over Adam's role as lord of the Earth. Things did not work out like the serpent planned. To this day there is enmity between him, and the descendants of Eve, this meaning all women.

When I hear stories of so-called "alien abductions" of human women carried out by so-called reptilian "grays", who subject them to all kinds of sexual "experimentation", I begin to wonder if there is more a demonic source for these events than an extraterrestrial one.

Chapter 12

Today's UFO Stories

Today's UFO stories fill up many books. In most bookstores around the world you will find a number of titles that deal with this subject. In researching this material, I also found at least five monthly magazines devoted to keeping the public informed about new revelations in UFO world. While there is a tremendous amount of questionable information out there presenting itself as authentic UFO reports, there are nevertheless three types of occurrences associated with UFOs that need to be examined.

First, strange lights and flying crafts have been seen in the sky by millions of people, from all walks of life, at all times of day and night. We will discuss these momentarily.

Second, there is a strange plague of animal mutilations where animals, usually cattle, are found dead in the fields with certain parts of their anatomy missing, apparently surgically removed by a means that baffles doctors. Many times the animal's blood is completely drained, and other carnivorous animals will not touch the carcasses. These events are definitely strange. A full examination of animal mutilations will again take us out of the topic of this work. However, I find it no coincidence that many of these animal mutilations are very similar in performance to certain blood rituals performed in satanic, black magic ceremonies. Unfortunately, these animal mutilations cannot be dismissed as the works of some secret satanic societies simply because of the technological methods used in the mutilations. Whoever has this advanced surgical technology must have knowledge of, and interest in, satanic ritual. Just as surgical technology cannot be learned anywhere or imitated, so too satanic ritual is very precise and intricate. One cannot just replicate it. One must learn it from a qualified, intimate source. To think that the similarity between animal mutilations and satanic ritual is mere coincidence is as illogical and foolish, as it is dangerous. However the most upsetting of UFO phenomena revolve around another set of suspicious events.

The third and strangest of all claims, again by a large number of credible people, is that they were somehow rendered helpless, and taken aboard one of these UFO crafts. While aboard they are allegedly subject to a variety of medical experiments. Most times these medical experiments have to do with sex. Men and women have claimed to have been forced to have sex with aliens, as well as with other strange men and women. Numerous women have claimed to have become pregnant through these experiments. Many times these women claim that the aliens come, and remove the growing fetus from their wombs. The number of reports makes these claims alarming and they are not going away. The number of reports from credible, rational, sane men and women is growing!

Let me proceed to document sources, and details regarding these matters. I will then attempt to correlate them to the material that is found in Jewish sources and try to offer an understanding, based on Torah sources, as to what may be happening to these people.

Chapter 13

Strange Lights in the Sky

The appearance of strange lights in the sky, and unidentified flying objects did not start in the modern era with the birth of science fiction. Throughout history there have been reports of strange lights in the sky. Most of these reports are cloaked in the religious languages of the cultures in which they were experienced. In other words, most people have interpreted these ancient UFOs as being spiritual observations, be they angelic or demonic.

Eric von Daniken, in his book Chariot of the Gods, goes so far as to interpret the prophetic revelation of the prophet Ezekiel in a most peculiar literal sense. Instead of Ezekiel experiencing a spiritual vision of the mystical "Heavenly Throne of G-d", von Daniken postulates that his experience is quite physical, and that what the prophet actually witnessed was an extraterrestrial UFO. Needless to say this opinion has no real basis in light of an accurate reading of the original Hebrew biblical text.

The vision of Ezekiel has been known from ancient times to be a step-by-step guide through the prophetic Kabbalistic meditative experience. Ezekiel's chariot meditative techniques are still practiced today regularly in the secret groups of Kabbalists. We know that this practice opens the doors to other dimensions of consciousness, but as yet, no one has bumped into any UFOs from outer space. So, in all due respect to von Daniken, his interpretations of Ezekiel's chariot experience is lacking. Von

Daniken's other biblical understandings can all be answered in similar fashion. Being that this present work is not intended to be a refutation of von Daniken, I shall not proceed to critique his book.

There are others who have written reinterpreting the biblical teachings to include an extraterrestrial component. These authors seek to interpret G-d as some kind of a super-astronaut from an extraterrestrial race, and that Adam and Eve were some kind of genetic experiment. Some go so far as to say the serpent in the Garden is the hero of the Bible story, and that G-d is really the devil in disguise (G-d forbid).

Due to the outlandish, imaginary, unsubstantiated wild contents of such works, I do not wish to even recite their titles or provide any quotes. The wild, imaginary tales that authors of this kind have spread is fine entertainment, for those who seek science fiction. However, I wish to deal with reality, and not fiction. Therefore, any serious and knowledgeable researcher dismisses the works of such authors and their so-called proofs because these authors make wild allegations based on faulty interpretations that are so clearly false to anyone with proper knowledge of biblical material.

The focus of this work is to cover the Torah's view of our subject, not to critique others. I comment on these works so that you, my reader, may know that Rabbis and Kabbalists alike have no respect for those who wish to enter unprepared into our area of expertise and foolishly misinterpret things in such an arrogant manner; expecting to speak with some type of credibility. We cannot, and will not extend them any authority.

Challenging the religious sacredness of the Bible is one thing; challenging legitimate biblical scholarship is another thing. One does not have to follow the Bible as part of an organized religion, however the choice to question the Bible does not give anyone license to reinterpret it in any which way, beyond the rigorous methods of certified scholarship. Biblical Hebrew and Aramaic are deliberate and precise. At a minimum, one must possess an extensive, thorough fluency of these languages. One cannot simply come along, and attempt to reinterpret biblical words in these languages to sustain wild imaginary ideas. The very words themselves contradict such wild attempts.

As I mentioned above, strange lights in the sky have been witnessed around the world throughout recorded history. Even the historian Josephus reported that prior to the destruction of Jerusalem in 68 C.E. there was an army of strange lights in the sky over the city. He said that they looked like an army of angels awaiting orders to defend Jerusalem. Alas for Jerusalem, those orders never came. At dawn the lights disappeared, and Jerusalem was left to her fate.

Associating these lights in the sky with UFOs did not however start with the science fiction writings about aliens from outer space. In the late 19th century there were numerous documented reports of airships allegedly spotted by many, over many portions of the United States.

Chapter 14

19th Century UFOs

Jacques Vallee, a serious UFO researcher, documents these 19th century airship sightings in his book Dimensions (Ballantine, NY, 1988). A point about these 19th century UFOs that I found most interesting is that their technology seems to be consistent with the times of their manifestations. The airships and their inhabitants appear to be very well suited for the 19th century.

Vallee quotes a report from the Houston Daily Post dated April 28, 1897. The report speaks of a heavy object dragging along with a rope attached that got caught up at a railroad crossing. The report continues:

On looking up they saw what they supposed to be the airship. It was not near enough to get an idea of the dimensions. A light could be seen protruding from several windows; one bright light in front like the headlight of a locomotive. After some ten minutes, a man was seen descending the rope. He was near enough to be plainly seen; he wore a light blue sailor suit and was small in size. He stopped when he discovered parties at the anchor (which was what was caught), and cut the rope below him and sailed off.

(Dimensions, Ballantine, NY, 1988, page 41)

Another sighting just weeks before was witnessed by the entire town of Fontanelle, Iowa. The April 13th, 1897 edition of the Chicago Chronicle reported, *"The airship was seen here at 8:30 tonight, and was viewed by the whole population. It... moved very slowly, not to exceed ten miles an hour. ...the vibration of the wings could be plainly seen. ...the working of machinery could be heard, as also the strain of music, as from an orchestra".* (ibid. pg. 41) Remember these reports were made years before the Wright brothers flew the first plane at Kitty Hawk. At this time, airships were supposed to be limited to the science fiction writings of the likes of Jules Verne. And since when do we have reports of UFOs playing orchestra music?

In the April 22, 1897 edition of the Houston Post there is actually reported a close encounter with one of the crew of the airship. A Mr. John Barclay had witnessed the airship and gives a rather thorough description of it. And then, *"the night was bright enough for a man to be distinguished several yards away, and when within about thirty yards of the ship he was met by an ordinary mortal".*

The following conversation ensued. Mr. Barclay inquired: *"Who are you and what do you want?"*

"Never mind about my name, call it Smith. I want some lubricating oil and a couple of cold chisels if you can get them, and some blue stone. ...Here is a ten dollar bill: take this and get us these articles and keep the change for the trouble".

After procuring the items, Barclay asked Smith from where he was and to where he was going. He replied, *"From anywhere, but we will be in Greece day after tomorrow".* He got on board, when there again the whirling noise and the thing was gone, *"...like a shot out of a cannon".* (ibid. pg. 42, 43).

The fact that the man refused to give his name is reminiscent of the biblical angels who responded in similar manner when their names were asked. But here is where the similarity ends. These airships make a lot of noise, and seem to need operating parts similar to 19th century technology. And though the ship takes off like it was shot out of a cannon (which by 19th century standards might still be subsonic) it will still take two days to get to Greece. A modern airliner travels this distance in a fraction of that time. No angel, demon or UFO has ever appeared so backward. There are no little gray men reported here. Rather the ships and sightings sound like the realization of something out of a Jules Verne novel. Maybe Verne's character, Captain Nemo, really did exist. Whatever the truth may be regarding these incidents, one thing is clear; they do not seem to be extraterrestrial by late 20th century standards.

The technology that today's UFOs and their inhabitants allegedly display is far more advanced than our own. If we do ascribe to the 19th century airship sightings an extraterrestrial dimension, then we must conclude that the aliens are advancing in their technology alongside the advancements made by mankind. This coincidence is highly questionable, and suspect.

If these incidents were not due to extraterrestrials or a real live Captain Nemo, then what were these mysterious airships, and where did they really come from? No one can really say, although Jacques Vallee believes that these encounters are not extraterrestrial, but rather from somewhere much closer, possibly a parallel dimension right here on Earth. Then again, even in those days the US government did have secret projects; the works of both Einstein and Tesla were known at that time. It is documented that in the mid-1890's, Nicola Tesla had a working model of a radio controlled robot submarine. Who knows what else he invented? Who really knows what was going on?

Chapter 15

Animal Mutilations & Satanic Ritual

At this juncture, I must return briefly to the matter of the animal mutilations, the second area of UFO phenomena that I feel needs further investigation. There is definitely suspicious satanic ritual to these phenomena. And to those who wish to dismiss these animal mutilations as the work of some secret government experiment, I ask the question, what is a secret government project doing knowing about and practicing satanic rituals? And let there be no mistake, satanic rituals are signature, meaning they are very specific. Nothing else is like them. Nothing else can be confused for them. Anyone with knowledge of the occult knows this to be true.

If the US government is behind these animal mutilations as some in the UFO community suggest, then maybe the secrecy surrounding this project has a lot more to hide than scientific experimentation. Being that I do not have any evidence to allege federal government involvement in a cross of scientific experimentation coupled with satanic ritual, I cannot proceed along this line of thinking. I will conclude however on one note. Scientific experimentation and satanic ritual have been used together in the past. The Nazis in the concentration camps were experts in the occult and ran their slaughterhouses and death camps in accordance to satanic ritual murder. These techniques are documented in a number of books as the real source of evil in

Germany's Third Reich. Interested readers should see the book, The Nazis and the Occult, by D. Sklar (Dorset Press, NY, 1977).

Chapter 16

Abductions & Experimentation

Now I must address the most disturbing of all UFO related phenomena: the abduction experience. As I mentioned above the phenomena of alleged abductions by aliens and subjection to medical and other experimentation are not isolated incidents. In recent books published, the number of credible people who have claimed to have had this experience is said to be in the tens of thousands. Whatever be the truth behind these phenomena it is, nonetheless, very frightening that something is happening to so many different people.

The first thing that must be acknowledged about these so-called alien abductions is that many of the cases can be explained as manifestations of a number of different psychological imbalances. In other words, a number of these so-called abductions are nothing of the sort, but rather an induced fantasy or projection, which is covering over serious psychological problems. However, while this might explain a number of the cases, there are still many more which cannot be so easily dismissed by saying that the person is out of his/her mind. Many of the people who experience these so-called abductions are sane people living normal lives.

Being that there is so much publicity in the popular media regarding alien abductions, any and all claims of such experience must be met with skepticism, but at the same time one must keep an open mind. John E. Mack, M.D., Professor of Psychiatry at Harvard Medical School, writes in his Foreword to the book, Secret Life, Firsthand Documented Accounts to UFO Abductions, by David M. Jacobs, Ph.D, that there might be upward of a million people who are abductees or experiencers. He writes:

The abduction phenomenon is, therefore, of great clinical importance if for no other reason than the fact that abductees are often traumatized by their experiences... I would merely suggest that if we could allow ourselves to reintroduce the possibility of a higher intelligence into the universe, and experience the numinous mystery of creation, this scenario is consistent with the facts of abduction phenomena.

Being that members of the psychiatric community are not dismissing the phenomena of alien abductions as nonsense, neither can we. An involved review of the abduction phenomena is beyond the limitations of this present work. For those interested in the reports of numerous cases, I highly recommend this book.

One major aspect consistent with almost all so-called alien abductions is the fixation on sex, especially with young women. Either women are seduced into having sex with an alien or are deceived into having sex with someone or something, all the while having a mental image projected to them that their sex partner is their spouse. Many women recall how there is a blurry image over the faces of their sex partners, at one time being their loved one, another time being an ugly old alien. While this might sound almost comical to some, to tens of thousands of women these are very real, frightening and life shattering ordeals.

We cannot dismiss the significance or reality of these episodes simply because we choose not to believe. I know that many people are afraid to believe that these occurrences could be real for the frightening conclusions that would then have to be drawn. Nonetheless, I believe these episodes are real. Just what they are, however, is something that the Torah can shed some light upon. Whatever the truth may be, we must take these matters seriously.

Abductees relate an enormous amount of information regarding their captors. The most frightening information is how helpless they are when taken and subjected to these experiences. Many abductees claim that the aliens were using them for breeding purposes. In other words, many felt they were being treated like cattle, with no regard for their morality, feelings, and human dignity.

The abductees walk away with a feeling that these aliens are conducting wide scale breeding experimentation on the human race for some concealed purposes. While I do not know the agendas of alien races, the sexual manipulations that these women have been subjected to sounds very similar to cases of demonic attacks that are described by Rabbi Yehuda Fatiyah in his book *Minhat Yehuda*.

Rabbi Fatiyah was a master at detecting the presence of spirits and demons and an expert in the art of exorcism. However, he also knew that people many times make up or imagine things to be that are just not true. He never simply accepted someone's word that they were in contact with a spirit or demon. In order to ascertain their credibility, Rabbi Yehuda would test them to see if the person really was having an otherworldly experience or not.

He relates (*Minhat Yehuda*, page 42) the tale of one married woman with children who claims that a male (demonic) lover would come to her, appearing out of thin air any time that she was alone, day or night. The demon was quite physical and by sheer force of will could make the woman submit to having sex with him anytime that it wished. She felt completely helpless to resist him. This sounds very much like the details of an abductee experience with one of the so-called aliens.

There are numerous tales told in Jewish folklore around the world of women who are kidnapped by demons and taken to live with them in their subterranean homes. There they are raped and forced to bear and raise for their demon masters mixed breed half-demon/half-human children. While most of these tales are told with a moral in mind so as to scare people into acting with righteous conduct, nonetheless their moralistic nature does not negate that something quite real and otherworldly has happened.

In all tales about demons, their subterranean homes are said to be quite opulent. The Zohar (1, 254b) reports that this same opulence belongs to the race of nose-less small creatures living under the Earth that I mentioned above. Aliens always claim to come from a place that is opulent, Utopian, and void of problems. I cannot definitely conclude from this similarity that the aliens are truly subterranean demons in disguise, but it does raise the possibility.

One of the most detailed Kabbalistic texts on demonology is the *Tzefuni Tziyuni* by Rabbi Menachem Tziyuni. Written over six hundred years ago, the *Tziyuni*, as it is popularly called, is perhaps the best source of information about how demons live, how their society is structured, and just what it is they want from mankind. After studying *Sefer Hasidim*, and the works of Rabbi Yehuda Fatiyah, Rabbis and Kabbalists have been in an excellent position to recognize demonic activity whenever it would rear its ugly head. There are a number of similarities between UFO abduction experiences and known demonic activity. Before I draw any conclusions, allow me to document for you the words of the Rabbis, and put them alongside the experiences of the abductees.

Throughout David Jacob's book, Secret Life, mention is made of the peculiar interest that these so-called aliens have shown towards human sexuality, specifically to get humans, mostly human women, to perform acts of intercourse. Why, we must ask, would aliens from another planet be interested in sexual intercourse with females of what to them would be a lower species. It would be similar for a human to want to have sex with a gorilla. Does this sound familiar? Did we not earlier mention that the Bible relates the story of the Benei Elohim (sons of G-d) coming to Earth and taking human wives? In Genesis 6:2 we read that *"the Benei Elohim, the sons of G-d saw the daughters of men, for they were good, and they took for themselves wives from any that they would chose".* Is it possible that demons today are still doing the same thing?

Why would the demons want human women? The answer to this I have already introduced. I have previously mentioned the teaching from the Talmud, b. Avot 5:6, that the original demons were created without stable physical forms, and that since then they have been trying to get bodies for themselves. In *Avot D'Rabbi Natan* 37:3, we have learned that demons participate in sexual reproduction. Can they then sexually bond with and reproduce from humans, male and female alike? The *Sefer Hasidim* and the *Tziyuni* (as well as all other Jewish sources such as the Talmud, Midrash Rabbah, *Hesed L'Avraham*) answer with a frightening yes! Both the *Sefer Hasidim* and the *Tziyuni* give examples of these phenomena, and why and how this occurs. In order to comprehend this fully we must delve into the holy Talmud to understand the origins of human-demonic cross breeding.

Chapter 17

Demons Becoming Human

Talmudic tradition (b. Erub. 18, Gen. Rab. 20:11) relates that in response to the murder of Abel by Cain, Adam decided not to have any more children and separated from Eve. In Genesis 5:3, it states that *"when Adam had lived one hundred and thirty years, he begot in his own likeness and his image, and he named him Seth".* It is said Adam's separation from Eve lasted the entirety of this 130 years. During this period, female demons came to Adam and male demons to Eve and bore them hybrid half-human, half-demonic children. This is why the verse specifies that Seth was in Adam's "likeness and image," something the hybrid children were not. It was in this way that the original non-body demons were able to acquire bodies for themselves. The master Kabbalist, the Ari'zal, in the Sha'arei Kavanot (Derush Pesah 1) reveals that these demonic souls incarnated into human bodies three different times, first as the generation of the flood, second as the people who built of the Tower of Babel, and third as the citizens of Sodom and Gomorrah. It was to trace these descendants of Adam that the Bible relates these episodes.

Regarding these spirits Maimonides writes the following:

And [Adam] begot [a son] in his own likeness and image. You know that whoever is not endowed with this form [i.e., the human form]... is not a man, but an animal having the shape and configuration of man. Such a being, however, has a faculty to cause various kinds of harm and to produce evil that is not possessed by other animals. For he [the demonic human] applies the capacities for thought and perception, which were to prepare him to achieve perfection that he [the demon] has not achieved, to all kinds of machinations entailing evils and occasioning and engendering all kinds of harm.

(Guide, 1:7)

The *Tziyuni* (49b) writes that the demons are still practicing their special breeding program to this day. He goes on to say that the children of such unions, who are essentially demonic in nature, are given the positions of leadership. These hybrid children enable the demons to become physical. Therefore, breeding with humans is highly prized. Does any of this sound similar to the abduction experiences? It most certainly does!

One other point that may be significant: David Jacobs records in Secret Lives (page 51) that *"at the beginning of the nighttime abductions, the Beings enter into the room through a light source coming from a window. ...Although abductees frequently report going directly through walls and ceilings, the Beings appear to seek out a window".* The *Sefer Hasidim* (Tzava'ah 20) writes that it is the nature of demons to travel through windows. Jacobs also mentions (page 50) that some abductees experience these so-called aliens in the form of a menacing animal. *"One abductee said she saw a wolf in her bedroom one night. The wolf was standing squarely on her bed looking in her eyes".* Other abductees have seen these so-called aliens as a devil. The she-demon Lilith is said to commonly take on the appearance of a wolf (Hebrew Myths, page 68).

Chapter 18

Masked Appearances

If the abduction experience is truly of demonic, and not of extraterrestrial origins, why then do these beings go to all the trouble to make people believe that they are from outer space? Why don't they present themselves in some other more acceptable form? Rabbi Yehuda Fatiyah answers this question for us without ever knowing of the modern, so-called extraterrestrial phenomena. He writes about what powers the demons have:

There are demons who are called "pious demons" (Zohar, Bamidbar 253a). These have a different way about them. They make themselves appear as the ancient [biblical] prophets, or as the Talmudic sages. There are those who make themselves appear as the judges of Israel and as great famous rabbis who have passed on to the other side. They all appear with great beards and crowns upon their heads, like the righteous and the pious. Sometimes they say that they are Avraham, Yitzhak or Ya'akov, or Elijah the prophet or the like. [These demons] can do even greater things than this. They can show to a person the image of the heavens, the image of the throne of glory, and the angels of heaven. [These demons] are careful not to frighten a person.

Minhat Yehuda (Miqetz 47)

Rabbi Fatiyah reveals to us that it is the way of demons to present themselves in whatever forms that people will find acceptable so as to have less of a spirit of resistance. Demons can appear as angels, holy men, and the like. They can show people an image of Heaven or of the Heavenly throne. Uneducated human beings, not knowing the spiritual reality of things, will easily be duped into believing that a demonically produced cheap copy of the original is the real thing.

We do not know what real aliens look like, or act like. So if a bunch of demons were to come and say that they were aliens from another planet, how would the average person be able to tell the difference between the truth and the lie? Wouldn't the amazement of being involved with a close encounter of the third kind excite a person to want more? Little do they know what it is that they are involved with. As Carl Jung has properly pointed out in his Flying Saucers, A Modern Myth, mankind has always looked for salvation from the skies. Extraterrestrials are just the newest form that this psychological projection has taken.

Another interesting point is that any and all encounters that people consciously have with these so-called aliens are always a positive and uplifting experience. Abduction experiences are quite the opposite. For one, they are all in repressed memory. No one remembers anything clearly until hypnosis is performed and the unconscious mind is allowed to release its terror. Why are all the alien encounters that can be remembered friendly, whereas the ones which involve sexual and medical experimentation are always erased from the conscious mind, as if by some form of mind control, exactly like the abductees in Jacob's book feel they were subjected to?

It is the unconscious mind that connects us to our soul, that spark from G-d within us. It does not forget, and it is not deceived. When going into the unconscious realms, all of a sudden these alien encounters become depraved, immoral, and monstrous. Abductees speak of screaming within themselves, but of being totally powerless to stop the proceedings, which include the manipulations of their bodies. The case for identifying alien abductions as really being demonic activity seems to have some serious validation. But establishing this to be the case only creates more problems than it solves.

The Rabbis and Kabbalists teach us that demons can come in all shapes and sizes. Therefore, we can perceive them in whatever form we so choose. This might explain why some people are seeing rather human looking aliens; the likes of which Rabbi Horowitz tells us do not exist. Are they demons in disguise? Personally, I cannot definitively say. I have not participated in any sightings of humanoid so-called aliens. However, from the reports that I have read, they are most definitely suspect. And for sure, the people who are claiming these extraterrestrial visitations know nothing about the ways of the demons. It would be the easiest thing in the world for demons to deceive such uneducated simpletons of the spiritual worlds.

If the aliens are really demons, and the demons live in subterranean caverns beneath the surface of the Earth, does this mean that the UFOs are coming to us from the subterranean realms? I am not the first to ask this question. Dr. Raymond Bernard Ph.D., in his book The Hollow Earth (Citadel, NY 1969), devotes an entire chapter to this subject. He says that the UFOs are coming from humanoid subterranean civilizations that are concerned about surface man's detonation of the atomic bomb.

According to the Jewish sources, there are such human-like races living under the Earth. Most likely they have some form of technology that is appropriate for their needs as our technology serves us. Are these human-like beings the fallen angels of whom we have spoken of above, whom the Zohar teaches now live underground? If they are not one and the same, then perhaps they know of one another or are somehow aligned with one another.

After all, if there is an Inner Earth then its surface is not as big as the Earth's outer surface. The fallen angels and their demonic cohorts, who possibly are behind these abductions, live and commune together down there. It is not too far an assumption to then say that if there are other civilizations beneath the Earth, maybe the fallen angels and demons also attempt to plague them as they do mankind? Regarding matters of this nature, we have no answers, we can only speculate.

If the so-called aliens were the ones performing animal mutilations, the fact that they are really demons would certainly explain why the mutilations are in correct satanic ritualistic form. If the aliens were truly the half-breed children of humans and demons, it would explain how they could be physical and non-corporeal at the same time. Most abductees ascribe this ability to almost all the aliens that they have encountered.

One way to ascertain the origins of the so-called aliens and test them for demonic origins is to interpret the communications and information they are allegedly giving to mankind. Whether in abduction experiences or in the now famous close encounters of the third kind, where aliens meet consciously and willingly with humans, the aliens are talking a lot, most specifically and curiously about religion and spirituality.

Almost all people receiving this information believe it to be far superior to anything that we on Earth have heard, or listened to, before. I believe it is important that I document what is alleged to be alien teachings on spirituality and religion. As always, I cannot ascertain the legitimacy of these accounts. I can only write what others are claiming that the aliens are teaching. I admit, the credibility of many of these sources is greatly suspect.

Chapter 19

Aliens & Religion

Religion is supposed to be teachings that we claim either come from G-d or speak about Him, revealing relevant truths about the nature of the entire universe, including wherever it is that the aliens come from. Given that we accept the fact that there is a Divine Creator, then it is He, G-d that has created the aliens as well as mankind. If these aliens are from a society that is more technologically advanced than ours, then surely they would know more about the truths of the universe, and they should be on a higher spiritual plane as well. This is the argument put forth by those who are allegedly receiving religious messages from these so-called aliens.

Rabbis and Kabbalists not only have faith in their religion, some even possess direct prophetic communication with ancient powers, which the Bible identifies as being the guardians of G-d's universe. So if and when an alien race comes and make proclamations regarding religion, these Rabbis and Kabbalists express keen interest as to what in reality is the source of these so-called new religious beliefs. The credibility of most of the sources for the alien teachings is rather dubious. Nonetheless, it is important to document them, and analyze them.

Chapter 20

How to Stop a Negative Close Encounter

While researching this material I came across a magazine entitled Alien Encounters (Vol. 2, No. 1 GCR, NY, 1995). In it is an article entitled *"How to Terminate a Negative Close Encounter,"* written by Wayne Laporte.

Laporte proceeds to outline what he claims are step by step instructions on how to kick out unwanted aliens that are disturbing your sleep or other activities. I was very surprised to learn that there was such a technique. I was under the impression, as are many, that these so- called aliens beam into a person's home, or room, with a Star Trek type of technology, physically pick up the person using a technological form of mind control, and then kidnap them in a very physical way to their very physical UFO. How is it then that Laporte can develop a method that the average person can use to overcome, and thwart such an advanced and seemingly unbeatable technology? Laporte's techniques shed much light on the true identities of these so-called aliens who are kidnapping, and abusing human beings with their so-called advanced technology.

Laporte's article reports the claim of one woman who said that unseen entities began coming late at night, making weird sounds outside her house, and sometimes even throwing small stones at her window. She learned that she could drive them away by reading aloud from her Bible. This sounds more like demonic activity than friendly extraterrestrials. Why else would they be afraid of the Bible? The woman proceeds to relate how she was taught an occult ritual to help battle negative entities. Are we to conclude that the aliens are negative entities, and possibly from Earthly origins? The author of this article is not the first person to make this assertion. Laporte mentions another article where it is claimed that inter-dimensional entities, connected with the Earth, were using *"the dragon power, something that is a part of all energy, but not a specific energy, at fault lines to materialize into and out of our world"*. Again, this does not sound extraterrestrial, at all!

Laporte continues to tell more of the story. The woman relates that late one night she heard a disembodied guttural growl come from the middle of her room. Looking around, she confirmed that she was alone. She cast a circle of white light around herself (the above mentioned occult ritual), and went to sleep. Later she awoke suddenly and with terror. Though she was wide awake, she was paralyzed, and she heard again the disembodied voice. She fought as hard as she could just to slowly turn her head, where just outside the circle of light that she visualized around herself she could see a floating alien head, human in appearance, swirling in an emerald-green energy. She started to mentally chant "In the Name of G-d I command you to return from where you came and don't return". Each time that she did this formula the floating head grew smaller and smaller until it finally faded away completely. When it was gone so was the paralysis of her body. The woman concludes by saying that she jumped out of bed to notice that the time was 3:00 a.m., what she calls the "magic witching hour" which is the same time that many UFO and paranormal events occur.

Many people were said to be able to successfully terminate negative close interactions in this religious manner. This sounds like a scene from a horror movie, yet this woman claims this is what her extraterrestrial experience was like. Both Laporte and this woman do not seem to realize this type of alien encounter appears very much to be an alien encounter of the demonic kind.

Laporte relates further examples. He tells the episode of Emily, who would be paralyzed by these entities. She would resort to an intense mental struggle to free herself from them. *"Furthermore, she learned that if she could move even a toe or finger she could break the paralysis and the creatures would instantly vanish".* He further tells of Lori Briggs, and her episode when *"one night, white skinned, large headed small humanoids suddenly materialized"* in her bedroom. They proceeded to transport her through her bedroom wall to a hovering craft.

Laporte relates still other people's experiences:

One night in the mid-1980's Melissa awoke paralyzed. Standing near her bed was a dark, but indistinct, human sized figure... she began calling on the chief warrior against all dark spirits - the Archangel Michael - to protect her. Immediately the dark shape vanished". Jean described an extraterrestrial as "Almost like an electronic force, trying to pull me out of my body. She confided in her grandmother who confessed that she too had problems with similar visitors. Jean found out her grandmother combated the intruders via the use of prayer.

As can be seen by these examples, the so-called extraterrestrial abduction phenomenon definitely has a demonic element to it. Maybe these abductions are not being carried out by aliens, but by demons disguised as aliens. Or are aliens the ones disguising themselves as demons? Maybe the inter-dimensional demons actually do inhabit another planet, and are thus both extraterrestrials, and demons.

Whatever the truth may be, these entities appear to be bad news for human beings, and they appear to be evil. The forces of good always vanquish the forces of evil. There is no greater force of good than the power of G-d. These examples clearly show that the power of faith in G-d seems to override the "advanced technologies" of these so-called aliens.

Would this be the case if these people were dealing with real physical entities using real physical technological devices? Laporte answers no, that real entities would be unaffected by such trivial things as prayer, and Divine invocations. But even Laporte recognizes a higher power and a spiritual technology operating in these circumstances.

Laporte gives people the advice that they should pray to G-d, use a banishing ceremony, and use a religious artifact to wave off an attack. He then concludes by going directly into the practices of magic to outline a technique of psychic self-defense very well known to every practicing occultist. Laporte teaches the use of the ceremonial dagger. Being that I do not wish to support, or encourage the use of magical ceremonies, I will not describe the ritual usage of the dagger. However, Laporte does describe in detail how the dagger is to be used. This shows that Laporte obviously has knowledge of occult magic.

The question is: why does occult magic have an effect upon alleged extraterrestrials? The answer to this I have already proposed many times throughout this work. There are negative, evil entities out there from whatever source, and their intent is harmful to mankind. At this point it does not matter if they are from another dimension, or from another planet. What matters is that we recognize that these experiences are real. What matters is that these experiences are not new.

Chapter 21

Deeper Kabbalistic Teachings: The Fallen Kings of Edom

As I mentioned above, one area of Kabbalistic studies involves discussions on the pre-Adamic worlds symbolically referred to as the *"seven kings who reigned in the land of Edom, prior to there being a king in Israel"* (Gen 36). The Zohar, and especially the writings of the *Ari'zal* are full of lectures upon lectures about this amazing topic. Interestingly, the world of the seven Kings is called Olam *Hatohu*, the world of emptiness, based on the reference in Genesis 1:2.

An involved explanation of this matter would take me far off course from what I wish to relate here. Also, due to the cryptic nature of the subject matter, any rendering into English would never do justice to the original Hebrew, and Aramaic texts. This is one of those topics that if someone wishes to research in depth, they had better be well versed in both Rabbinic Hebrew and Aramaic. However, I will briefly cover those points, which are relevant to our topic.

Sefer Etz Haim of Rabbi Haim Vital comprises the vast majority of teachings that he received from his Kabbalist teacher, the *Ari'zal*. Based mainly on the Zohar, Rabbi Vital expounds, in the name of the *Ari'zal*, on the entire order of creation, beginning with the original desire of the Creator to create a world, and finishing with the Creator's lowest creations.

To sum up the teachings on these matters, Rabbi Vital relates that were three distinct levels of creation. These creations were not exclusively a creation of physical places, but rather they are epochs in time and space, which outline the order of spiritual evolution.

The first of these three worlds is said to "emanate from the mouth of Adam Kadmon" (Primordial Man). Adam Kadmon is not a person, but rather a symbolic metaphor used to describe the Divine Will. It is also referred to as the first sefirah, Keter.

At this level, it is said that all Ten Sefirot came forth from the Supernal (symbolic) Mouth, encased together in one vessel. This was the primordial beginning of the differentiation of light and its container, the vessel. This initial creation was the creation of form. For prior to this, all existence was exclusively G-d's light. Nothing independent of G-d could manifest, for it had no form through which to manifest. Form, therefore, had to be the first creation, for without it, there would be no differentiation, and nothing would be able to maintain an independent identity. Without form, nothing in creation could be recognizably different from the Creator. This then was the first creation, or world. It is called the "Realm of the Bound" (Olam HaAkudim).

The second creation to manifest from the Primordial Man is said to have come forth from his (symbolic) "Eyes". However, the light of the Eyes of Adam Kadmon did not shine out of the Eyes, but rather shone from below the (symbolic) Waist. Many reasons are given to explain why this occurred, but these reasons are not relevant to our present discussion. It was at this level that G-d's ultimate light diversified into what we will call "the shades of color". This was the creation of diversity. The duality of force and form, soul and body, was thus firmly established. In this realm, the light of G-d's ultimate Being was able to exist within the arena of creation without it overwhelming creation, and thus nullifying it. This was accomplished through the formation of vessels, which would act to filter G-d's ultimate light. These vessels are the primordial forms underlying all creation. These vessels are the Sefirot.

One thing is certain, whenever diversity exists, all existence within the diversity must have its proper place so that all aspects of diversity can become manifest, and perform their given function. When all is one there is never any conflict, for there is nothing to be in conflict with. With the creation of diversity, there arises the potential for conflict. If one claims or usurps the place, role, or identity of another then the two struggle. This struggle is a given feature within any dimension of diversity.

In order to do away with disorder, there has to be the creation of order. Yet, before order can be established, it must be defined. In other words, order must remove disorder, which by definition means that disorder must precede the creation of order. And so it is that we find that prior to the creation of light, the world is void and empty, and prior to their being a "King in Israel" (order) there are "Kings in Edom" (chaos). This is speaking about the Kabbalistic secret of the creation of evil, the breaking and disorder of the primordial vessels, G-d's creation of chaos.

It is out of chaos that order is born. The Kabbalists teach that when the Sefirot came forth for the first time, each in its own unique vessel, the vessels themselves were not in their proper order. The light of G-d shone forth, expecting to shine into each and every vessel, but when the vessels were not in "the right place" to receive the light, they no longer had the ability to survive by themselves. The vessels, therefore, broke and shattered, scattering their pieces over all of creation. This was the creation of the primordial chaos.

As the prophet Isaiah (45:7) has said, G-d creates evil. Evil was created so that good can come forth from it. The Bible itself subtly hints at this process. The first act of creation was the creation of light, but where did the light come from? The Bible is clear; the light came forth out of the darkness. The darkness existed prior to the light, and the light was created to illuminate the dark. The number of vessels that were shattered was seven. Thus Genesis 36 speaks about seven "Kings" who reigned in the land of Edom (the realm of darkness) prior to there being a "King" in Israel (the realm of light). These seven primordial worlds existed long before Adam. Adam was to be the one who was to restore order to the universe. Adam was the symbolic "King of Israel". This is humanity's collective legacy too this day. Yet, there is more to tell about the seven primordial kings, for these worlds of chaos were the previous cosmic Sabbaticals spoken of above.

Many modern students of Kabbalah, even within the Orthodox circles, have never penetrated into the true heart of the teachings of the *Ari'zal* and Rabbi Haim Vital. For Rabbi Vital details the falling of the primordial Kings by saying that each one came forth, reigned for a while, and then died. He is quite clear that there was a fall in the lowest of the Sefirot, Malkhut, which is the force that manifests corporeal reality.

The energy of the Sefirat Malkhut (*Malkhut d'Asiyah, Etz Haim*, 50:1) is that energy described above as nefesh, libido, or orgon energy. Many of the Kabbalists today teach that the fallen Kings were spiritual worlds, totally non-corporeal. This, however, cannot be so, for Malkhut is corporeal. If the original "King" of Malkhut had fallen, then there was a "King," i.e. a physical realm, which had arisen and fallen. Many modern Kabbalists wish to object to this point, yet the evidence is quite clear, Rabbi Vital documents that the "King" of Malkhut had fallen. Therefore, the breaking of the vessels occurred in the physical world, as well as in the spiritual. This point is important to emphasize, for many Kabbalists do not believe that the fall of primordial Malkhut to be physical. They are unfortunately mistaken. In order to understand the relevancy of the fallen Kings to our topic of extraterrestrials, I must delve deeper into the exact meaning of the fall.

Chapter 22

Sefirotic Interactions

It is known that the Sefirot are a type of spiritual DNA. In the process of their emanations, each Sefirah builds upon the others that have preceded it. Each individual Sefirah has within it all of the others. Each individual Sefirah is thus a micro-pattern for the whole.

The pattern of the Sefirot divides them into three columns, referred to the right side, left side, and center. The Sefirot are energy. The energy is intentionally polarized into right and left columns, representing primordial male and female energy. The two are always in a constant state of friction. The center is where they meet and merge. Kabbalistic activity requires the Kabbalist to activate the powers of the supernal male and female, right and left sefirotic columns, and to unite their energies in the center column.

Between the union of male and female, there is the passion of bonding; this is the ecstasy of the prophetic Kabbalistic meditative experience. With the union of male and female, there is the impregnation, gestation, and eventual birth of life. This is the role and function of the Sefirot. They are collectively called the Etz Haim, the Tree of Life. This pattern is their state of order; however, prior to their order was their chaos.

Originally when the first arrangement of Sefirot "emanated from the Mouth of the Primordial Man," the first three Sefirot, which form the first triad, corresponding to the (symbolic) "brain," came forth in proper order and arrangement. A problem then arose. The following seven "lower" Sefirot, those which correspond to the (symbolic) "body," instead of emanating in the form of the columns, as previously described, and as did the first triad, emanated one after another in a "straight line". This rigidity of form did not allow the light within the Sefirot the necessary movement to maintain life. As each Sefirah emanated forth, not in its correct polarity, be it right or left, the light within the vessel was too strong for the vessel to handle. Not being in their right "place" weakened the vessels ability to properly serve as a body for the light to shine within it. The light therefore withdrew. The vessel, being left empty, collapsed, and "died". This episode was the fall of the seven Kings.

One point that Rabbi Vital makes must be emphasized here. The Breaking of the Vessels (Sheviray HaKelim) occurred at the micro-pattern level, as well as on the grand scale. In other words, each of the Ten Sefirot had within them Ten Sefirot, the top triad of which remained intact and did not die, but the bottom seven of each of the ten fell, and died. What remained in the original pattern of the Sefirot, was both order (the upper triad) and chaos (the lower seven). G-d allowed the lower seven to come forth in this blemished manner, knowing that they would die. In this way, G-d created the chaos, which we would come to know as evil, and darkness, so that He could afterwards create order and rectification. The seven lower Sefirot within each of the Sefirot, therefore "fell and died" by the deliberate act of G-d. These are the worlds that G-d created and destroyed prior to our own that are mentioned in Genesis Rabbah.

Chapter 23

Interdimensional–Intergalactic Pre-Adamic Humans

Each of the fallen Kings was a complete world made up of the four realms of the spiritual, mental, emotional, and physical. The upper triad corresponds to the spiritual-mental aspects of those worlds; the lower seven to the emotional-physical aspects of those worlds. The physical-emotional realms are what were destroyed.

Being that no destruction is spoken of regarding the upper triad, it is implied that the life forms corresponding to it did indeed survive. As I mentioned above, there are a number of references throughout Jewish Scriptures that speak about the pre-Adamic generations. For some Kabbalists the question as to what happened to the pre-Adamic peoples is not a question at all. In their opinions, the realms of the fallen Kings were entirely in spiritual, non-corporeal worlds. They say there was no physical aspect to creation prior to Adam.

However, the minority opinion of these Kabbalists is not considered binding. For as in Jewish law, Kabbalah can have varying, even mutually exclusive beliefs, and all of them can still be correct. For as we say, "elu v'elu divrei Elohim Hayim", (both are the words of the living G-d). Therefore, according to the Rabbis who held that the pre-Adamic civilizations did exist, the question must be asked: what happened to them? Where then did they go?

There is not one book in print that I have found that even attempts to offer an answer. Yet, this does not mean that no answer exists.

The Talmud (b. Hag. 13b) speaks of the 974 generations before Adam. Many commentators, as referenced above, interpret this event to be quite physical, and not simply non-corporeal. There are a number of sources that speak of pre-Adamic humans. Although their civilizations were created in imbalance, and therefore fell into chaos, we have, nonetheless, learned that there was a remnant. This surviving remnant corresponds to the "head of Esau buried in the lap of Yitzhak". Esau's head is "buried" in the Cave of Makhpelah in Hevron, the same cave which is the vortex doorway to the Garden of Eden, and the astral plane. This realm is the home of the Ishim angels.

As we have learned above, the Ishim are the only group of angels that have some type of humanoid form. Although they are astral beings, they seem to be quite able to appear human at any time. When an Ishim angel appears as a human, he is quite indistinguishable from any other person, until he so decides to "reveal" himself.

There are two people of whom we know from the Bible (and more from later sources), from this Adamic race, that have ascended above and joined the ranks of the Ishim. These personages, of course, are Enoch and Elijah. Both have "ascended" above and became angels. Enoch became Metatron, of whom we have spoken of earlier, and Elijah became Sandalphon.

In the words of the Talmud, and the Kabbalists, both Enoch and Elijah were originally angels who incarnated and were born as men. They ascended above death, and returned to their previous abodes. Rabbi Moshe DeLeon, a master Spanish Kabbalist of the 12th century, and a codifier of the Zohar, is reported by Rabbi Moshe Cordevero (Pardes 24:14) as saying that Elijah was never born as a man, but rather he descended to Earth as an angel (without human birth, or human parents), and returned in the same way. Rabbi Cordevero also quotes a section of the Zohar that says the opposite of Rabbi DeLeon.

Sefer Likutei Shikha U'Peah 23b states that Enoch-Metatron is the head of the Ishim. We thus see that there is a direct relationship between translated human beings, and the Ishim angels, who are the "princes of the Teli," the rulers of the stars. Enoch was rewarded for his righteousness, as was Elijah. Both did not taste death, but rather they ascended on high and joined the ranks, and leadership of the Ishim angels.

It is possible that these Ishim, the ones who are so similar to human beings were, in fact, human beings, who like Enoch and Elijah were rewarded for their righteousness, and have ascended above to rule the stars. This ascension should not surprise us, for as Rabbi Aryeh Kaplan quoted above said that the reward of the righteous of our world is to, after the resurrection, travel to the stars, and rule there. The resurrection seems to be a prerequisite for our intergalactic travels and ascension to inter-dimensional authority. Enoch and Elijah's translation into bodies similar to the Ishim are the bodies that are given to the resurrected. Thus the bodies of the resurrected and the bodies of the Ishim are identical. Thus they are of one, and the same race.

Chapter 24

The Resurrection

The resurrection is not something that is in the far-off distant future. Rabbi Avraham Azulai writes in his *Hesed L'Avraham* 27a that with the advent of the Mashiah (the true Mashiah) the righteous of the land of Israel are to be translated similar to Enoch, Elijah, and the angels. This translation was originally published in my work, *Yikrah B'Shmi* (1993).

Know, that it is an accepted tradition in our hands that on the day that King Mashiah will come with the ingathering of the exiles to the Land of Israel, there will be found in the Land only seven thousand of the Children of Israel. On this same day, the dead of the Land of Israel shall be restored to life. On that same day also, the walls of Jerusalem shall be removed, and rebuilt from precious stones and pearls. Then, at the time, the dead of the Land of Israel shall be restored to life; they shall be new spiritual creations. Also, the seven thousand who shall be left alive at that time, they too shall be new creations, all of them with spiritual bodies, similar to the body of Adam prior to his sin, and the body of Hanoch, Moshe our teacher and Eliyahu. They shall all float in the air, soaring like eagles. This shall be seen by all the people ingathered from the exile.

Notice that Rabbi Azulai uses the metaphor of the resurrected beings "soaring like eagles". This is the same metaphor used by Rabbi Aryeh Kaplan, in the name of the Zohar, that speaks of the resurrected beings traveling to the stars to govern alongside the present governors, the princes of the Teli, the Ishim angels.

Chapter 25

Ishim Angels & Extraterrestrials

What can be learned from this teaching? There are a number of points that seem to fit together. The reward of righteousness is resurrection, (or translation). One so blessed receives a body of light similar to the Ishim angels, and like them, travels to the stars to govern.

So what happened to the righteous remnant of the "fallen Kings of Edom," the survivors of the pre-Adamic races? Did they like Enoch and Elijah, like the righteous to come on the day of Mashiah, ascend to Heaven; become the Ishim and the rulers over the galaxy? While no Kabbalistic text say this outright, it is clear that this is implied! The Ishim are the translated survivors of the pre-Adamic human races. It is they who inhabit the inter-dimensional, intergalactic realm. It is they, who, as the angels of G-d, are destined to come back to Earth and be the conquering armies of the Mashiah, as it is written, "And YHWH my G-d shall come, with all His holy ones.

(Zech 14:6).

There are extraterrestrial humans in outer space. But they have evolved far beyond what we understand to be human. They live in the non-corporeal realm of the Teli and they are what we will be in the future. They were what we presently are.

G-d's entire universe thus proceeds in cycles, even as the doctrine of the Shemita teaches. These pre-Adamic translated humans, who are now the Ishim angels are very much involved with human affairs. They are very much our guardian angels. They are very much our Watchers. G-d has placed them to be responsible for us.

In Kabbalistic meditations there are specific formulas, which are used which enable us to communicate with the "princes of the Teli". These formulas have never been published. Corporeal extraterrestrial entities, and non-corporeal astral entities (angels and demons) are often one and the same thing. At some point intergalactic reality crosses the inter-dimensional line, merging two realities together as one. The apparent separation, therefore, between the corporeal and non-corporeal (the physical and the astral) must be redefined. With the present growth in modern quantum physics and chaos theory, this is beginning to occur. Kabbalists, however, have been aware of these things all along.

Chapter 26

Conclusion

The UFO experiences of people nowadays are all part of G-d's plan to make us aware that there is a greater world surrounding us, more than what the eye can see. Many of the UFO stories are nonsense. Many UFO sightings are really secret military projects, which the government has every right to keep top-secret. Many close encounters with extraterrestrials are really encounters with other inter-dimensional beings, most likely of a demonic nature. Some sightings, stories and encounters are the fantasies of deluded minds. Some sightings, stories, and encounters might very well be of real extraterrestrials that have a G-d-given right to be here, to conduct whatever business it is that G-d has given them to do. No matter what the source is, no matter what the truth, there is still only one underlying reality beneath all these phenomena.

When we look out upon our universe, and explore everything there is to be explored; once our minds have examined all things and we rise to be true masters of the physical universe, we will find as the last and most ultimate discovery that which legend instructs that the ancient master Avraham found some 4,000 years ago - there is only One true existence and only One true reality.

This reality is the consciousness of the universe. It is above and beyond the universe as the soul is above the body. This reality is the true Being and awareness of all. This reality is above the universe itself. Above and beyond, while at the same time, below and within. This reality is G-d, the one and only True Source. G-d can never be removed from us, no matter where we go. G-d is ever guiding our footsteps back to our true spiritual home.

There is only one thing left to learn. King Solomon said it best, so with his words shall I conclude.

The end of the matter, when all is said and done: Have awe of G-d and keep his commandments; for that is the whole duty of man. For G-d shall bring every work into judgment, even every secret thing, whether it be good, or whether it be bad.

(Eccl 12:13, 14)

PART THREE

G-D, ANGELS, & HUMANITY: REVELATIONS & INSIGHTS ABOUT OUR COMPLICATED RELATIONSHIP

This section was written as an independent book originally distributed within the Orthodox Jewish community. References herein will reflect Orthodox Jewish traditions and beliefs.

Chapter 1

The Dominant Rule of the Name Elohim

In numerous places within Torah literature, the different names of G-d are said to refer to different aspects of revelation of the Divine within creation. Within creation, there are numerous dimensions and universes. To simplify matters we can state that there are two relative dimensions in creation. These dimensions are the realms of the natural and of the supernatural.

Within the realms of the natural, G-d is referred to as Elohim, the Creator. This is because as the Creator, He established the laws of nature and allows the universe to be governed by them. Indeed, the name Elohim is in gematria equal to the Hebrew word for nature, "HaTeva".

The realm of the supernatural, however, is different; it is when G-d wishes to intervene in creation above and beyond the limitations of the natural laws of physics that govern a relative place. When G-d performs this intervention, He is referred to by His name YHWH, the ultimate Being, and Essence of the universe.

Throughout the TaNaKh (Bible), we have numerous examples of Divine intervention into human and natural affairs. The exodus from Egypt, the parting of the Sea of Reeds, the crossing of the Jordan, and the stopping the movement of the sun are just a few of the miracles which occurred when the name YHWH was revealed in the natural universe. YHWH can be considered an internal or higher aspect of Divine revelation, whereas Elohim simply connotes G-d's latent and concealed presence throughout and within nature.

The name YHWH does not always manifest itself in creation. Since the days of the destruction of the First Temple over 2,500 years ago, the name YHWH ceased to manifest itself entirely. With this concealment, many things happened. Prophecy ceased to exist. The Holy Temple was destroyed. The Ark of the Covenant, and the ancient treasures, were concealed and thus lost to future generations.

For millennia now, we have lived under the dominion of the Divine revelation inherent within the name Elohim. This name not only correlates to the forces of nature, it also manifests the element of Divine justice and severity. This explains why the laws of physics are so strict. They cannot be compromised with as much ease as can be human laws.

It is clear and evident that the Jewish people and nation have suffered tremendous hardships since the destruction of Solomon's Temple and the loss of our national treasures, the Ark, prophecy, and the Divine Presence (Shekhina). Yet, this was not the greatest loss to be suffered by the Jewish people.

With the destruction of Solomon's Temple, we lost our most precious possession, our "face to face" relationship with G-d that manifested to our nation His Divine mercy through His name YHWH. With the destruction of the Temple, not only was our relationship with G-d severely altered, His "innermost" name was concealed from the world. No longer would we call upon the His name YHWH; instead, we today call upon the name ADNY (Adonai – meaning L-rd). While this too is a holy name, it still represents an aspect of G-d that operates within the natural realm similar to the name Elohim. With the loss of Solomon's Temple, we lost the ability to receive supernatural intervention into natural affairs.

Although miracles have continued to occur from time to time, some great, some small, they all nonetheless, emanate from a much lower source than the name YHWH. In essence, all miracles since the days of the destruction of Solomon's Temple have been veiled within the occurrence of natural events. The stories of Purim and Hanuka are two such examples.

The story of Purim and the book of Esther is the prime example of the change that occurred after the initial exile began. The striking remarkable fact about the book of Esther that separates it from every other book in the TaNaKh is that the book never makes any mention about G-d, angels, or Divine intervention. The book of Esther was written to make the entire story of Purim read like a tale of political intrigue instead of like the rest of the TaNaKh, which always emphasizes Divine intervention into human affairs.

Since the days of Purim until today the only way to solicit and receive, Divine blessing in the natural world is by doing natural things. In other words, unlike in the old days, those who today rely and wait upon miracles are usually sorely disappointed. The new way of things in the days of exile follows the natural order. This lesson was taught to us well by Mordechai and Esther.

Those who take matters into their own hands, as did Mordechai and Esther, provide for G-d the tools of practicality, through which Divine blessing can come. Those who plan, prepare, and execute action with wisdom, deliberation, and discipline express the greatest of G-d's gifts, the use of human intellect and resolve.

In essence, the exile has been for us a blessing in disguise. No longer are we to rely upon our Heavenly Father to extricate us from our own messes. Now, we must take responsibility for ourselves. What we create is what we have, be it for good or for bad. G-d has given into our hands the powers of blessing and curse. When we look upon our world and upon our personal lives, we can no longer blame G-d, the angels, or any other supernatural power for whatever goes wrong. What we create is what we have.

Granted, it is a tenet of faith to acknowledge that G-d is the true author of all things. It is true that nothing transpires in the natural world that is not in accordance to the Divine Will. Yet, we mere mortals are far from understanding the Divine plan.

All too often, we attribute to G-d's Will the failures in life that we ourselves have created. In other words, when something goes either very right or very wrong we attribute this to being the Divine Will. Ultimately, this is of course true, but the Divine Will can manifest in various different forms. It is not necessarily G-d who chooses to manifest His will in the way it does. Human choice plays a great role is what aspect of the Divine Will becomes manifest in the natural world.

This concept that I am describing to you now is one of the most difficult of human attributes. It is a unique and special gift from G-d. We call it Human free will.

Chapter 2

The Role of Free Will

Free will is the fundamental gift of G-d. It allows us to be fully human instead of pre-programmed robots. Free will enables us to choose between good and evil. This choice enables us to merit reward or punishment, blessing or curse.

We can choose! Yet, this makes us responsible and liable for our choices.

Apparently, good and evil are not limited in definition by moral directives. There are natural forces in the universe that must also be considered. In other words, the ramifications of our actions affect far more than the moral dimension, they affect all areas of our life and environment.

For example, the development of technology is a man-made choice inspired by human creativity and our desires to make our world a better and easier place. Pollution is also a man-made choice, a by-product of our technology. While technology is a good development, pollution is a bad development. Technology can make all our lives much easier. Pollution can ultimately snuff out life all together.

Therefore, shall we call technology a blessing and pollution a curse? Can we call technology good and pollution its evil twin? Do we say that technology is from G-d, and pollution from the devil?

Let us not get G-d and His angels involved, and hold them responsible for a man made quagmire.

Granted, G-d gives intelligence to man. Mankind then uses his intelligence, curiosity, and tenacity to discover the foundations of the laws of physics. What man discovers is what the Creator has placed in His universe from the very beginning. Like a child, mankind is looking a puzzle and only now recognizing that the many pieces fit together and form a greater picture.

Mankind does not need a devil or demons to create for him havoc. Pollution is the prime example. The devil did not create pollution. Mankind did. The devil did not create pollution in order to hinder man's technological growth. Mankind created pollution by not being intelligent and caring enough to see the long-term effects of his actions, upon himself, and his world.

G-d allows pollution to exist, simply because mankind allows it to exist. Pray as hard as you like. Prayer will not remove pollution from our environment any more than from within the human soul. Man created pollution and in order to dispose of it before it kills him, he must use his G-d given brain to devise a way to neutralize it. If not, do not expect G-d to miraculously intervene and clean up the environment. These are the blessings and curses of free will.

Free will can be a real blessing and a real curse. Yet, there is also the Will of G-d. G-d does ordain and predestine certain things to be. Therefore, how far can free will go? The Talmud answers this question for us with a most remarkable story.

In the Talmud (b. B.M. 59b), a discussion is recorded between Rabbi Eliezer and the Sages regarding whether a certain type of oven is to be considered kosher or not. When the vote was taken to decide the law, the majority sided against Rabbi Eliezer. In response, Rabbi Eliezer called upon supernatural powers to enforce his opinion over that of his colleagues. Rabbi Yehoshua, representing the Sages, rebuked the supernatural forces and disallowed their influence over rational legal decisions that decide matters in the natural world.

In frustration, Rabbi Eliezer invoked G-d Himself to intervene on his behalf. Indeed, a Voice speaks out from Heaven declaring that the law is in accordance to the view of Rabbi Eliezer. At this point Rabbi Yehoshua speaks out and quotes a verse from the Torah that states "it is not in Heaven" (Deut 30:12). This verse is interpreted to mean that Torah Law is decided by the majority opinion of the court. The implication is that man decides the Law, not G-d. In essence, Rabbi Yehoshua, however politely, told Heaven to mind its own business.

This is such a shocking story. One would expect Rabbi Yehoshua to be in deep spiritual trouble with G-d and His Heavenly tribunal. One would expect a Heavenly thunderbolt, with Rabbi Yehoshua's name on it, to strike at any minute. Yet, this was not the case.

Days later, one of the Sages present at this debate encountered the prophet Eliyahu. He asked Eliyahu, what was going on in Heaven when Rabbi Yehoshua stood up against the Heavenly voice. Eliyahu said that G-d laughed. G-d said, "my sons have defeated me". In other words, G-d admitted that Rabbi Yehoshua was correct in telling Heaven to mind its own business.

According to the famous psychologist Erich Fromm, this story embodies the highest goals of human freedom expressed in the Torah. In his work, You Shall Be as Gods (Henry Holt, NY, 1966, page 79) Fromm writes:

The very fact that man has made himself independent and does not need G-d any longer, the fact of having been defeated by man is precisely what pleases G-d. It is in the same sense that the Talmud says: 'The character of mortal man is such that when he is conquered, he is unhappy, but when the Holy One is conquered, he rejoices'
(b. Pes 119a).

While mankind, of course, needs G-d, as does the entire universe, nonetheless, the implication here is that G-d has given man certain responsibilities. Man, therefore is obligated to uphold those responsibilities and not depend upon G-d to do that which man himself is required to do. Man's free will, as can be seen, entails a great deal.

Chapter 3

The Influence of the Watcher Angels

While free will gives us a tremendous amount of choice, it also gives us a tremendous amount of responsibility. One might conclude from this that destiny and fate are what we individually decide for ourselves. In other words, one might conclude that there are no other outside supernatural forces that have any influence over our decision-making. Yet, according to Torah, nothing could be farther from the truth. In the universe of natural things, we most certainly are not alone.

While fantastical life in outer space has long been a popular part of the general culture, there is no acknowledgment of any scientific proof of there being any real extraterrestrial life. Yet, every culture in history around the world has stories of otherworldly beings, be they angels, demons, spirits, or whatever. Most people in modern societies dismiss their stories as pure myth. Yet, in spite of this opinion, numerous millions of people around the world do believe in these otherworldly beings, with a substantial number of reports from people who claim to have made contact with them.

Taking for granted that there really are such entities as angels take a moment and ask yourself, just what is an angel? Where do they come from? What do they really look like? How do they transport themselves? What do they do with their time? Do they eat, sleep, or perform any other type of behavior similar to humans?

If angels are anything other than myth, they must have some type of life, and they must live in some type of place, but what and where?

While religion will answer these questions with faith and theology, there is no actual scientific evidence to validate or dismiss anything. All that we can say is that angels must be extraterrestrials simply because they are not of this Earth. This does not imply that they are "little gray men" traveling on "flying saucers" from another planet. Nonetheless, according to certain Rabbinic opinions, there is a definite relationship between angels and other planets.

The Bible and later Jewish literature relate that angels and demons play extremely important roles in human lives. The Sages teach us that there is never a moment, ever, that we are not in the presence of both types of these alien beings. Yet, we must question, what do they want from us, why do they care to be here instead of minding their own business. The answer to these questions might be very unsettling to many people.

In the biblical book of Daniel, we find that individual nations are under the guidance, leadership, and protection of specific angelic governors. Torah literature outlines that not only does each nation have its angelic chief; each and every individual has their own personal angel, and besides this, their own personal demon.

One aspect of Torah literature endeavors to de-personalize these otherworldly beings and say that they are merely aspects of human psychology. One's personal angels have been associated with the Yetzer HaTov (good inclination) and Yetzer HaRa (evil inclination) within the human psyche.

However, the majority of views, especially that of the mystics, is that these entities (including the two yetzers) are real, external extraterrestrial beings, that are invisible to all normal natural senses. More so, they are here for a reason. In the book of Daniel, these angels have a special name. They are called the "Watchers".

The Watcher angels are described in merkava literature as being a specific species of angel whose job it is to run things here on Earth as G-d's messengers. Indeed, the Hebrew word for angel, malakh, literally translates as messenger. While G-d is Ruler over all creation, the day-to-day affairs He has handed over to this "civil service". This is the order of things under the name Elohim or ADNY.

Indeed, the Watcher angels are also referred to elsewhere in the Torah and later literature as the "Benei Elohim" angels. The Benei Elohim are the "sons" of Elohim. They execute the edicts of the laws of nature ordained by Elohim. When the name YHWH is revealed in the natural world this means that G-d takes personal control of matters, overriding the rule and role of His servants, the Watchers.

The Watcher angels are charged to maintain creation and the continuing function of the laws of nature. The Watchers also have the job to influence the minds and hearts of men. Yet, as mentioned above, the personal angel that we each have is accompanied by a very real and personal demon, who itself is in reality another Watcher angel.

Therefore, while we as mankind boast of our independence and free will, we have still to contend with invisible outside Watcher influences that endeavor to direct our thoughts and mold our behavior, all in accordance to the Divine plan.

The existence of an outside influence over human decision making capacities may or may not be a good thing. For although free will is a universal constant, the decisions of free will reveal the variable element in creation. In other words, as long as there is free will, almost anything can happen, for either good or bad.

Unlike what is taught in spiritually immature cultures (idolatry), there is no great war going on in the universe between G-d and "the Devil" battling for possession of our souls. For although there really is a Satan, the Hebrew word/name Satan actually means prosecutor. While the term Satan does refer to a specific angel, it also refers to a class of angels whose job it is to act as officers in G-d's Heavenly tribunal. The Satan is not a judge. He is a prosecutor. He is by no means of equal status, power or authority with the Heavenly judges, even more so is he less than the Creator Himself.

Judging from the biblical book of Job, the Prosecutor angel also acts to create "sting operations". The Prosecutor, through his Watcher agents endeavors to cause man to use his free will in ways that are detrimental to himself and others. If any individual falls for these tricks, the prosecutor immediately ascends before the Heavenly tribunal and brings accusations against the individual and then acts as witness against him/her. If found guilty, the Heavenly tribunal can enact edicts that can have the most severe consequences upon an individual's life.

Although many wish to dismiss this invisible drama as mere myth, the ramifications of its reality are no less diminished. Terrible things happen to good people on an almost daily basis. There seems to be no rhyme or reason to what happens in the world. Yet, there is an order to everything in the universe. The universe does follow a divinely ordained comprehensive, rational program. The rhyme, the reason, and the program however, are totally invisible to the majority of us.

This is where faith comes in. One is to believe that whatever happens is for the best and serves a Higher Cause. Yet, faith can also be abused and used as an excuse for one not to take personal responsibility for certain matters in life. Instead of one recognizing his/her own faults, one blames G-d and/or his individual sins for his personal misfortune.

Although the Watchers watch, we can still exercise our full share of free will and operate with the minimal of Watcher influence and intervention. However, this is much easier said than done, as we shall soon see.

Chapter 4

Watchers & Man: A Relationship of Enmity

Free will, what a grand concept! Watcher angels, what a frightening concept! Put the two together and what do we get: the present turmoil of human morality and human thinking.

One should not think that Watcher angels, because they are closer to G-d than are we, that they are perfect "angelic" beings. This notion is unfortunately not the case. As we recall from Genesis, a group of these angels "fell" from Heaven, came to Earth took wives for themselves, bore giant children, who created so much havoc that G-d (Elohim) had to send a flood to wipe them all out (along with all other life on Earth).

Did you ever stop to ask why an angel would want to descend to Earth, take on a lower form of existence and then cohabit with females of a foreign species (human)? We humans are all attracted to the beautiful members of the opposite sex. Yet, when was the last time a human was aroused to cohabit with a chimpanzee, a baboon, or a reptile?

Angels, even their lowest rank, the Benei Elohim, are far above present day humans on the evolutionary scale. Why then would an angel want to come down here and play with (what are in his eyes) the apes?

In order to understand this we must delve into Jewish legend. For thousands of years, there have been many stories that have accompanied and explained the biblical stories. Stories about the beginning, specifically about the days from creation to the flood, abound. They are often detailed and relate to us a side of history most profound and most disturbing.

According to these stories, G-d's creation of man was not met with full support by the already previously existing angelic races. Indeed, great controversy arose when it was revealed that a superior race of beings was to be created. One angelic race challenged the decision outright and refused to pledge loyalty and cooperation with this new species to be called "Adam" (man). Representatives of this race claimed before the Heavenly court that for whatever reason man was chosen to be created; they could fulfill that purpose better than could the new race.

YHWH told this angelic race that they did not have it in them to perform the tasks that man was to be created to perform. Thus, enmity arose, from the beginning, even prior to our creation. Yet, we can live with enmity. However, what happened next is what affected us the most.

A representative of the race decided to take matters into his own hands. He decided that he would show YHWH the flaws in His newly created "man" and thus hope to influence the Divine plan more in his own favor.

This angel disguised himself and succeeded in confusing the newly created man (and woman) into violating their prime directive. This is the fall in the Garden of Eden. The angel proved himself right, but because he thwarted the plan of YHWH, he was severely punished. This angel today is the one we know as the Satan. Those of his species who follow in his philosophy and actions are the ones we today call demons. Yet, be mindful, there are other races of entities here on Earth, also referred to as demons, which are vastly different in origin and nature from these rebellious angels.

Yet, now we must ask, can an angel really thwart the plans of G-d? For that matter, can man do the same? As we have learned previously, G-d's plan is rather complicated. It apparently took into account with forethought all the rebellions and problems which were to come.

This raises the question, if G-d knew that Satan was to rebel and man was to sin, did He not plan for all this from the beginning? The answer to this conundrum is both a confusing yes, and no. G-d foresaw the potential of these actions and enabled the universe to be able to absorb these behaviors. The universe did not need these acts to occur. Another, even more efficient plan would have transpired if the behavior in creation was different. Thus, there was no destiny or fate that guided events. Events transpired randomly, with the universe responding in accordance to pre-set Divinely ordained laws and guidelines.

Why was a lofty member of such a sublime species intimidated by the creation of lowly man? The answer to this, revealed to us by the mystics, is that when Adam was created he was far, far different and superior than terrestrial man is today. Originally, like the angels Adam too was created as a highly evolved being of light. The initial Adam was not a corporeal being as we are today. Adam's initial state was one of pure mind.

Indeed, G-d's purpose in creating Adam was so that the Adamic species would serve to unite and integrate the two realms of creation, the natural with the supernatural. G-d's original design was for Adam to accomplish this task working essentially from the supernatural side, reaching downward into the physical. The sin in the Garden confused Adam into thinking that if he first descended into the physical universe, he would be able to rectify it quicker and better. Alas, for Adam, he was not ready for such a descent.

The eating of the forbidden fruit was Adam's descent and experiment with the physical universe prior to his being ready and able to do so. We are all suffering the consequences of this action. For once Adam descended below, he became stuck. He only too late realized that "he was naked" of the spiritual power that enabled him to arise and come and go as he pleased.

Adam became stuck in corporeal reality and the saga of present human history began. This story explains why man, as a species is always so restless. Humans, more than anything else are explorers, wanting to learn and know new things. Once the spirit of adventure has left a person, that individual has become more like an ape than like a true human created in the image of G-d.

The Watcher/Benei Elohim angels who maintain the operations of natural law look upon fallen man with disdain. The lofty, high and mighty Adam has fallen and devolved. Instead of being an entity of light like the angels, man has become like the monkey, an entity of flesh and blood. When it comes to the daily operations of creation, these angels, therefore, care not to give any leeway, to fallen man. Their attitude is simple, if man has fallen, let him pick himself up. Man will receive no special favors from the Benei Elohim.

Until YHWH intervenes in creation, fallen man is left to his own devices. While there are other, higher angels who do look benevolently upon man, these guardian angels are limited in the scope of their power. We thus find that, in the invisible realms, politics and intrigue are not too dissimilar than they are here in the physical, natural world.

Apparently, human free will, as grandiose as it is, from time to time comes into conflict with the Watchers and their plans. Although everything that happens to people comes from the Will of G-d, in the state of exile where the name Elohim rules, severity rules. Mankind is advised how to act in order to avoid conflict between himself and the forces underlying nature. Unfortunately for man, he seldom listens to what is best for himself. Thus, an elemental cause of human suffering comes from supernatural causes. Yet, these too can be controlled by man's choice, specifically by his actions.

Chapter 5

Of Angels & Man: Differences & Similarities

In spite of any and all supernatural interference, man is still ultimately responsible for himself and his behavior. Although G-d might allow or even ordain for one to stumble along the way, nonetheless, one cannot use stumbling as an excuse for improper behavior. Remember Job.

As fallen man, we are in a very difficult position. While we are unaware of our true human status, the higher species (angels) are very well aware of it. More and more as the individual man/woman cultivates him/herself and grooms his/her behavior; the surrounding angels take notice. Some welcome the growth. Others resent it. Some wish to encourage man to find his lost hidden self; others wish to hinder his growth.

Learn from this that there are numerous species of angels. RaMBaM enumerates ten different types, but no one knows in detail the specifics. Angels are races of beings, far older than man. Being that the title "angel" is a generic term for G-d's messengers, we use it to describe numerous types of beings, with numerous types of tasks. In other words, not all angels are alike.

In order for us to grasp the slightest insights into angelic nature, we have to have a basic understanding of the multiple dimensions that exist in our universe, both the natural and the supernatural. These insights also shed a great deal of light onto the true nature and potential of man. In other words, when we understand the nature of the universe we understand our own nature. The opposite is also true; understand man and you understand the universe.

As discussed previously, we can divide the universe between the natural and the supernatural. The natural, we know as the universe around us with all its physical laws. The supernatural is the generic term we use to describe everything else. Thus, in order for us to attain insight we will have to go beyond the generic and diagram the multiple realms that we call the supernatural. We will begin this discussion here and continue it in upcoming lessons.

The supernatural realms are all interconnected to and intertwined with our physical universe. While the realms are separated, they are not separated by space or by time. They are however separated by perception. In other words, what is extra sensory or supernatural for one is very natural and sensory for another.

This fact is not only true among angels and men; this is also true of many physical animal species. It is documented science that elephants and dolphins have audio abilities far beyond that of man. For us these species have extra-sensory audio perception. From their points of view, they must think man is rather deaf. This same comparison can be made between man and angels.

There are angels who dwell in this physical universe of ours. However, unlike man, the physical makeup of these entities is far different from our own. Our bodies are composed of elements in combined solid, liquid, and gaseous states. The angelic races of this universe apparently do not share with us a solid or liquid state. We have no record of them being of a gaseous state, however there is yet another element.

The fourth element beyond the gaseous state has traditionally been called "fire"; the "energy" state or plasma. While the vast majority of Rabbinic scholars believe that angels have no corporeal element within them, there is a single, rather old opinion, that claims the lower angels have a form composed of this fourth element, fire. According to this singular opinion, this explains why angels often appear to have a body of light, or some type of glowing or burning form.

Whatever be the composite of advanced intelligent beings, one thing is certain; their construct defines for them their perception of the universe. In other words, as with the example above of animals, an entity views the universe in accordance to its senses. A human can only see so much because human eyes can only perceive light within a certain scope on the spectrum. Granted our technology has spread out that scope. Yet, we are far from seeing the entire spectrum.

There are other entities whose structural makeup enables them to perceive entire areas of the universe invisible to the physical human eye. Yet, does this mean that man has no access to these areas, or must he simply use other senses to access them? We believe that even fallen man has hidden within him all his lost potential, waiting to be rediscovered and released. If such reawakening were to occur, man would be able to "see from one end of the universe to the other". In other words, man's mind would be able to grasp and comprehend all things in creation, regardless of its dimensional origin and position.

The human mind is a most incredible thing. We only know its most surface level, what we call consciousness. Yet, we also know that there is something called the unconscious. No one can say for sure what lies in the unconscious, for if they could it would be conscious.

Here is where the great difference lies between man and angels. Man has an unconscious wherein resides the vast majority of his knowing. Angels have no such thing. Man's mind is split and thus so is his compression of the universe. With angels, there is no such thing. Man's mind can expand and grow to infinite levels. Angels are what they are; they cannot evolve beyond their present state. As we can see, to be an angel or to be a man, both have their advantages and their disadvantages.

Unlike humans, angels are not curiosity driven. Angels live in realms and areas of the natural universe that from our limited sense of perception we call the supernatural. Yet, we must remember the supernatural only refers to those realms that relate to the holy name YHWH. Granted there are the angels of YHWH, but these are not the Watcher/Benei Elohim. In essence, the angels of YHWH are as above the Watcher/Benei Elohim as the Watcher/Benei Elohim are above mortal man.

Mortal man, limited in perception as he is, cannot perceive with his senses the existence of any type of life form not of solid structure. Mortal man, therefore, cannot perceive or experience the presence of angels. Mortal man, therefore, could not tell the difference between a Watcher/Benei Elohim angel, and a Cherub angel, or a Seraph angel. The differences between these species are great. They clearly recognize the differences between themselves. We on the other hand are totally oblivious to their existences, much less their distinctions. As different as they all are, man in his higher state, prior to the fall, was greater than them all.

Angels differ and so do the places of their dwellings. As non-solid life forms, their places are not physical locations, as we understand the concept. Angels differ in character and in degree of closeness to the Creator. As lofty as they are, still they lack one ability unique to the Adamic species, the free will to choose between good and evil, to thus merit reward or punishment.

Chapter 6

The Role & Limitations of Guardian Angels

What is the role and power of a Guardian Angel? Can they intervene in our lives to provide for us good? If so, then they should also be able to intervene in our lives to protect us from harm. Alas, judging from all the bad things that happen to good people, either our Guardian Angels are rotten guardians, or simply there is a limitation to the amount of their intervention. In order for us to be able to answer this question, we must endeavor to understand it from the angel's point of view.

It is easy for us to judge something we know nothing about. Being that they are invisible, we can judge spiritual beings any which way we like. We can never know if we are right or wrong.

It is just as easy for us to proclaim a statement of faith about something that may or may not be true. We can all proclaim that G-d is just and true. Still, we must ask why G-d allowed a million young and innocent children to be murdered by the Nazis. We can claim that man allowed it to happen and G-d watched, and "cried". We can claim that the souls of these children were "destined" to be martyrs. One opinion claimed that the murdered souls were reincarnated sinners who were paying back their debt to G-d. In our present human condition, we can never know the answer to questions like these.

Who are we to judge? Even if we were to judge and declare G-d cruel, what good would it do? Do you really think that G-d is willing to change His Divine plan and practice based upon human shortsightedness? If we declare G-d just and true and that we are the sinners, then how bad must our sins be to have deserved the horrors that we humans have faced throughout history?

Do not let religious fanatics answer this question for you. For each group that proclaims that it alone has G-d's true message and all who reject it are going to hell, each one of these groups have had horrible things happen to its members that no sense of justice can justify. They proclaim a message of faith, but for those suffering, words of faith are little comfort for heart wrenching anguish and grief.

So, where does this leave us? To try to understand G-d's plan with limited fallen human intelligence is impossible. Yet, G-d's plan continues, regardless whether we like it or understand it or not. Rather than look upon G-d's plan from a human point of view. Let us endeavor to penetrate behind the spiritual veil, ever so little, to grasp a glimpse of what is seen in the angelic realms.

The Talmud (b. Pes. 50a) records an episode about one Rabbi Yosef who once fell extremely ill. During his illness, he had some sort of vision and/or out-of-body experience. When asked by his father what he saw, Rabbi Yosef claimed he ascended to Heaven and saw there an upside-down world. That which is great in this world is small there, whereas that which is small here is great there. In other words, that which we humans consider important is insignificant in the eyes of Heaven, whereas that which we consider insignificant is considered great in Heaven's eyes.

Life and death are of those things whose values are viewed oppositely in Heaven than on Earth. In G-d's Eyes, there really is no such thing as death. In His eyes, all human souls are before Him, always, whether in a body on Earth or in spirit in Heaven. G-d sends a soul on its journey, both in this world and in the next, for purposes known in His Divine wisdom. Apparently, G-d sends our souls to Earth because both good and evil reside here. We are thus given the opportunity to use our free will to choose a course of action for ourselves, with the accompanying reward and blessing or punishment and curse.

Even a lifetime of suffering in G-d's Eyes exists for only the smallest fraction of a second when looking at eternity. As our souls are eternal, an entire human lifespan is insignificantly short. Whatever happens to us only matters from the point of view of how we deal with it. Heaven views the present state of fallen man to have caused us to become overly attached to the physical world and to almost entirely forget the reality of the higher realms and dimensions. Life and suffering are thus sent to us as teachers to remind us where our true priorities should lie.

With regards to Guarding Angels, their purpose is clear. They are sent to fulfill G-d's task for us, not to serve us, as we would wish.

Terrible things have happened to decent and good people throughout history. Evil and rotten people have built themselves up upon the flesh and blood of numerous victims, have lived lives of pleasure, and die in grand old style. There just does not seem to be any justice in this system.

Alas for eyes, our eyes only see the smallest portion of life, the portion when the soul resides in the body. Our religions tell us what happens to bad souls after leaving the body, but ask yourselves, is this truly a consolation for those who have been victimized? Hitler, and other evil fiends, have murdered millions of people and paid no price for their hideous crimes. What justice can we call upon them? What could G-d do to their souls that would appease the millions of their innocent victims?

The question is whether it is important for G-d to appease the victims, as we here on Earth would demand. Maybe the victims once relieved of their physical life understand their experiences in a different light? This might not help those of us who are suffering here and now. Yet, maybe the purpose of our present suffering is a test to see how we react. Remember Job.

G-d is the ultimate Teacher. All things in creation serve Him, one way or another. Even we humans with our free will, who choose to rebel against G-d and Heaven, are still playing a role in G-d's master plan for the universe. Remember that our physical universe operates by quantum principles. Contradictory laws can and do abide simultaneously. There is always a random element underlying even the most stable of natural laws.

Guardian angels serve their Creator not their charge. Part of a Guardian Angel's job is sometimes to lead his charge into adversity, so that the individual will struggle, persevere, and eventually overcome adversity. This was the case with Yosef in Genesis.

The Torah tells us that Yosef was sold into slavery by his own brothers. He descended into Egypt, spent 13 years as a slave before "fortune" shined upon him and changed the course of his life. Yet, just how did Yosef's brothers lay hands of him? The Torah records that Yosef was lost, wandering in a field, when all of a sudden a man appeared and directed him to his brothers. The commentators relate that this so-called man was none other than an angel, Yosef's Guardian Angel. Yosef's angel set him up, led him to his brothers, and thus into captivity.

Nice angel! Yet, we cannot blame the angel; he was only doing what G-d commanded him, to fulfill the higher purpose of what the rest of the book of Genesis relates. Yet for all those years that Yosef suffered, do you think that he ever considered that it was an angel who sent him to meet his fate and that G-d ordained his present suffering? It was not until later in his life, when he stood before Pharaoh that everything became clear to him, but for all those years, what was he thinking?

This is how it is with us today. Many of us suffer. Some of us suffer as a result of using our free will and making poor choices. Others of us suffer because we do not use our free will with enough resolve and end up becoming victims to other forces around us, which we could have avoided. The job of our Guardian Angels is not to get us out of trouble. G-d gave us enough intelligence to help ourselves. The angels are there to make sure the Creator's Will be done, whether we approve and like it, or not.

Free will, making the right choices, therefore, becomes ever the more so important, when we recognize just how far reaching the consequences of any small action can be.

Chapter 7

The Future of Man

What would our lives on Earth be like today if Adam had never fallen in the Garden of Eden? This question is much more than worthless speculation. For although we cannot undo what has been done, we can and do, nonetheless, pick up the pieces that have been broken and repair them. In other words, the destiny of mankind, as outlined by the Divine plan, is to restore that which has been lost and to go beyond it to fulfill the purpose for which we were initially created.

The entire history of mankind reads like the turmoil that goes on inside the individual mind. This should not surprise anyone simply because society as a whole is only made up of all its individual members. We are on the outside what we are on the insides. In spite of all of society's attempts to conceal the true inner nature of our species, both our humanity and our depravity always seem to glaringly come to the forefront. Beneath this all our free will, used or abused, merges with the Divine plan.

A good example of this is the story of Yosef. Through no fault of his own, he was sold into slavery, falsely accused of adultery, and thrown in jail on false charges. He thus wasted thirteen good years of his life. There was nothing he could do about his circumstances. All he could do was choose how to respond to them. It was his response to circumstances beyond his control that merited him the title of Tzadik (the righteous one).

278

Yosef is the classical example for us today. Like Yosef, we are all subject to circumstances beyond our control. G-d has a plan and an army of angels at His command to assist Him in carrying it out. Free will aside, we cannot control G-d's Will, nor can we manipulate an entire army of angels. Therefore, we are subject to the Divine plan, be it for good or for bad. This is another reason why bad things happen to good people. Yet, there is a Divine purpose in all this that is invisible to eyes.

We must take it for granted as a logical conclusion that G-d only wants what is best for us, His creation, as a race and as individuals. We humans do not understand how sufferings in the end manifest a higher good. Many really do not care. Many simply want the sufferings to end. Somehow, I believe that G-d also wants our sufferings to end, but His idea of how to stop them and ours differs sharply. G-d sees things in the ultimate Divine light of things, whereas our vision is limited to our Earthly points of view. In other words, we cannot see, grasp, or comprehend the "big picture". As such, we are subject to the big picture and judged how we react in relationship to it, just like Yosef.

Biblical prophecy outlines that inevitably man will grasp the big picture with the event known as the coming of Mashiah. Yet, until this event occurs, we live as we do. The coming of Mashiah is a pivotal event for mankind, for this event signals the return of YHWH influence over nature, as discussed earlier.

Mankind has a destiny; this is the future in a nutshell. Whether we foresee it or like it or not, we are destined by Divine plan to fix what we as a race have broken and move on with our original purpose. Yet, in order for this to happen a huge number of changes must first occur.

When Adam tasted the forbidden fruit in the Garden, he accidentally entered into physical space/time before he was psychologically and emotionally prepared to do so. Fixing this means that mankind must evolve emotionally and psychologically to the point of becoming unattached to this physical world that has become our prison. This is no easy task, even for G-d. Free will makes things all the more difficult when we can choose individually or collectively to flow against the Divine plan seeking to delay, postpone or cancel it. Oh, what foolish mortals we are.

The split between the natural and supernatural worlds must be mended. Human shortsightedness, living in only one-dimensional plane at a time must be repaired. The separation between body and soul must come to an end. Death as we know it must cease to exist. There must come about a full integration of consciousness with the unconscious, unlocking our minds, enabling us to perceive the truth of the greater realities in which we live.

Granted, there is one opinion that states that the only difference between present and messianic times will be the reestablishment and perseverance of the Davidic monarchy and the Kingdom of Israel. Yet, in light of modern current events, this task might prove as difficult as all the supernatural events mentioned above.

The future of man is integrally connected to man's past. Our collective destiny runs in a circle. We must come back to the beginning and to start again. Biblical prophecy outlines that this is exactly what is to happen. For almost six thousand years, since the days when Adam walked this Earth, man has been simultaneously creating beautiful arts and sciences and acting beastly towards himself and others, destroying the advancements that he has made.

Man encompasses the potential to be either angel, or ape. This split must end. A choice must be made. Mankind as a whole, and each individual in particular must choose, whether to become fully human or fully animal. Biblical prophecy states that the Divine plan calls for mankind to go through a period of trials and tribulations. During this time each individual will finally have to decide once and for all, does he/she wish to remain a creature created in the Divine image or embrace the animal within and leave the human race entirely.

Remember the lesson of Yosef, he went through extremely trying times, and only then, possibly because of them, did he merit ascending to the heights of the world. We are no different. We will not be able to influence that which is destined to soon come upon us. Yet, we can use our Divine gift of free will and choose how to respond to adverse circumstances. Will we rise up and be like a Yosef, or will we sink down to the depths of depravity? Time will tell. Each of us will be judged accordingly. The Watchers are watching and the clocking is ticking away.

Chapter 8

Armageddon of the Inner Mind

A fearful yet popular topic discussed today in all mediums is the subject of the End of Days and the Apocalypse. Every culture around the world seems to have its "doomsday" prophecies with focus on their fulfillment in our days and in the next few years.

While current events do appear to be a modern fulfillment of biblical prophecy, still, no one knows exactly what is going to happen. More so, no one knows when.

Our world is truly in great turmoil. There are so many competing ideas, systems, philosophies, and religions fighting for dominance one over the other. Rather than all mankind seeking a way to live and work together, each group seeks to destroy all others and establish a world created in their own image. Needless to say, all such endeavors are doomed to failure. The problem is that so many innocent souls get caught up in fights that are not their own and suffer accordingly.

There is only one way we as a race can ever stop the up-coming apocalypse and that is by first averting the psychological apocalypse that is presently destroying our individual minds. Again, before we can change the world, we must first change the people in the world.

Herein lies the problem, how can we change everyone? The answer is that we cannot. Therefore, the upcoming apocalypse is unavoidable. G-d has only so much patience with fallen mankind. We have a collective destiny to fulfill. G-d's plan has allotted to man only a finite amount of time for us to get our collective act together. There is an appointed time when G-d Himself will personally intervene in human history and set the record straight.

Why must there be an apocalypse? Why must there be such great suffering for everyone prior to the birth of a new world? The answer is that there does not have to be such a rude awakening. All we have to do is awaken ourselves. Yet, alas, we are all sleepers. We enjoy being mentally, and psychologically lazy. Instead of making efforts to work with those so different from us, we seek to conquer them and subdue them. Needless to say, this leads to strife where one nation defeated by another will seek revenge, regardless of how many centuries it takes. This is what is happening now in current events and will eventually blow up into a full scale World War III.

Ask yourselves, where are all the Guardian Angels and Watchers while this is going on? Are they not here to help us and protect us during these dark times? The truth is that many of the Watcher angels, specifically those Divinely assigned as national princes, are the ones instigating the battles. The book of Daniel makes quite clear the role of angels in the wars of men. The angels are the ones stirring up the pot, at the behest of the Almighty, to create for us so much havoc, that we will have no choice but to call out to YHWH to save us from ourselves.

The only reason why an apocalypse is coming is to awaken us from the slumber that we fell into when our souls in Adam became overly entangled in this physical world. We are all too awake to our physical selves, whereas at the same time we all lie asleep with regards to our spiritual selves. Our spiritual side is a real and active part of our being. We have just kicked it out of our lives and delegated it to the realm we call the unconscious.

Well, our spiritual side does not like to be pushed around. It wants its equal share and say in our lives. After all, our universe is not merely the physical space/time that we see and experience. There is far more to creation than this. In order for us to awaken to see the truth of a greater world, we will have to be rudely awakened if we so choose not to awaken voluntarily.

So now, what is to happen to those who seek awakening in the world that wishes to continue its slumber? Remember G-d has His plan. Six people can be in a car that gets involved in a horrible accident. Five people in the car can die, whereas one walks out without a scratch. How does this happen? Read the daily news and you will see that events like this occur often. One person in the middle of a disaster survives rather unscathed while everyone else around him/her is wiped out.

This is how it will be with the coming apocalypse. Those who are prepared to move forward in life will not be so much affected by the world falling apart around them. Those who are psychologically and emotionally strong, rugged men and women with strong resolve and righteous action will weather the upcoming storms. Being that their spirit is different from those around them, they will somehow find their way out of the muck and mire of a world gone haywire with war.

Yet, these folks are not going to be saved by miraculous event and Divine interventions. Those who will make it through the hard times to come will do so because they have made proper preparations, because they are internally strong enough not to break down and most importantly because Heaven will smile upon them.

This does not mean that Heaven is going to perform miracles for individuals. This may or may not happen. Miracles at best are unreliable. Those who pray for miracles and then wait for them to happen usually perish when they do not occur. The best adage here is the words of Benjamin Franklin. These words are not in the Bible, but they should be. Franklin said, "G-d helps those who help themselves".

Anyone who believes that they can stand in front of a moving train without being hit is a delusional fool. Thus, anyone who believes that they can make it through trying times without proper internal and external preparations is likewise mistaken. Granted, a one in a million miracle might occur. I am sure all the people who died in the Holocaust, especially the religious ones, all believed in miracles. Alas the miracles that did come were few and far between, leaving everyone else to fall into the pit.

Armageddon is coming because it is already going on inside the human mind. All of us individually and collectively are in such turmoil and confusion about religion, spiritual matters, morality, and the like. Today our society openly flaunts behavior that at one time was not only immoral, it was illegal. Today, law and so-called "human rights" protect illicit behavior.

No one will listen to either you or me teach them about morality. I guess that those individuals will have to be taught directly by G-d through his agents of worldly upheavals, wars, illness, and suffering. I wish this did not have to be the case, but what can any one of us do? If individuals and society as a whole decides to embark on a path contrary to the plan of G-d, then it will be G-d Himself, and not religious devotees, who will do something about it.

All we can do is move out of the way of the out-of-control train. What this will require of us we will have to discuss at another time.

Chapter 9

What Does G-d Want From Us?

With everything going crazy in the world and with all the chaos in our personal lives, one might rightly ask, just what is it that G-d wants from us? If you are asking this question, then I am sure G-d is proud of you, for this is exactly what He wants of us first. He wants us to ask. For only by first asking and then being open to the answer can we ever expect to do what we are supposed to do.

Every religious system claims to speak for G-d and, therefore, will have a different answer for you as to what G-d wants from you. Some will tell you that G-d demands of you certain daily acts of piety. Some will tell you that G-d demands your children become martyrs for the cause. Some will tell you lots, others will tell you little. It has never ceased to amaze me how many people rush to the forefront claiming to be speaking for G-d.

I must tell you that I cannot make such claims. Although I have had many spiritual experiences in my life, I have never been directly approached by G-d Himself, and given a public message for me to share in His name. I am, therefore, thankfully, not a prophet! I say that I am thankful of this because I do not feel that I need for G-d to speak to me directly today. Sure such an experience would be the greatest thing in the world, but it is just not necessary.

G-d has already spoken to me, to my soul that is, when along with all the other souls of Israel I stood (or hovered) at Mount Sinai to receive the Torah in the days of Moshe. Of all the religious texts in the world, only the Torah includes the words, "Thus says the L-rd G-d". In other words, instead of Moshe writing down his own words and interpretations of what G-d said, he merely wrote down G-d's own words. The prophets followed in his footsteps and that is why we call the Bible, the "Word of G-d," and not the words of the prophets.

Therefore, if I want to hear G-d's Voice today, I go back to the source and read what He has already said. How can I expect to hear G-d speak anew, when I have not yet listened to what He has said of old?

G-d is not a human being, nor does He think or act like one. Granted we, as the children of Adam were created in G-d's image, but that was the image before the fall. Now, we are closer to monkeys than to G-d. Any recent review of human behavior in your daily news will unfortunately validate this all too well. What G-d asks of us is repeated clearly numerous times throughout the Bible. Here is just one example that is most fitting to our conversation:

Which of us can live with the consuming fire? Which of us can live with the eternal conflagration? One who (1) walks with righteousness and (2) speaks with truthfulness, who (3) spurns extortionate profit and (4) shakes off his hands from holding a bribe, who (5) seals his ears from hearing of bloodshed and (6) shuts his eyes from seeing evil. He shall dwell in heights, in rocky fortresses is his stronghold, his bread will be granted, his water assured.

(Isaiah 33:14-16)

It is plain and clear what G-d wants from us. Theses six simple, but not so simple things are said to sum up the entire Torah (b. Mak. 24a). G-d wants us to act humanely towards one another, as creatures created in and worthy of His Image.

No mention is made of doctrines, or creeds. G-d knows that the mind of man has been blemished by the fall in Eden. He knows that our doctrines and beliefs about Him have been tarnished and compromised. No matter, G-d does not judge us by what we believe, but rather by what we do. Do the right things and the rewards become self-evident.

If we act like humane human beings, we will be treated as such. If, however we choose to act like animals, with disdain and disrespect towards others, G-d will act that way in kind with us. In other words, how we act with others, is how G-d acts with us. It is no wonder then, why we only experience G-d's severity and judgment and not His mercy. Do not ask why G-d does not shine His face upon us; ask rather why you do not shine your face upon others?

The greatest exercise of human free will is to be like G-d. This does not mean that we should become gods, with everyone else worshipping us. Remember that all other humans also have free will. Each of us must come to act like G-d, together, jointly, in peace. Only then can we unleash the Divine nature lying dormant in the unconscious side of the heart within us.

What does it mean to become like G-d? It means to mimic G-d's actions. As G-d is just, so must we be just. As G-d is merciful, so must we be merciful. As G-d is wise and understanding, so must we be so. The examples of this are found on every page throughout the Bible.

If you really want to know how G-d acts with man, read the history of it. A good daily Bible study, where you just sit and read the good book, the Torah, the Prophets and the Writings (TaNaKh), will open your eyes and deeply touch your heart. You do not need to read as an academic exercise. You do not need biblical commentaries to help you digest every word. You simply need to read and get in touch with the spirit in text, and then the words of truth will echo in your heart.

Almost every culture around the world shares elemental human values. Basic concepts of right and wrong appear to be universal and somehow engraved within the human mind. Our problem is we all too often forget that which is written on our hearts and attempt to rationalize immoral and criminal behavior. People do not like to read the Bible because it reminds them of the truth; the truth that they know deep within themselves that certain behavior is wrong and harmful.

What does G-d want from us? Do we really need to ask? Do we not already know? Who are we trying to fool? G-d is not fooled, the angels are not fooled, the only ones apparently fooled are ourselves. What fools we are, if we endeavor to fool all and end up fooling only ourselves. Free will is such a great treasure, but like any other, it can be abused to no end. Thank G-d, He cares enough about us to not let us remain in our self-made muck and mire forever.

Alas, the temptation of physical sensations continues to blind the eyes of many, even the wise, and we all continue to suffer because of it. We will discuss more about the power of temptation and deception as we proceed.

Chapter 10

The Image, the Breath & the Call

So, G-d wants us to do the right things? He wants us to act morally and responsibly towards one another. This apparently makes good sense. After all, a world without order is a world in chaos.

Order, rules, and responsibility make society stable and life enjoyable to live. Chaos, on the other hand, can unravel the fabric of creation and undo G-d's "hard work". What else would the Creator want from His creation other than to safeguard and upkeep the system? Granted, G-d has angels to do a good share of the work, but apparently man also has his share to do.

I can understand G-d ordaining rules that outlines our behavior towards one another. Not to murder, not to steal both sound like good stable advice. No one would wish to be a victim of these acts. It stands to reason, therefore, that in spite of an individual's cravings or desires, such acts should be outlawed. If we do not wish to be robbed or killed, then we should not do it to another.

Yet, is this really the way of the universe, of physical law? Why should we not say, "might makes right" and anything that I can get away with is fair and good? Do not tell me about things in life having to be fair. Everyone knows life is unfair. The laws of nature certainly do not consider fairness when dealing with human beings. Why then should we not learn from nature and not be fair either. After all, only the "losers" lose in the end, and who cares about them anyway? They are powerless and insignificant. What difference does it make if life and "the powers that be" are fair?

Which of the two above ideas do you agree with? What do you really FEEL deep inside? I already know what you are going to answer. You will say that we humans have a heart. We feel for our fellow man, and therefore, want to do right by him, as we want others to do right by us. If you are of this opinion, then I have news for you – you (your soul) is originally an alien of extraterrestrial origins. Let me explain.

Adam (and thus all the souls of mankind) was created in a place called the Garden of Eden. In case you have not noticed, that is no place around here. Mystically speaking, Adam was originally created in a body of light and not of flesh and blood. The Garden, therefore, was also a spiritual place, not indigenous to our Earth. This does not mean that Adam and the Garden are from a different planet, but rather from a different dimension. They might have been from right here on Earth, but a different dimension of Earth than that which we know.

Adam's form was created in the "image of Elohim" and thus it is subject to the laws of form. This "bodily" side of Adam, however spiritual or physical, is ruled by whatever laws of physics that rule the place where he resides, be it the Garden or Earth. This is why the "body" of Adam, created in the image of Elohim, was created from the ground of the Garden. The body is thus subject to the laws that dominate the Earth.

On the other hand, YHWH, the supernatural power over the laws of nature, breathed into Adam the spirit of life, making him alive. Although created in the image of Elohim, Adam was not considered alive until he received a portion from YHWH. Therefore, Adam is a combination of both Elohim and YHWH elements. In other words, Adam (and thus all mankind) was created with both natural and supernatural components.

Even as a spiritual entity with life from YHWH, Adam (from the Elohim influence within him) was still subject to the physical laws of his environment. Nonetheless, as having within him the breath of YHWH, Adam shared with his Creator something the rest of creation did not have. Adam had a conscience. He had an internal barometer that enabled him to know the difference between right and wrong.

With the fall in Eden and our descent into this world, our internal moral barometer has lost much of its sensitivity, but that does not mean we have lost it all. Although we often deceive ourselves much to our own harm, most know deep down within their hearts the differences between right and wrong. This sense of morality is our inheritance from father Adam. It resides within the heart of every true human being.

This is why we do not simply rule human society with the coldness of machine logic, regarding not the feelings of our fellow man. Something inside us tells us that there is a thing called morality.

Granted, in our present fallen state human morality is a blurred as everything else is blemished. Nonetheless, it is still there, unfortunately all too often deceived and manipulated by the forces of evil to perform their lowly bidding.

What so blinds us from clearly seeing and DOING the right thing? Although most of our intentions are good, there is an old saying: "the road to Hell is paved with the best of intentions". In others words, the greatest evils ever perpetrated on Earth have been done with some convoluted rationalization that what was done was for a greater good. Without G-d's Word as our guide, how would we ever know right from wrong?

If we humans were created without the YHWH element within us, we would not have developed a spiritual element such as conscience. After all, no other creature on Earth has a conscience, no matter how intelligent they are. Angels are no different. This may be one reason why a certain race of angels is called the Hayot, which is the Hebrew term for animals.

We humans do have a conscience; this is the remnant element of our otherworldly origins. This is what separates man from beast (and from angel). The human conscience acts as the receiver and tuning fork for the spirit of YHWH. Alas, our conscience resides within our minds, which also houses such a large portion of animalistic tendencies. The animal side of our minds causes the manifestation of the Elohim/physical law aspects in creation, with all their severity and limitations. When we elevate our thoughts and thereby redirect our actions, we reveal our humanity and along with it the YHWH element in creation.

This then is the secret of the humanity in man. As we discussed in our past essay, an apocalypse is coming. Great chaos and upheavals are about to hit us like never before. How to avoid these things on an individual basis depends upon our actions. We have to do the right things. Yet, it is not easy always knowing what is the right thing. Human logic is still blurred. We all too often make mistakes, and are held accountable for them.

For this reason, to assist us is fine-tuning our inner moral compass, G-d send upon us trial and tribulations. He creates circumstances in our lives and sends his angels to whisper in our ears how to handle them. If we listen, then it will be well and good for us.

As we mature in spiritual responsibility, the angels cease to whisper in our ears. Then, using our free will and G-d given intelligence, we take responsibility and control, making moral decisions, and thus embodying the image of G-d in which we were created. Yet, there is another step to be taken after we straighten out the Elohim side. We must strive to embody the YHWH side.

Speaking about this and the upcoming apocalypse G-d spoke in the biblical book of Zechariah (13:8,9), *"And it shall be, in all the land, says YHWH two parts in it shall be cut off, and die, but the third shall be left in it. And I will bring the third part through the fire, and will refine them as silver is refined, and will try them as gold is tried, he shall CALL UPON MY NAME, and I will answer him. "*

To embody the YHWH element within us, we must "call upon His Name". Calling upon the Name of YHWH is not just praying to Him, it is hearing His Voice in return. While many individuals out there today believe that G-d talks to them daily, they are hearing nothing other than their own inner voices telling them what they want to hear. They claim they hear from "the L-rd," yet none of them know YHWH. How can they, when they do not even know His Torah?

We will discuss more about the "Voice of YHWH", the "Voice of Elohim" and what hinders our hearing them as we proceed.

Chapter 11

The Prison of the Spark of Good

We have within us the human potential to unleash miraculous powers. Using our human resolve and free will, coupled with our righteous actions and clear intelligence we can actually unlock our latent, sleeping YHWH element lying dormant within the recesses of our unconscious minds. Granted, this is a difficult thing to accomplish, but it can be done! In light of current events, it must be done!

Yet, in spite of all our inner potential and all of G-d's promises, something within us always seems to get in the way and thwarts our spiritual development. Before we start throwing blame and pointing fingers saying "the devil made me do it," let us first look and see what we are doing ourselves, and why. In order to understand the reality of the problems facing human nature, we need first review some basic facts of science. We will soon see the correlation.

It is the nature of physical matter to be very confining and constricting. This is the nature of physical things; there is a lack of freedom of movement. More than this, any movement in physical things has to be relatively slow. For something to be material and physical, its particles must move slower than light. Once particles move faster than light, matter turns into energy and is no longer physical. All things moving slower than the speed of light, therefore, comprise the natural/physical world.

Angels, as we know are entities of light. This is why they do not exist in our universe in material form. Their makeup is above physical matter. Adam too, was originally a light being; only he fell and became entangled here in our physical universe.

Our spiritual side is a vestige of our original Adamic stature. However, our spiritual side is from a light universe, where movement is always at hyper-light speed. Once entrapped here in the physical universe, our spiritual side is severely limited in movement. This is why our spiritual potential lies latent in our unconscious mind. For the unconscious mind opens us up to a realm of thought, far beyond the binding limitations of physical space. Anyone ever having a dream knows this reality all too well.

As beings (in Adam) originally created to inhabit a universe of light, our collective descent into the physical has left us with a sense of collective unconscious claustrophobia. Deep within, we humans always feel constricted and seek ways to expand ourselves. Here in the physical world, this is usually manifest in the pursuit of wealth and power. This is where the problem begins. Unfortunately, this is not where it ends.

Claustrophobic man always endeavors to spread out, and he always runs into the same oppositions. Man always runs into the realities of practical limitations. There are never enough physical resources to manifest all one's most grandiose dreams. Therefore, resources must be acquired. Herein lies the conflict.

Resources are usually unequally distributed between many peoples. If one group wants more resources than what it has, they have to be taken from another. If they cannot be acquired through a mutually agreeable form, then often they are taken in a manner less than agreeable to the losing party. What I have just described here is greed, jealousy, theft, and war. In other words, the grandiose desire to expand outwards like the spiritual beings we once were is what deeply motivates us to commit all kinds of crimes.

Herein lies a bizarre secret. That which makes us great in the spiritual pursuits makes us evil in the physical pursuits. This is because the laws of nature that govern the two universes are extremely different. If one wishes to expand and broaden one's horizons in spiritual pursuits, there are no limitations to what one can accomplish.

However, when one wishes to expand and broaden oneself in the physical world, the limitations of physical nature impose boundaries. Frustrated by these limitations of free movement, man intends to fight the boundaries and often breaks them. While the damage in doing so is great, man is usually blinded by his short-term goal of self-expression. He, therefore, pays no attention to the ramifications of his actions. Others are hurt. The Heavenly forces are outraged. The natural forces follow their course. To every action there is an equal and opposite reaction. Man's greatest plans are eventually foiled.

This then is what we have to deal with. We have a spark of good encased in a prison that limits its operations. Rather than seek the proper escape through the door of spiritual development, man chooses to attempt to break down the prison walls. Alas, these prison walls are the forms and laws of nature. Man cannot break them; he can only bend them, and bend them he does. This is why our world is in such bad shape and in need of such repair.

In the words of the Mystics, the walls that surround the human mind and heart in the world are called husks, or shells (klipot, in Hebrew). Enclosed within them is a spark of goodness, which unfortunately all too often manifests in a shortsighted and thus harmful manner. This is the source of evil.

Our dormant spiritual stature is not just asleep, it is imprisoned, and in need of rescue. A wall of limited perceptions surrounds us, our minds, our emotions and our actions. These perceptions are the prison, the husks and the shells that keep us imprisoned and bound. They pervert the flow any of internal goodness within us. They cause our free will to act in a harmful manner. These husks bring us into conflict with the laws of nature and the Watcher Angels who are charged to safeguard them.

Our prison is only partially self-imposed. The prison of the mind and heart is a byproduct of living in a physical world with all its natural limitations. Naturally our spiritual soul is stifled and seeks release. Unfortunately, all too often the easiest choices of release are also the wrong ones. Before we call upon the Name of either Elohim or YHWH, we must first find the right door out of our mental prisons. Only in this way will our calls be heard and responded to.

Chapter 12

To Stand Up for Oneself

Have you ever been wronged by someone? Have you ever become angry because you have been denied justice? I have a feeling that every one of you will answer yes to all these questions. Now, let us ask what can we do about it?

One religious philosophy tells us that when wronged one should "turn the other cheek". In other words, one should forgive and forget. There is wisdom in this philosophy, to a point. One should not hold in stress and anger because these can harm an individual almost as badly as a physical cancer. Yet, merely to forgive and forget a wrong does not address the issue of justice.

If someone wrongs another, one can emotionally forgive him/her, however this does not mean that justice is thereby fulfilled. The laws of our society do not work like that and neither do the laws of our spirituality. If one commits a crime, our justice system does not forgive and forget, even if the person regrets his/her deeds, expresses remorse, and makes restitution. Granted these acts of contrition might lighten his punishment, but punishment he will receive, regardless of his repentance. This is how our society works. Why then should we as members of society expect anything less from our fellow individuals?

If you cause harm or damage, you are required by the laws of the land, the laws of morality and by the Laws of the Bible to make appropriate restitution. Even though one may "turn the other cheek," the principle of "an eye for an eye, a tooth for a tooth" is still in force.

The biblical "eye for an eye" principle is a metaphor for demanding appropriate compensation for losses incurred. No one ever really poked out another's eye, or knocked out a tooth. Remember that G-d ordained this law. It is meant to be enlightened and just, not barbaric.

Today many people have a problem demanding justice for themselves, especially in everyday personal matters and interactions. Today many people do not speak up for themselves because they are afraid of the responses from others. This fear and timidity breeds internal, often unconscious anger and frustration which serve as barriers, disabling one from properly reaching out to G-d.

The solution to this dilemma is not to "turn the other cheek" as some suggest. This faulty logic only makes the problem worse. The true solution, the one outlined in G-d's word is for one to embolden oneself and to speak out and tell the truth. One may indeed offend another with one's honesty and boldness. However, when one is in the right and is willing to discuss and defend his/her position, he/she is "getting off his chest" a burden that might otherwise bother one and haunt one for years to come.

The removal of psychological and emotional burdens is one of the most important tasks we face as human today. We will never be able to rise to our spiritual heights all the while that we are chained down to the Earth. Simply making believe the chains are not there will never unchain us. Unless we make the efforts to first acknowledge our chains and then make all efforts to break them, we will never become free from them.

The chains that enslave us today are our misconceived ideas, attitudes, feelings, and behaviors. In others words, we are all in need of total makeovers, not the cosmetic external type, which is like a new coat of paint over a rotting surface, but rather an overhaul of the entire structure of our personalities.

We have been timid, weak, and silent for too long. We tolerate and swallow everything; even deceiving ourselves into believing that when bad things happen to us it is because G-d wants it to be this way. Stress and anxiety are not from G-d. Stupid people doing stupid things are not from G-d. (Yes, there really are stupid people in this world. This is not a judgmental statement; it is a statement of fact. Admit it and deal with it!). Being silent and not standing up for your rights is not from G-d. Always being wrong, or for that matter, always being right, is not from G-d.

Before one can call upon the name of G-d and expect to be answered, one's spiritual inner tuning must be properly calibrating in order to hear the Divine "Voice". However, how can one hear a Divine "Voice" when one's inner mind is so cluttered with so much confusion? How does one expect to distinguish and differentiate?

The first step is that one must first get rid of all the clutter. To begin this process, tell the sources of stress and anxiety in your life to mind their own place, a place that is outside of you. In doing this, one must still be careful to do so in a manner that best manifests one's humanity and not one's animal characteristics. This means that one must be confrontational, but in a cool and calm manner. One must be rational and logical, forceful, and straightforward.

Now ask what does this psychology talk have to do with our topic of spirituality, mysticism, and serving G-d? The answer is that it has everything to do with these things.

Remember this lesson well, for it is the basis of all mysticism: spirituality is psychology; psychology is spirituality!

When I refer to psychology, I am not referring to the secular godless forms practiced by the vast majority of people today. Secular psychology and psychiatry are like ships lost at sea without compass or maps. Being that such philosophies and their practitioners deny G-d, and His authority in one's life and mind, they have no sense of moral baring how to guide a person. Both of these pseudo-sciences fail miserably to alleviate human sufferings.

While psychiatric medication is a blessing from G-d in that they help to alleviate psychotic symptoms, nonetheless, all the drugs are is a "Band-Aid" over a festering wound. Psychologists and psychiatrists today who do not guide their clients into a relationship with G-d are missing the point of their service. Indeed, in many cases they often take their clients further away from G-d by manipulating their thoughts into believing that G-d is not real, or that G-d accepts whatever it is that the individuals wish to give Him. They teach their clients that if they are happy, that is all that matters. In a world so full of strife, many people fall for this deception, thinking that happiness is the only way to be free of suffering.

True inner happiness can only come about once one is totally honest with oneself and with G-d, pledging to living up to the mindset and lifestyle that G-d has ordained for us. This is what it means to fulfill being created in "His Image". Without this commitment there is always a piece missing from one's soul. Whether one denies it or not, there will always be something missing in one's life all the while that G-d is not a part of it.

Part of free will means to stand up against those who would wish to rob you of it. Today, there is such a war of ideas, against anything religious, against anything holy, against anything having to do with G-d. Yet, rest assured this too is part of the Divine plan. A warrior is only honed on the battlefield. A righteous individual is only defined as one once one stands up against the forces of Godlessness in our society.

Do you want to draw close to G-d? First, separate from that which opposes G-d, and which G-d Himself opposes. It is a lot easier making the voyage to G-d's side not carrying a tremendous wasteful load.

Chapter 13

The Rider & the Horse

The holy Sages have said, *"The rider controls the horse, not the horse the rider"*. The Bible says, *"That which is in your hands to do, do with all your strength"* (Eccl 9:10).

These two sayings exemplify what we have been discussing about the proper use of free will. It is true that we are inundated and surrounded by spiritual barriers that retard our spiritual maturation. These barriers are both self-imposed and externally imposed by G-d and His angels. Indeed, G-d Himself instructs His angels to place impassable spiritual barriers before us to prevent us from drawing too close to Him. This is the proverbial "sword of fire that guards the path to Eden".

Why would G-d do such a thing? He knows that in our hearts that we love Him and want to learn more about Him. Why would He block our minds from understanding? The answer to this is G-d's Divinely ordained laws of physics. Just like we humans cannot walk on the face of the Sun without serious protection, so we cannot experience certain aspects of Divine reality unprepared. To do so is more than dangerous, it is deadly. Remember that G-d is a consuming fire (Deut 4:4). Fire only burns those things that draw near unprepared. At present, we lack a spiritual form of asbestos.

G-d is no mere intellectual concept. G-d is the living force of the universe. The Elohim aspect of G-d is much easier to approach than is the YHWH aspect. In order for one to experience an aspect of Elohim all one need do is remove the barriers of wrong deeds and behaviors from one's life. In other words, one must live a righteous and moral life. With this accomplished one will be defined as a good person. Nature or "fate" will shine upon such a person granting them a good life. This is all one can expect from the Elohim aspect.

If one wishes to go further to experience the YHWH aspect of G-d, then there are further barriers to be removed. Being that the YHWH aspect of G-d is the supernatural aspect, it resides outside our physical world. In order to bring it into our physical world we must have a place where it can safely reside. Being that we are dealing here with a non-physical tangibility, we cannot speak of any physical place. We must find an ethereal place for an ethereal thing. The place ordained by G-d for which His YHWH aspect can manifest in physical space is the human mind.

However, in order for the human mind to be able to properly be this lofty receptacle, it first must be clean and ready for use. Alas, most of us have cluttered minds and, therefore, do not have the mental "space" to receive YHWH.

The meaning of calling upon the Name of YHWH means that one must prepare one's mind, cleaning it from all clutter, and making it accessible for YHWH to enter. This is what it means when it says those who call upon the name of YHWH will be answered. In other words, if we take the first step and prepare the place, G-d will come and fill it.

While all these words are well and good, how does one practically go about doing this? The answer to this is the two sayings quoted at the beginning. The emphasis is on taking control and responsibility for things in life. One must be like the horseman who directs the horse, and is not directed by it. When an opportunity arises one must grasp it; with "gusto" doing whatever it is one does with passion and strength. This is the secret of success, no matter what it is in which a person endeavors.

Herein lies the problem. We spend much time and effort in our spiritual and religious pursuits. Many are happy with their level of religiosity and are convinced that they are "OK" in G-d's Eyes. Yet, is our human criterion of judgment the same as that used by G-d? Although we are satisfied with our spiritual pursuits and accomplishments, can we honestly say that G-d is also satisfied with us? Judging from the amount of suffering in our world and in our personal lives, we should not rush to answer these questions so affirmatively.

When tragedy strikes we all ask what we did to deserve what has happened to us. Maybe we should stop and think before disaster strikes what we are doing, both right and wrong. We know what G-d wants from us. What we apparently do not know is how to give it to Him. We lack the passion and the "gusto" in our spiritual pursuits. As long as we remain lazy by not cleaning up our "inner" shops from all the clutter with "gusto," YHWH cannot rest therein.

The secret of spiritual success is for us to not only do the right things, but to do them with passion. Without passion, even the greatest of deeds and spiritual pursuits will lack the necessary "gas" to make the proverbial engine work.

One of the greatest problems facing spiritual pursuits today is the false belief that merely performing religion by rote is satisfactory in G-d's Eyes. Granted, by exerting the minimum amount of effort, one does fulfill the most external form of law, nonetheless, without appropriate efforts, the spirit and thus essential element of action is missing. This can be compared to a body without a soul, or with an extremely weak life force, that leaves one almost comatose.

The message throughout the Bible is clear. A lack of commitment is viewed in G-d's Eyes as outright hypocrisy. Expressions of religious or moral devotion devoid of true sincerity serve to distance one from G-d, not bring one closer. One should never be so arrogant to say that his/her behavior is so good that G-d must find nothing wrong with it. The one who believes this is usually too far beyond help.

Passion is an emotion. Beyond the human mind, emotions exist independently of us. Angels are said in many ways to be (bodiless) personified emotions. Therefore, the cleansing of one's emotions enables one's soul to properly calibrate into the frequency resonance of the angels. Once this process is accomplished one can work on clearing one's mind and thus approach YHWH, and begin again to manifest His presence in physical space. This is the role and job of man.

Do not underestimate the value of the heart in the path towards G-d. G-d commanded us to love Him with all of our hearts, not our heads. He commanded us that His words be placed upon our hearts, not upon our minds.

The Watcher angels look down upon humans specifically because our hearts are not pure. They do not hold what we lack in our heads against us, but they see into our hearts, in a manner similar to how we read a newspaper. When we are hypocritical we fool only ourselves, we harm only ourselves, we damn only ourselves.

Many people simply want to learn more about religion because they find it intellectually stimulating. Yet, with all this knowledge, has one the heart to "digest" it properly? If the answer to this question is no, then one has a long way to go on the path to G-d.

Chapter 14

Angels & the Mind

How does an angel see a human being? I do not mean how does he see us emotionally or spiritually, I mean how we appear to him in his "physical" eyes.

We know that angels are not physical beings by the standards that we measure and define physical reality. We know that unlike us, angels can visually see their own dimension and ours. When one angel looks at another, he sees another member of his species in his own dimension. Let us say that one angel sees another with the same ease that we see one another. Yet, we humans are a different type of dimensional being. Metaphors aside, what type of visual apparatus do angels have and how do we appear in their field of vision?

You think these questions cannot be answered? Maybe you think that these questions are unimportant. However, they can be answered and the answer is very important. We regularly interact with these angelic entities. As we know they have a great influence over everything in our lives. If we wish a glimpse into the greater world, then we had better start with the science of vision and learn how to look and how we appear. One definitely affects the other!

Angels are referred to throughout Judaic literature as Sekhelim Nivdalim (separate intelligences). Simply, this means that angels are generally considered to be disembodied intelligences. What forms these take in their own dimensions, no one can say for sure.

Although the Bible describes angels in Heaven (Isa 6) and in G-d's "chariot" (Ezek 1) as extremely alien creatures, we are also told that these descriptions were exclusive to the eyes of the individual prophet in his meditative/vision state. In other words, just because the prophet saw an angel in a certain form does not mean that is the absolute form of that angel. Rather the form visualized by the prophet was a form that his mind helped create in order to assist him in physically perceiving a non-physical entity.

The secret to understanding angelic form is in the word "Sekhelim". The angels are considered "intelligences". In essence, they are thought forms, unique and separate from one another. This might be hard for us to understand, but let us look at it like this. We are all familiar with the thought form of love. We all know what it feels like to love. We also know all too well the thought form of hate. We all know what it means to hate.

When we think of love and hate all types of images come to mind. When we think of love, we think of beautiful things, sunny days, flowers, softness, and sweetness. When we think of hate, we imagine hell, fire, and brimstone. Yet, love and hate have nothing to do with the images we ascribe to them. Those images are our way of expressing love and hate. In other words, our images are the vessels or the thought forms through which we manifest love and hate.

Angels do not need such metaphors to express the emotions they embody. They are the embodiment of such emotions. Remember now that emotion, which we ascribe to the heart, is actually also a part of the mind, however conscious or unconscious. When we refer to the heart, we are not speaking about the physical heart in one's chest; we are speaking about a deeper side of the human mind, where emotions originate. The word "heart" is merely a metaphor.

Angels are thus intelligences, or focal points of emotions. This explains why we have angels of love, angels of healing as well as angels of anger and angels of destruction. In essence, when G-d wishes to send an angel on a mission, He merely thinks the thought that He wishes and an angel is thereby dispatched. Thought therefore is a very powerful thing.

It is rather difficult for us to understand with our limited minds, life forms so different from everything we have ever known. Yet, this does not mean that they do not exist. Angels and the other spiritual beings see human beings not as we view ourselves as physical entities. Rather, angels view us by seeing our minds. In angelic eyes, our thoughts and feelings are like "colors" to them. They can tell right away with a mere glance whether an individual is righteous, evil or any combination of both. Apparently our thoughts, feelings, and behaviors color our souls. Thus, without any possibility of deception angels see clearly who and what each of us individually is.

Angels communicate with us from disembodied mind to embodied mind. From the perspective of angels, the existence of our physical bodies is a mere vessel that houses our true selves. Therefore, when angels wish to communicate with man, they do not communicate with our bodies, but rather with our minds. Our problem is that we often do not understand that we are receiving a transmission. The reason for this obliviousness, as we have discussed previously, is due to all the clutter we have in our minds that blocks our clear reception.

Cleansing the mind therefore is not only a valuable psychological exercise; it is also a spiritual imperative.

We are all being watched at all times. Not only are our deepest darkest secrets publicly broadcast to all angelic beings, they are also known to other non-angelic spiritual beings. This is simply the nature of the laws that govern our two dimensions, the physical, and the non-physical. This phenomenon also explains why psychic events happen and why certain people seem to know a great deal about unknowable information. Being that the spiritual world is the realm of the mind, anyone able to tap into this source of information will be able to know almost anything about almost anybody.

We are all surrounded by a greater reality, which encompasses numerous other races of intelligent beings, which are different from us in the most elemental way. Those who we call angels are the representatives and agents of G-d. However, they are not the only ones who inhabit this greater unseen universe of ours. There are other races of beings out there not so chosen to perform Divine tasks. Of these races of beings are those most malevolent to us humans. They also see us individually for what we really are and take advantage of this at every turn.

G-d has taken steps to protect us from these malevolent beings and gave us instructions how not to attract them to ourselves. Alas, who listens any more to the biblical edicts of old?

It is with good reason that G-d ordained the Laws that He did. Not only does the Law establish for us a sound and stable society, it also mystically protects us, by cleansing our souls, so that we do not become too attractive to those malevolent entities that suckle off our filth. More about this needs to be discussed as we continue.

Chapter 15

The Nature of Evil

Do you believe in Evil? Do you think you can recognize it? Can you detect its presence? If you say yes, are you really so sure?

Evil is NOT merely the absence of good. Evil is a created entity ordained by G-d (Isaiah 45:7). It has its proper place in the general scheme of things. Our problem arises when we allow evil to move from its place outside of us and invite it into our minds, our feelings, and our behavior. To be fair, most people invite evil into themselves because they do not recognize evil for what it is. Therefore, in order for us to avoid evil, the first step is for us to recognize it.

Ask yourself the question: what is the definition of evil? Can we define evil as the intentional harming of another human being? If so, then capital punishment would be evil because it inflicts intentional harm. Yet, capital punishment is ordained by G-d (Gen 9:6). Is one so arrogant to condemn the Word of G-d as evil? Certainly not! Also, is evil only limited to the realm of human contact? Is there no evil with regards to anything other than man?

The definition of evil can be debated in long philosophical discussions; the likes of which I have no interest in or desire to pursue. I simply look at the Bible and interpret my definition from there. In the story of creation, G-d saw all that He had made and called it all "good". As logic dictates, good is the opposite of evil, and therefore, I can now define what is evil.

Evil is the opposite of good. Good is the work of creation, the establishment of G-d's handiwork and plan. Evil is the destruction of creation, the ruining of G-d's handiwork and the thwarting of G-d's plan. In other words, the definitions of good and evil do not revolve around man and human philosophy. Good and evil are inherent definitions and existences prescribed by the Creator and present throughout all of creation. Yes, good and evil exist on other worlds and in other dimensional planes. As sorrowful a statement it is, evil is not indigenous to Earth, nor is it limited to here.

The Mystics explain in great detail why G-d created evil and what purpose it serves in creation. We do not have to concern ourselves with mystic revelations. We merely need to understand two points. One, evil exists. Two, it is a danger to us. With this foundation, we can proceed to discuss what we can do to defend ourselves against this inherent danger.

G-d created man to serve Him in His purpose of perfecting creation. Evil seeks to thwart the perfection of creation. Therefore, evil seeks to thwart the development of man.

Evil is not some nebulous dark cloud floating around the universe. It is an intelligent life form that seeks manifestation in the physical world even as good does. Spiritual entities seek physical hosts to embody them so as to manifest their influence in the physical world. For example, evil could not have entered to the Garden of Eden to seduce Eve and Adam if it did not first embody itself in the Serpent. Once entrenched in a physical host, evil drives that host to follow its dictates. In this way evil is manifest and numerous others are victimized.

Why one invites evil into oneself is best understood only once we understand HOW someone would open him/herself to be its agent. Remember that our human minds are clouded from the sin in the Garden. Through Adam, we all ate of the forbidden fruit of the Knowledge of Good and Evil. Consequently, our minds and our souls became possessed with both good and evil. Due to the mixture within us, we lost the ability to clearly distinguish the difference between them.

Herein is the dilemma. We often avail ourselves to become agents of evil because we do not realize that that is what we are doing. We deceive ourselves and start a journey down a long dark path. At first, we convince ourselves that we will not walk too far. However, with every single step, return becomes more and more difficult, until return is all but impossible. At such a juncture, one has become a complete agent of evil. Even the attempted good deeds that such an individual does are tainted.

The only solution for such a negative influence is removal and cleansing. This is why G-d ordained capital punishment. When a soul becomes overly drawn towards to forces of evil, it must be withdrawn from its body to prohibit evil from using that body to manifest any further harm. Once extricated from that prison of the contaminated body, the soul can be reeducated and enlightened. It can be taught how to avoid further contamination.

However, there is one condition. The soul has to be willing to separate from the evil. If not, then once it has been removed from its body, it only seeks another body to continue to perpetuate its harmful influence. This is the foundation of what we today call "demonic possession".

In essence, the victim is not possessed by a demon, but rather by an evil soul. In actuality, the evil human soul once disembodied acts without regard to the Image of G-d in which it was created. As such that soul loses that Image and indeed becomes what we call a demon.

How then do we attract evil to ourselves, however knowingly or unknowingly? The answer is inherent in evil's spiritual origins. Evil is not physical, it has no form of its own. It needs a form through which to manifest. The forms most conducive to the manifestation of evil are thoughts, feelings, and behavior. Through these modes, evil can become most manifest.

In the spiritual world where all our thoughts, feelings, and behaviors are open books visible and exposed to all, likes attract likes. There is some sort of a magnetic pull between likes, the opposite of physical law where opposites attract.

When one thinks an evil thought, or feels an emotion of evil, even more so behaves in an evil fashion, the forces of evil take note of a kindred soul. They are opportunistic and naturally attracted to such an event and stick around for a while, with the hope of further influencing that soul to become an agent for their influence. If one stops oneself in his/her tracks, and does not repeat the evil expression, then the forces of evil become bored and leaves, seeking better game. This is the process of repentance. However if one does not repent of the evil, one thing leads to another, until evil dominates.

Chapter 16

What is Evil, What is Good? I'm So Confused!

There is only one reason why Evil exists in the world and that is because it exists in the heart and minds of men. We are all victimized daily by those who manifest evil in their thoughts, feelings, and behavior.

We cannot escape Evil because we cannot totally remove ourselves from people, which would have to include ourselves. What then can we do to protect our loved ones and ourselves? The answer to this question I can put into a few simple words. However, the doing of what I suggest will require an entire overhaul of human civilization

In order to eradicate evil, we must first recognize it and then have the courage to proclaim it as such. Then we must courageously confront it. This is not only true with regards to society and others; it must start at home, with each of us looking within ourselves.

Do you have any aspects of Evil in your soul? If you say no, then you are the best candidate to serve an evil purpose. Those who believe that there is no evil within them have a blind eye to the truth. Therefore, the forces of evil can most easily manipulate such a person to perform their dastardly deeds whilst the person is totally oblivious to the evil his/her thoughts, feelings or behavior manifest.

What do you think is Evil's greatest weapon in its war against man? No, it is not lies, anger, or hatred. While these weapons work well, most are able to recognize them as evil. The greatest and most deceptive weapon Evil possesses is the weakness in man to be more than he/she is or to crave more than his/her share. It is our own true and sincere desire for growth that is most often used against us to the harm of ourselves and others.

As example of this, let us go back to the beginning to the biblical story of the Garden of Eden. Remember, G-d said to Adam do not eat from the Tree of Knowledge Good and Evil. Adam said OK, conveyed the message to Eve, and went about his business. Along came the Serpent and struck up a conversation with Eve. Here already was the first mistake. Eve was open to dialogue about a forbidden topic when she should have known better.

The Serpent told Eve that if she ate from the Tree her eyes would be open and she would become "like" G-d. There is no inherent crime in either of these things. We all seek enlightenment and who would not want to be "like" G-d with great knowledge and ability, all to do good, of course.

This then is the second mistake. The deceiving Serpent did not lie to Eve. He told her the absolute truth. When she ate of the Tree, her eyes were opened and she did become "like" G-d. The Serpent did not deceive her; he merely told her what she wanted to hear. The greatest deception is always the right truth at the wrong time.

Once convinced that the Serpent was telling the truth, specifically a truth that she wanted to be true, Eve proceeded to eat of the forbidden fruit convinced that "the truth would set her free". Unfortunately, in this case, the truth did not set her free, instead it imprisoned her.

Eve's third mistake was that she thought herself wiser than G-d. G-d did not tell Adam or Eve why He did not want them to eat the forbidden fruit. He simply gave the order and waited to see if man (and thus woman) would use his free will to be obedient or rebellious. Eve rationalized that because her intentions were good that everything would work out fine. She wanted to eat of the fruit and she wanted to believe that there would be no consequences in doing so. Alas, for her, G-d had other ideas.

Once fallen, Eve's first act is to topple Adam after her. She knew that her "eyes had been opened". In other words, Eve knew that she had fallen and she intentionally gave Adam to eat knowing full well that he too would join her in the fallen state. The Serpent never spoke to Adam about eating from the Tree. G-d never spoke directly to Eve about eating from the Tree. Everything happened in a roundabout way. G-d spoke to Adam and he never took of the forbidden fruit by himself. The Serpent spoke to Eve, although G-d never did, and she listened to the Serpent and not G-d (through Adam).

Do you see the confusion here? It is very subtle, but very real. The results have devastated us ever since. This is the way of Evil, to blur the differences between itself and good. Evil presents itself as good and presents good as evil. In this way, the human mind, wanting to do good, instead is convinced and dedicated to its "noble" cause. Unfortunately, many times those convinced that their noble cause is good are actually the perpetrators of the greatest Evils.

All this occurs whenever one strays from obedience to the higher calling. In other words, when one begins to question G-d's Word and biblical wisdom, believing that today we have a "higher" understanding, this is the beginning of the unraveling of the fabric holding together creation. Once an individual opens him/herself to dialogue with a thought process or emotions that contradict the Divine order and the greater human good, like a spiritual magnet "likes attracts likes" and that soul is swept along a course which can lead only to perdition.

It is often said, "the road to hell is paved with the best of intentions". How well we all know this to be true. What I have described here is only one form in which Evil takes advantage of fallen man.

What we must learn from this is that as long as we can be deceived, we will be deceived!

We must therefore take whatever measures necessary to safeguards our minds. Only when our minds are protected can we be assured of proper protection for our feelings and our behavior. The Sages of old have said that nothing enters the heart before it enters through the eyes. In other words, no one can desire something that they know nothing about. If we open ourselves to see or contemplate that with which Evil tempts us, we can cultivate a desire for it. Once a desire is planted, like a weed it can grow, eventually choking and killing all the good plants.

Evil is real. Our minds are real. Internal spiritual/psychological battles are real. The war for our souls is real. G-d is real. Heaven and Hell are real, however, their reality lies more within our minds than elsewhere. In other words, Heaven and Hell are states of minds more than places of being.

Evil wants to undo the fabric of creation for its own designs. Man's job is to uphold creation and reinforce the process of continual growth and renewal. Alas, mankind's destructiveness is the ultimate expression of the Evil flowing through him (us). We all have a share in this, however great or small, whether in thought, word or deed.

If we wish to cleanse the world of Evil, we have to start at home and first cleanse our own minds, feelings, and behavior. This task is the hardest of all. Until we take the time to look deep into ourselves, we will only see the Evil being perpetrated by others. We will never see the evil being perpetrated by ourselves, although others scc it all too clearly.

Chapter 17

The Struggle Against Religious Insincerity

Within a world that surrounds us with Evil, how can one free oneself from its influence? It is easy to say that we must cleanse our minds, feelings, and behavior. Yet, practically speaking how does one do this?

One cannot answer and say by becoming religious one is protected. Unfortunately, we see all too many religious individuals who, in spite of their religious practices behave in horrible fashion. This, of course, is not the fault of the religion itself; it is the fault of the individual who hypocritically cloaks him/herself in religion all the while maintaining evil in their personalities. In order for religion to transform a person, the transformation must come from the inside out, and not the other way around.

Many people not raised religious end up becoming religious later in life. Usually these adult decisions are sincere. However, after many years involved in a religious community many sincere devotees lose their passion and simply adapt the status quo of religious observance of their communities. Religion, therefore, become a matter of rote and no longer a pursuit of human excellence accompanying a relationship with G-d.

Then enters Evil and replaces true heart felt religion with external, social, political convenience. Their peers, who observe all the externals of religion, but at the same time have G-d far removed from their consciousness, often disappoint sincere devotees to spirituality in religion. These externally religious types believe themselves to be the best people in the world. However, in the eyes of G-d and the Watchers, these poor fools are worthy of nothing but scorn.

In order for one to manifest Divine mercy in the world through the name YHWH, one must have a personal, living relationship with G-d. When all one gives to G-d is the most external aspects of religious observance, G-d in turn only reveals to such an individual His most external aspect, the name Elohim. This concealment of G-d's inner essence from the human mind, soul, and experience is the definition of exile.

The Laws of G-d are many and each of them teaches an aspect of inner personality transformation. Without prior inner observance, all external observance is incomplete. Without one's heart being right with G-d (and man) all one's religious observance is impure in the "eyes" of those who see from above. Since the insincere are not afforded any type of spiritual protection and thus succumb to the forces inherent within nature.

Spiritual sincerity in religion is the key to coming close to G-d, or better to say, G-d coming close to you. Yet, how does one acquire religious sincerity? Is not it enough that one performs all the commandments that one can? Is it not better to do the right things, even for the wrong reasons, rather than not do the right things at all?

Most religious leaders will tell you to do the right things regardless of your motivations or intent. I would generally agree with this advice. However, there is still an inherent danger in religious observance without sincere devotion. This is the danger of hypocrisy. While we may interpret our fellow religionists to be very sincere, Heaven sees things as they truly are, for good or for bad and judges accordingly. We do not know the secrets that lurk in the hearts of man, but the Watchers know them.

Remember that our innermost thoughts and feelings are clearly open and revealed in the spiritual realms to all the beings that reside there. While here on Earth it is easy to hide religious insincerity, in Heaven this is an impossible task. Whatever is in your heart for real is known to all above and you are judged accordingly. What a frightening thought! We are judged in accordance to what our truly lies in souls regardless of whether or not we are aware of it.

Cultivating sincere spiritual devotion in religion has been a challenge to the religious since biblical days. Indeed, G-d allowed His Holy Temple in Jerusalem to be destroyed specifically because of the lack of spiritual sincerity. With our lack of spiritual sincerity, we lack the ability to experience G-d's innermost nature, His supernatural essence YHWH. Yet, we are not left abandoned. G-d has revealed to us how to cultivate spiritual sincerity.

Spiritual sincerity was always in the hands of the prophets. Granted we do not have prophets today, in spite of claims otherwise, nonetheless, the message of the prophets has not been lost. It is recorded for us in the Bible. Spiritual sincerity in religion is a required prerequisite for religious observance. This is how one can cultivate it.

It is written, *"I place G-d before me always, He is at my right hand, I shall not fall"* (Ps 16:9). This verse from Psalms contains a secret of the mystics. This verse teaches us how to cultivate an awareness of Divine mercy (YHWH) in our lives and how to elevate our souls.

In order for one to clear their mind, one must simply replace bad thoughts and clutter with good thoughts and clarity. This verse in Psalms teaches us how to do this. We are to mentally visualize G-d's name YHWH at all times. This simple act is the most basic form of meditation. Thus, by keeping aware of the continual presence of G-d, one disables unlike thoughts from coming into one's mind. The spiritual rule that "Likes Attract Likes" works equally for good or for evil. When one does evil, one attracts evil. When one does good and tries to draw G-d close, one attracts good and does draw G-d close.

Drawing G-d close, into one's consciousness on a regular basis, is a process that takes a long time. This is not because G-d wants it to take so long, rather because we humans have such cluttered minds, it takes time for us to learn how to focus and concentrate.

There is also a warning I must share with you. Visualizing G-d's name and cultivating an awareness of His presence in your consciousness can be a dangerous thing. The dangerous matter in visualizing G-d's name is that His spiritual light shines in your unconscious and makes you very uncomfortable with the mistaken thoughts, feelings and behavior that you cling to. The light of G-d shines into your mind and begins to realign your inner feelings to correspond to the proper workings of the order in creation.

Visualizing G-d's name is also the calling upon His name mentioned in Zechariah 13:9. This is how one makes peace with G-d. Clearing out the clutter of the human mind and preparing ourselves for spiritual evolution are no easy tasks. In spite of the difficulties, we do have the freewill to choose where we wish to go. Try as we will though, there are always forces hindering our growth. We must learn more about them in order to neutralize their influence.

Chapter 18

What Keeps us Distant From G-d?

To think about G-d continuously is a great way to keep negative thoughts out of one's head and bad feelings out of one's heart. To talk to G-d in one's head or verbally is a great way to accustom oneself to G-d's presence. Both of these practices help us become more aware of a higher reality and to live up to it accordingly.

However, I have heard from a number of people that they do not have the time to be thinking constantly about G-d. Frankly, they tell me, they are too busy, with so many other important things on their minds. Nonetheless, they assure me that they are good people who live moral lives and observe G-d's commandments. As long as they do what is expected of them, they feel that they do not need to do anymore. In other words, enough is enough for them when it comes to religious matters.

I accept what I have been told by these certain individuals. I have no response to them. Frankly, I do not believe that they are open to anything that I would have to say. Sometimes being silent is the loudest comment one can make. I often practice speech through silence. I allow nature to take its course and for G-d to act as He sees fit in His Divine wisdom.

What I see is that in many cases these people who are too busy to think about G-d often fail to see that G-d in turn acts "too busy" to think about them. I have seen all too many cases of family problems, economic woes, and health issues amongst these types.

Yet, in spite of all their problems they claim that they are doing enough and whatever ill befalls them it is G-d's Will and they are willing to accept that, no matter what the loss. Thus, people suffer and blame G-d for the fruits of their own deserts. I see this all the time and I remain silent, knowing that my voice is not accepted, and my words of advice not received.

There is an old joke about a man dying from an illness. He prays to G-d for a cure and out of Heaven, the Divine Voice responds to Him, "I will heal you". Jubilant, the sick man cries out 'thanks to G-d' and awaits his healing. A moment later someone knocks at his door. The man opens it to see a doctor. The doctor says that he is a specialist and has the ability to heal his illness. The man closes the door on the doctor, saying, "no, G-d will heal me as He has promised". Moments later, there is another knock at the door; this time it is a surgeon, who also claims to be ready and able to heal the ill man. Again, the man rejects the surgeon, waiting for the Divine Hand to heal him. Not too long afterwards the man dies of his illness. He ascends to Heaven bewildered and angry. He stands before G-d's Throne and asks why G-d did not fulfill His promise to heal Him. G-d responded and said, "you fool, I sent you two healers, what more did you want?"

Although we chuckle at this story, its message is most important and applicable. G-d provides for us things in very practical manners, in accordance to the laws of nature that He Himself has ordained. In our present state of spiritual exile, events are not going to occur outside of the norm. Indeed, our Sages of old have taught us not to rely on miracles.

Nonetheless, people still live their lives with G-d far removed from their hearts and they still expect G-d to be at their beckon call whenever they are in need. What is wrong with this picture?

Let us ask the question, what other important things are on people's minds that keep them from thinking about G-d. The answers are many and include business, career, money, prestige, sports, other people, family members, fashion, and expensive adult toys. All these things are what most people spend the majority of their time and energy pursuing. In one way or another, we all have something of this physical world to which we cling at the expense of our spiritual selves.

The reason why we become so attached to physical objects is because that is what we see all around us. One will not see G-d or anything spiritual unless one makes the effort to look. All physical attachments act as barriers to our seeing the spiritual reality underlying our lives. Even the physical aspects of religious observance can act as a barrier to deeper spiritual introspection. In other words, often when one is observing a certain set of religious rituals, that one believes that said observance is all that G-d requires and there is no need for further self-improvement. In such a case religion performs the opposite effect of what it is supposed to.

In truth, there is nothing wrong with physical attachments all the while we live in the physical world. We do need to eat, sleep, work, and otherwise provide for ourselves and loved ones. Working hard is certainly not a sin, neither is being wealthy. It is not the possession of things that causes us harm; it is our relationship to said things that can cause the harm. In other words, attachment is fine. Over-attachment is wrong and harmful.

How then is one to distinguish between healthy attachment and harmful over-attachment? This then is the great question and may take a lifetime for one to answer. To make matters even more confusing, the right level of attachment differs from person to person. What might be healthy for one person can be a deadly poison to another. Unhealthy attachments are what separate us from G-d. Therefore, it is no wonder then that G-d assigns the Watcher angels the job to direct our lives to separate us from that which separates us from G-d.

People can become attached not only to physical things, but also to ideas, concepts, and feelings that also blur one's spiritual vision. These also the Watcher angels are employed to correct in us. This very truth underlies the entire human experience.

There is something very deep within us that guides our daily path in order to bring us to a higher revelation about life and reality. Our free will enables us to embrace the truth once it is revealed us. The opposite is also true. Our free will enables us to deny the revelations of truth. When this rejection occurs, the Watcher angels accompanied by our inner selves must work harder to bring into our minds and realities that truth which we seek to hide and deny.

Our denials and dishonesty are the cause of human suffering. In other words, when we suffer, it is for a reason, not haphazardly. Therefore, when sufferings come upon a person the most important task one has to perform is to investigate oneself to see what it is within oneself that could have caused or allow a tragedy to occur.

Chapter 19

Detach From That Which is Unhealthy

Picture this: you are standing in between two horse drawn chariots, with one arm tied to each. The horses are trying to pull away and as they do, they are tearing you in half. Did you ever get the feeling that this is how life feels? Feel it or not, this is how life is. We are always split in our desires, passions, and allegiances to opposing forces.

There is the spiritual element within us (the soul) that is continuously seeking expression so that it can manifest the Divine plan in the physical world. Opposing it is our physical element, our daily aspect of being, which simply wants to do what it needs to do to get through the day and enjoy as much of it as possible.

Pursuing daily physical sensations and expressing higher lofty spiritual goals often come into conflict. Yet, unlike conflict between peoples, who can be separated by distance, where can one go to hide from an inner conflict within oneself?

As composite spiritual/physical beings, we have exposure and access to both the natural and supernatural worlds. Our conscious mind deals with the natural world, our unconscious mind deals with the supernatural. Yet, due to its nature the unconscious and the supernatural do not exist in the natural/physical world and many have come to ignore them. Indeed, many have entirely forgotten about anything beyond what their senses can ascertain.

While certain realities can be pushed out of the conscious mind, this does not mean that they go away. On the contrary, whenever we push something out of consciousness that belongs there, it sticks around and haunts us like a ghost. Our minds, therefore, are regularly plagued by repressed thoughts or emotions. These sometimes can take on a life of their own and attract like spiritual entities. Just as there are real demonic entities outside of us, so are there are own personal self-created demons. The latter type is most certainly more dangerous than the former.

Human beings were created in G-d's Image to exist simultaneously and equally in both the physical and spiritual worlds. However, because of Adam's eating the forbidden fruit, we his children, lost focus of the spiritual side of our existence. While we acknowledge its existence and feel something spiritual from time to time, we are nonetheless in a state of grievous imbalance between the two levels of our being.

The major struggle for us as human beings since the time of the fall is to realign the lost balance between the physical and spiritual, between the natural and the supernatural. G-d gave us a helping hand thousands of years ago when He spoke on Mount Sinai and later to the prophets. Yet, we still do not listen. We still do not do what we already know deep down is best for us.

In many ways, as adults we never give up acting like little children. In many ways, we want what we want when we want it, and we cry and act up when we do not get what we want. Like children, many of us are enamored by possessions. Like children we become possessive of our adult 'toys" and refuse to share. When we lost the equilibrium with our spiritual side, we lost the ability to become mature human adults.

Our attachments to our physical surroundings hinder our reattachment to our spiritual surroundings. Because of this disconnection, the Watcher angels act in our lives to realign us, by force if necessary, with our lost spiritual halves. Indeed, our repressed inner spiritual half takes on a life of its own. Many times when we dream that a horrible ugly monster is pursuing us, the monster is not actually something bad, but rather only something that our mind interprets to be bad, although in reality it might be good.

Our minds play tricks on us and not everything that we think, dream, or perceive is an accurate perception of true nature. Our mental vision has become clouded by our collective fall. Until we individually address this issue and review of thoughts, feelings and behavior, we will remain in the fog of confusion.

Detachment is a helpful path when one desires spiritual growth. Now remember, detachment is not supposed to be absolute. We do require a certain amount of attachment in order to survive and in order to fulfill G-d's plan.

Most people who possess a large quantity of things are usually happy with their acquisitions and vehemently refuse to part from them. These individuals identify themselves by what they own instead of who they are. To have or to be, this is the question.

Who are you? Ask yourself to define yourself. Who are you? Most likely, you will answer that you are a doctor, lawyer, or something else. You are a husband, wife, father, mother, or something else. In other words, all you have told me is your occupation and a statement about your relationship to others. What you have not yet said is who are you?

You are more than your occupation. The proof of this is that if you ceased to be a doctor, lawyer or what have you, you would still be you. If you ceased being a husband, wife, father, or mother, you would still be you. These forms of identification identify what you have, meaning your occupation or relationships. They do not define who you are. The definition of your essence goes far beyond what you possess. Yet, most are totally oblivious to who and what they really are because they identify themselves so much with what they have that their entire definition of self is defined as what they have instead of who they really are. This error is the greatest level of delusion and deception possible for man.

Do not think that the spiritual powers that be are willing to accept being blocked out and denied. The reason for most human suffering is our conflict with our own inner selves. Even when accidents occur, it is often not too hard to find what we could have been done to avoid it in the first place. In those events when tragedy occurs for absolutely no rational fault of our own, still there is something deep inside us that allowed this to happen. If one would only take the time and contemplate, they would see that even life's most tragic events all have a purpose and a moral connected to them.

This insight describes the true nature of things. Everything in life has meaning and a purpose. G-d, His Watcher angels, our unconscious minds, and our spiritual soul all gang up on our conscious selves in order to educate us and open our eyes to a greater world. These higher forces have no interest in or care for the attachments that we make for ourselves in this world. In the eyes of these higher beings, our physical attachments are merely illusionary nuisances, which should only be removed so that one can come to attach to the real things in the real universe.

Chapter 20

Prayer & the Power of Faith

The power of the human mind is truly phenomenal. If we as a race were only able to unleash our collective inner mental powers, we could change the entire universe. Man's destiny, as outlined by biblical prophecy, indeed includes our accomplishing this lofty goal. Eventually, we will collectively realize our inner spiritual needs and we will make the necessary efforts to align them in healthy balance with our physical natural lives.

Whether we like it or not there actually is a cosmic conspiracy committed towards the betterment of man. Although we live today in exile and therefore do not see the spiritual realm around us, it is nonetheless teeming with activity. The forces that we call good and evil are in actual war for control here in the physical universe. Yet, when all things look so haphazard, we must remember that there is still the One Force that rules over all.

Indeed, G-d has given us free will. We can make terrible mistakes that we will have to live with. True, we are surrounded by very vicious spiritual and psychological enemies who can invade our very thoughts and cause us harm in many ways. With all that appears to be going against us, let us not forget the invisible Force of G-d that referees all.

As human beings, we have ability apparently unique to any species on Earth, and possibly unique even amongst the angels. We have the ability to pray. Prayer is not merely saying words or reciting texts from a book. Prayer is the communication of our souls with their source.

In spite of all the barriers that separate us from G-d the connection, although blurry has never been broken. Indeed, the apparent difficulty in our communications with G-d is actually only one-sided. In other words, we humans view ourselves as having the problem communing with G-d. Yet, G-d has no such problem; G-d communes instantaneously and continuously with our souls. In reality, in spite of our collective fall in Eden, our spiritual connection to G-d has never been broken.

Here then is the key to our individual and collective redemption. G-d has given us intelligence and has constructed things so that we use our ingrained ability to think to solve our problems. We are commanded to make best use of all the tools that G-d has given us. Yet, with all of our best efforts, sometimes they are not enough to get the job done (whatever job we have to do). When we have done our best and things still fall short, this is where G-d comes in and fills in the gaps.

Prayer is not words; it is a state of mind. In this state, one looks to G-d with human pride and humility together and says, "L-rd, I've done my best, may You bless the work of my hands".

G-d, for example, provides for us wheat. Yet, we must plant it, harvest it, grind it, prepare it, and bake it into bread. G-d provides the wheat, the rain, and the force of life to make it grow. Yet, all that, as essential it is, is not enough. Without our contribution, the work does not get done and we therefore could starve. Just remember, although we do all of our chores, unless G-d does His share we all labor in vain.

In order to pray one must possess an important prerequisite. One must have faith. The Sages of old have said that the entire biblical message is summed up in this one word: faith. The definition of righteousness is one who lives by faith. Faith is clearly very important yet just what is it?

Faith is NOT the blind acceptance of a creed or statement of beliefs. Faith is NOT mere adherence to one's religious doctrines.

Faith is NOT what you believe. Faith IS what you do. Faith IS how you act upon what you believe. Faith IS what you do in time of crises when no other criteria are before you to tell you how to act. Faith defines who you truly are, what you truly believe and where you truly stand, in relationship to G-d and to yourself.

Human intelligence is limited. There is only so much that we can figure out. Human emotions are extremely fragile. With too much pressure, the best of hearts turn insensitive. Faith is what you do once your head and heart can no longer help you decide what is best. This is why faith is so difficult.

When given a choice it is always easy to choose that which we know or feel is best. We simply rely on the past and act the same way in the present. In this way, we do not have to make the effort to think or to feel. We already know what to do and do it almost by rote, knowing that it is the right thing to do. Life like this is easy. There are not too many challenges.

What happens however when the rules change, when entirely new circumstances in life present themselves, when we cannot recognize what is or is not the right thing to do. This is where faith begins. Faith begins when I can no longer rely on the past, when I can no longer see the future, and when the present is before me like a complicated maze, all too rich in possibilities. What do I do now?

Fear will not help one now. Insight, caution, wisdom, all these, and everything else are of no value at this moment. Faith is when you must rely upon the Higher Power to guide you through. With faith, you take the next step, not knowing if you are walking into Heaven or into Hell. With faith, you place your entire security, your future and your well-being into hands other than your own. With faith, you make the conscious choice to surrender your free will and rely upon the Higher Will of Another.

As can be seen an act of faith even more so a life of faith is a frightening thing in and of itself. This is why we have so few people of faith in this world. We have enough trouble believing that there is an Invisible Force in the universe, all the more so placing our security into Invisible Hands. Yet, at the moment of crises, be it physical or psychological, what choice does one have?

Prayer is the true communication of one's united head and heart with G-d at such a moment of crises. When illness cannot be treated by the doctors, when the bills are not getting paid and there is no work to earn money, when others troubles arise that appear to offer no way out, these are the tests that mold the character of men and women. How we act at these times defines for us and for G-d if we are truly human created in His Image or whether we are just some sort of smart monkey.

Those who have been through a moment of crises and have cried out in their hearts to the Higher Power know exactly what I mean. Somehow, in some way, when all hope is lost, when there is nothing more we as individuals can do, something manages to pull us through. The secret here is faith.

Faith is the open doorway through which the Higher Power can intervene in our lives. This does not happen every day, but when it does happen it is a personal miracle and a revelation of Divine mercy. This is a step in the direction of world redemption. For how can a world be redeemed other than by first redeeming its inhabitants?

Chapter 21

The Nature of the Supreme Being

With all of our discussions about faith and spirituality, we have as yet failed to understand the most important of elements. We must understand who and what is G-d.

G-d is NOT some little old man with a long white beard sitting on a cloud somewhere. This is a myth perpetuated by European art. Yet, in reality, G-d is not a man, nor does He have any semblance to human form. When the Bible says we were created in G-d's Image, it is speaking about a spiritual/psychological Image. In other words, our minds are created in the Image of the Mind of G-d. The description of our physical bodies is not applicable here.

G-d is about as close to man as is possible, whereas at the same time G-d is as alien from man as can be. This irrational contrast explains why G-d at times seems so close and yet so far. We must understand that when we talk about a Supreme Being, we are talking about a type of life form so radically different from everything else that it itself is the definition of life itself. That is probably the best definition we can ascribe to G-d with our present limited human understanding. G-d is the life force and consciousness of the universe.

When we say that a consciousness pervades everything in the universe, we are saying that everything in the universe is in one way or another is connected. More than this, everything is the entire universe is, as if, aware of everything else. At some level of connection, everything has the potential or ability to influence or affect everything else. In other words, G-d created His Universe as a concentric whole.

In mystical literature, it is said that the universe is in the metaphorical shape of a man. In other words, like in the human body, so everything in the universe is interconnected and interacts. The more modern science and cosmology marches forward the more this interconnectedness is being proven accurate. As mystical as all this might sound, it should help us to understand how G-d can be aware of everything going on in the entire universe all at once. Nonetheless, it is impossible for us to imagine a Conscious Intelligence of this magnitude.

From our human side, the problem is not that we have such a hard time imagining such a Divine Being. Our problem lies in that we have a problem imagining that such a Being would have anything to do with us. While different spiritual philosophies from around the world acknowledge man's higher potential and destiny, none other than the Bible seems to place man square in the proverbial middle of the universe with a unique relationship with the Creator.

Unlike other religions, the Sages of the Torah have expressed their opinion that there are other beings existing on other planets. Way back in 1797, a great Rabbi from Vilna, Poland, Rabbi Pinhas Horowitz, wrote a book entitled *Sefer HaBrit* (The book of the Covenant) in which he discussed scientific discoveries in light of biblical teachings. He mentions the possibility of life on other planets and emphasizes how different from us they would be based upon the environments of their respective planets.

While we have no absolute proof of life in outer space yet, the possibility of it is high. Regardless of what is or is not out there, we humans still have a unique place in the scheme of things. We cannot comment about the role or place of others in the great scheme because we do not know anything about any others. If there are others, and many of them, we cannot say that our human role is more or less important than theirs until the Creator reveals such.

We know that there are angels. According to some biblical scholars, angels have long been associated with the planets. It is possible to offer an interpretation of certain old religious teachings to imply that angels might live on other planets. While this view is not accepted theology by anyone, it still can be a point of religious philosophical discussion. No one will know for sure what really is until such an insight is revealed in accordance to the Divine plan.

These ideas boggle the mind, and so they should. Yet, ideas like these should help us recognize that we are not alone in the universe and that there is a lot going on that we know nothing about.

Some modern philosophers have suggested that the G-d of the Bible may possibly be some technologically advanced extraterrestrial from another planet. Books on this subject abound and have been popular for decades. Only faith can respond to such arguments.

If someone wants to proclaim that there is no scientific proof of the existence of a Divine being, we will have to admit, whether we like it or not, that this assertion is correct. There is no scientific proof that I know of that absolutely proves the existence of G-d. However, this does not mean that no proof exists. Indeed, life and the structure of the universe is good proof that things did not just happen haphazardly. Life is far too complicated for mere chance to be responsible for it. Scientists know this but they hate to admit it because, in their eyes, this would be like having to admit that there is a Creator, a Creator that they as scientists cannot measure. Therefore, if the idea of a Creator is outside of scientific understanding then there cannot be a Creator according to science.

Yet, as we all know, as advanced or underdeveloped modern science is, it does not have all the answers. Indeed, as science advances farther into understanding the secrets of the laws of physics underlying our universe, the more they begin to sound like the religious mystics of old. One thing we can say is this; science and religion both seek an explanation of the true nature of existence. With this common goal science and religion can and should complement and support one another. All we need do is remove the prejudice and politics from both.

Inevitably, I believe science will catch up with religion and come to recognize that there is a Single Intelligence that gave rise to all of creation. When science discovers G-d, I am not so sure that He will be portrayed as religion has portrayed Him in the past. Maybe once our scientists touch the Divine, recognizing Him or not, maybe then they will take a cue from the Bible. Our Sages of old have taught us that our understandings of the Bible only scratch the surface. What wonders lie hidden within the biblical texts, only time will tell. We have a great future of discovery awaiting us.

In our present state of limited human knowledge, we call G-d a "Father" and a "King". These mortal concepts assist us in understanding G-d's role in our lives. If continuing these metaphors helps one to grasp some concept of G-d then let them stand. However, we must evolve our spiritual understandings. We must rise above a mere faith in G-d and embrace something higher. We must come to the awareness and knowledge of G-d's existence. Knowledge must supersede faith. For once we realize for real that G-d Himself is for real and that He is watching, only then will we take Him into account in our daily affairs. Only when we collectively turn our eyes to our Creator will we be able to finally see ourselves in the Eyes of the Divine.

Chapter 22

The Uniqueness of Being Human

What is the definition of being human? Should we limit our definition to biology alone? Shall we say that we are the species of Homo sapiens, and that alone defines what is human? I do not know one human being that can honestly ascribe to such a narrow point of view. We humans are far more than the sum of our biological parts.

We humans have essential ethereal, non-physical aspects to us that more or less totally define our being. I am not talking about anything spiritual or religious. I am referring to the human mind and spirit.

The mind exists within the human brain. Our minds define for us our individuality, our personalities, and our sense of being. Our minds are deep and tricky things. Yet, our minds are not our brains, although they inhabit them. Our minds are something that cannot be viewed or measured in a laboratory.

Even the science of the mind, so-called psychology, is so limited that in many cases it is a dismal failure. Psychiatry cannot address problems of the mind. All psychiatry can do is provide drugs that interact with brain chemistry encouraging or discouraging certain behaviors. Yet, psychiatry cannot cure mental illness and has never claimed to be able. The reason for this is that mental illness is a problem of the mind, not the brain.

Science cannot address the mind because it does not exist within the tangible parameters that science calls its home. No, there is much more to being human than biology. There is an ethereal side that experiences awe, wonder, love, and passion. The aspect of the mind called the heart has given rise to such beautiful art, poetry, and literature.

The imagination fires the mind, like fuel in a furnace. Yet, the imagination is not physical. Love is not physical, but it remains one of the strongest forces in the world. Why? These are the expressions of our "other" side, the side that science may one day may be able to manipulate, but never be able to control.

The greatest lie ever told to the human race is that we are nothing more than the descendants of monkeys. While there may or may not be any truth to Darwin's unproven theories of evolution, it really does not matter. For whether our bodies evolved from monkeys or created from the dust of the Earth by G-d, either way we humans possess something that Darwin and later scientists cannot understand. We human beings have a soul.

When we humans are looked at as being no more than a very complicated machine, then the entire element that makes us human is overlooked. Not everything is controlled by genetics and brain chemistry. Although these two forces have successfully been manipulated by science, they are far from being under control. Indeed, science will never be able to control anything that comes from the mind/soul, simply because this ethereal aspect of our being is not subject to scientific rules.

If one has a strong surge of water coming out a pipe or a hose, one can control the flow of that water by manipulating the release valve. One can thus release or hold back the water as one wishes. Yet, one thing is not accomplished by controlling the flow; the strength of the water surge is unabated. Indeed, if the release valve does not allow the water to flow out of the pipe or hose freely, but seeks to restrict its flow, greater and greater water pressure builds up until finally it explodes. The pipe or hose is thus destroyed and all means of control is lost. By not allowing the water to take its natural course, instead of improvement and control one creates only disaster.

This example of the surge of water is the story of the human mind, with all its desires, dreams, and passions. Natural law, as created by G-d, has ordained that we humans be who and what we are. We are not numbers that fit neatly into a place. We are not cogs in a machine that merely do our jobs in silent obedience.

Dwelling deep within us, often buried, often repressed, but never dead, is that which makes us truly human. It is our soul, the higher, thinking, psychic element within us that knows what is best for us and how we are best to live our lives. This and this alone separates us from the animal kingdom. It is this "otherworldly" nebulous non-physical mind/soul that makes our physical selves truly human. It is a crime against humanity to try to convince any human being that he is anything less than a lofty soul created in the Image of G-d.

There is an interesting opinion among the Sages that one day in the future, when mankind has rectified his inner turmoil; he is destined to travel to the stars. Legend says that in the World to Come, the righteous will each inherit 310 worlds. While most interpret this as a metaphor, one leading scholar asks the question if this teaching could be taken more literally. This biblical scholar opines that possibly in the distant future a spiritually transformed man will work in conjunction with G-d, acting as agents of the Divine throughout the universe. This should not sound so ridiculous to us in light of the biblical fact that the Watcher angels are doing this task right now.

Although in our present quagmire of troubles, life and the future look so difficult and gloomy, we must keep focus on the proverbial light at the end of the tunnel. We are not merely stupid creatures who lack the common sense to save ourselves from a global holocaust. Our personal and collective history is not merely a series of haphazard events. There really is a great effort on the part of countless "others" to enable us to realize our true inner potential. Yet, we have already learned what inhibits us from reaching our lofty goal of self-recognition. We have already learned that we are our own worst enemy.

What we must focus on is that we are also our own best friends. The Supreme Creator of the universe placed us here for a reason and with a purpose. We will meet our destiny for good, whether we like it or not.

How does one reach for the proverbial sky? The first thing one must do is to look up. In other words, if we place so much attention upon our biological sides, we will indeed confuse ourselves with our biological cousins. However, if we place our attention upon the side of the Divine within us, then we might begin to confuse ourselves with our spiritual cousins, the angels. If one has to be confused between being a monkey or an angel, which would you choose?

Eventually confusion passes and all that is left is the clarity of knowing that we are truly pearls in the rough. Our lives then become dedicated to shining up the pearls, waiting for the day, that the newfound shining pearl, will, be elevated to heaven to become a newly formed shining star. Is this a beautiful metaphor or some mystical truth about our future forms? Are we destined tomorrow to radiate as the angels do today? Only time will tell.

Chapter 23

Rosh HaShana, Everybody's Judgement Day

In the beginning of the biblical book of Job, we are given a glimpse into what goes on behind the scenes, spiritually speaking. Job is enjoying life with his family. He is a good man and lives a righteous life. The narration then "magically" switches us up to Heaven where the angels are having some kind of gathering. The Hebrew narrative refers to these angels as the Benei Elohim. We know them as the Watchers, the angels who have charge over the affairs of man.

At this gathering the Accuser enters. The Accuser is the angel better known as Satan. G-d asks him what he has been up to, Satan answers that he has been busy going to and fro over the face of the Earth.

Now, G-d challenges Satan and asks him if he has noticed Job and how good a man he is. Satan enters into debate with G-d claiming Job is only a good man because of all the good things he has in life. Take away his good things, Satan says, and watch what happens to Job. G-d agrees to test Job and the rest of the story makes up the next forty or more chapters of the book.

Why G-d allows Job to be tested and why He even brought up the challenge to Satan are difficult questions to say the least. Religious philosophers and mystics have debated these pointed for centuries. We do not have to follow in their footsteps with long and winded discussion. Rather than focus on what happened, let us pay attention to WHEN it happened.

According to biblical legend, the day that Satan stood before G-d and discussed Job was on the biblical holiday of the New Year. In Hebrew, this day is called Rosh HaShana. According to biblical tradition, the first Rosh HaShana is the day that G-d created Adam and thus is it was the first day of human history. This day is thus commemorated and observed as a sort of "Judgment Day". On this day, all living souls stand before their Maker, like they did on the first Rosh HaShana. Like Job before them, on this awesome day all souls are judged and have their destinies decided for the entire coming year.

Today Rosh HaShana has become a Jewish holiday, celebrated by Jews around the world regardless of their background. Yet, while the observance of this day is one of the commandments that the Jewish people follow along with all the rest, the day is not exclusively a Jewish holiday.

The Rosh HaShana Day of Judgment applies to all human beings, regardless of one's religion. This is G-d's time and G-d's business. Whether one believes in what happens on this day or not has no consequence or significance in G-d's eyes. Like Job, the Maker judges men at the time He has so ordained. Indeed, the Bible makes it clear that Job himself was not Jewish. He was still nonetheless judged on G-d's annual Day of Judgment, Rosh HaShana, the New Year.

While Jewish people celebrate Rosh HaShana with all kinds of biblical and other traditional observances, the rest of mankind has no such obligations. Nonetheless, while Jews are blowing the shofar (rams horn) in accordance to biblical edict, everyone including the Jews are being observed, reviewed, and judged.

Biblical and Jewish tradition refer to the time leading up to Judgment Day as the "days of penitence," during which each and every person looks into themselves to see how one can best improve one's life. This act of personal introspection should be universal and practiced by everyone, just as Judgment Day itself is for everyone, whether we like it or not.

Getting oneself right with G-d has nothing to do with Jews or the Bible. It is a universal principle underlying a universal truth. That truth is that whether we like it or not, we are responsible for our actions and behavior, we are being watched by a Higher Power and we are being judged by that Power. Fortune and misfortune do not happen haphazardly. There is a rhyme and reason to our universe and to our mortal lives within it.

One of the fundamental principles that we all should live by is the belief that good is rewarded and evil is punished. This concept underlies our entire system of justice, regardless of our differing cultures, religions, and lifestyles. We all share a concept of justice in spite of how we may differ in its interpretation. When we are wronged, we demand retribution. This is natural and normal. Natural law, as ordained by the Creator dictates that to every action there is an equal and opposite reaction. In other words, if there is a wrong, there must be a right to balance it out.

A major problem arises when one set of justice does not match up with another. When two individuals or peoples have different sets of values and different definitions of right and wrong great problems arise as to how to execute righteous judgment with which both parties will be satisfied.

With the laws of man, compromises can always be worked out, in spite of how difficult such negotiations might be. However, when it comes to Divine justice, G-d has His rules and we are subject to them, their rewards, and punishments, regardless of our individual beliefs, religions, cultures, or concepts of justice.

G-d has His ways of doing things. G-d has His times that He has so ordained to do certain things. G-d does not always reveal to us His thinking or His plans. Regardless, we are subject to His Will, even though we have free will of our own. Whether we like it or not, we are not masters of our fate. Yet, this does not mean we have no influence over what happens to us.

Bad things happen to good people. We all know this. People pray from morning until night, in every language and in every religion. Despite all our piety (or lack of it), we are all subject to the Forces that are beyond our control. Rosh HaShana is that one time ordained by G-d wherein which we can have a say in our destinies. Yet, our say, is not by our words, it will be by our deeds.

If you can honesty look at yourself in the mirror and say that you are the best you can be and that you have no room for improvement, then you are either a liar or hopelessly deceived. Our first priority in life should not be to ourselves, but for the betterment of the whole. Granted, we must provide for ourselves, for this too is G-d's Will. However, we should not be so selfish to think or say, "what's mine is mine and what's yours is mine (if I can get it)". Even to say "what's mine is yours and what's yours is mine" blurs the distinction and proper boundaries that G-d has ordained for us.

On Rosh HaShana G-d makes His decisions. Whether you believe this or not do you not think it worth your while to err on the side of caution. Just in case G-d does judge us on Rosh HaShana shouldn't you consider looking at yourself a little bit more honesty in the mirror. Shouldn't you begin to correct some of those old faults that you know have been hanging around inside your personality, festering like an open wound?

Just in case, the story of Job is true. Just in case there really is a G-d. Just in case that Rosh HaShana is His judgment day, maybe we should take this time a bit more seriously, and do something about it to better ourselves. Just remember this, if G-d forbid, anything bad happens to any one of you this year, it was ordained to be so from Rosh HaShana. We have the opportunity to make a difference. Why would anyone want to miss such a chance?

Chapter 24

Dream Messages

"In a dream, in a vision of the night... Then He opens the ears of men... that He may turn man aside from his conduct"
(Job 33:16, 17).

Dreams are such wonderful things. They can take us to places we have never been. We can do things in them that we could never normally do. We can see things and experience wonders in them unlike anything normal life can provide for us. Indeed, many great scientists and inventors have been inspired by their dreams to discover the secrets of the universe and to create the wonders of technology.

Dreams can be rather dreamy or they can be rather dense. Sometimes dreams are so confusing that they make no sense. Sometimes dreams are so real that upon awakening one is visibly shaken by what one has dreamt. Most times, however dreams come and go like a wisp of wind unnoticed.

In religious, spiritual and mystical circles, dreams have always been a means of communication with powers beyond our world. Even psychology recognizes that dreams contain within them messages from beyond the conscious mind. How far beyond the conscious mind depends upon you ask. Carl Jung believed in a collective unconscious while Sigmund Freud had a hard time believing in anything larger than his... well let's leave it at that.

Our old friend Job knew a lot about dreams. Job and his friends knew all too well that sometimes a dream is a message. This message originates from the Source of the human soul, from the Creator Himself. As the verse above states, G-d uses dreams as a means to communicate with man. Elsewhere in the Bible (Num 12:6), we find that G-d communicates with prophets through their dreams. Therefore, a dream has the potential of being a whole lot more than our personal wishful thinking or a result of eating too much ice cream before bed.

How can one tell which dream is a message from beyond and which are simply byproducts of a number of different elements? The answer we already know, although we might not know that we know it. Most of us have at one time or another experienced what I will refer to as a "strong" dream. This is the type of dream that shocks you into awakening, with you remembering every little detail. Something deep inside tells one that this dream has some type of message in it. Regardless of how rational or irrational the feeling, one somehow knows, intuitively, that the dream was important. More so, more people than not have a good sense about what their dream means and what the message is.

As dense as we wish to believe ourselves to be, our spiritual roots are alive, well and rather untouched, and unscathed by our lack of paying attention to them. Regardless of how secular or non-spiritual one becomes, one cannot escape from receiving an inner message. The more one wishes to ignore it, the harder it comes back. Dreams can be a real "pain in the neck" when one wishes to ignore their message. If G-d wants to get a message through to you, then that message will get through. If one wants a tap on the shoulder or a punch in the head, it is all up to how the individual receives the dream message.

The very same vehicle that receives dream communication also alters and perverts its original meaning. The conscious aspect of the human mind receives the dream messages; however, it interprets these messages in a most peculiar way. This is why dreams always appear to be a series of confusing, irrational, disconnected images. To our rational minds, the dream does not make any sense. However, to our unconscious mind, the mumbo-jumbo of dream talk comes through very loud and clear.

Our conscious minds think in a manner very different from our unconscious minds. Our conscious minds are best adapted to life in this physical world and therefore understand it best. Our unconscious minds, however, deal with the spiritual realms. As such, it views life in a very different light than does our conscious minds.

The language of communication in the spiritual world is almost the opposite of how we communicate here in the physical world. In essence, our conscious minds are like the tips of an iceberg. Our unconscious minds on the other hand are like a looming mountain concealed from sight. The unconscious mind is what guides our conscious minds, and as such, is what molds our entire lives.

The way and communication of the unconscious mind is so vastly different and foreign to us. This is why we hardly understand our own inner thoughts. This is why our dreams are always such a mystery. Our dreams are the communication between our unconscious minds and our conscious minds.

What for our conscious mind is a series of confusing irrational images is for our unconscious minds; the most direct and clear spiritual message. Something is wrong here. It is like our minds are speaking two distinct and separate languages. In our own minds, we simply are not speaking the same language. What are we to do about this inner confusion? The answer is most simple. One side of the mind has to learn the language of the other side.

Being that we are only aware of our conscious minds and have absolutely no affect upon our unconscious minds, it behooves us to consciously learn the language of the unconscious in order to be able to understand what on Earth we are saying to ourselves. Do not underestimate the importance of this necessity. If one continues to be in darkness about their own inner needs, the voice from within can become louder and louder. Eventually that inner voice can force one to listen by becoming heavily involved in one's personal life, to the point where life can become a living hell, if one does not understand and heed the inner message.

Job learned that G-d speaks to us in dreams. Yet, as dream language is so bizarre according to our conscious minds, most of us would never recognize whether G-d was talking to us, or whether we are listening to our midnight snack, our inner fears, or our secret desires. There is a lot at stake when it comes to dreams.

The book of Genesis relates that in ancient Egypt, Pharaoh was warned by G-d in a dream about upcoming economic disaster. Yet, Pharaoh did not understand his dream, although he dreamed it twice. In his dreams, he saw gatherings of sheaves of grain, and a bunch of cows. What do these have to do with years of plenty, and years of famine? Could not his dreams be a little bit more direct, and to the point? The answer is that the dreams were direct and to the point, but in spiritual language, not physical language. Pharaoh therefore needed a spiritual man in order to interpret for him "spiritualeze".

Yosef proved his value to Pharaoh by his being able to understand "spiritualeze". Now once Pharaoh heard Yosef's interpretations of his dreams he could not rationally prove them right or wrong. Yet, something deep within him recognized that Yosef's words were true as opposed to those spoken by his other wise men. Such an interpreter of "spiritualeze" is worth his proverbial weight in gold.

Therefore, Pharaoh hedged his bets, and placed a young Hebrew slave upon the throne of Egyptian lordship. For a master of "spiritualeze" knows how to balance the conscious mind with the unconscious and the physical world with the spiritual. These special men and women are what we call prophets. Not only can they understand Divine messages; they know how to communicate them to us. They are not spiritual "holy-rollers," but rather rational, practical men and women, who have an inner ability to balance one's spiritual side with one's physical side. As such, they are a profit to all.

So then, what can one do to cultivate this inner ability to speak "spiritualeze"? This we will discuss in our next essay.

Chapter 25

How to Speak "Spiritualeze"

Dream language is most bizarre. Yet, in spite of the numerous dream interpretation books available none of them can successfully interpret our dreams for us. This does not mean that dreams cannot be interpreted, for indeed they can be. However to interpret dreams we must have the right keys to open them.

Dream keys are not an accepted group of interpretations with specific symbols meaning specific things. If this standardization was the case, one could open a dream interpretation book, interpret symbols, and become fully aware of the dreams and their meanings. Anyone who has ever tried to interpret dreams through a book knows this is not what happens.

There are very old dream interpretation manuals based upon reliable biblical and Rabbinic sources that outline alphabetically symbols and their meanings. Rabbis have used these texts for centuries, but have always known their limitations. One famous ancient Rabbinic text on dream interpretation, *Pitron Halamot*, was actually used by many of the original pioneers of dream psychology, including Sigmund Freud. Unbeknownst to most practitioners in the mental health field, but much of modern dream psychology actually is based upon ancient biblical, and Rabbinic sources.

Nonetheless, the number of symbols interpreted in these books is only a small portion of the symbols that people actually see in dreams. While portions of dreams can be understood using reliable ancient texts, this does not mean that entire dreams are hereby interpreted. Therefore, even the best and most legitimate of dream interpretation books are very limited. There is more to a dream than the symbols therein. The biblical personages Yosef and Daniel knew this truth all too well. They are the ones who taught it to the court wise men of Pharaoh in Egypt and Nebuchadnezzar in Babylon.

To understand a dream in full one needs more than just a written book. The Bible gives two examples of excellent dream interpreters, Yosef, and Daniel. Both were able to plummet to the depths of a dream's meaning, when all others who tried failed. Both lacked dream manuals or any professional training in dream work. Yet, both Yosef and Daniel shared very important common characteristics; they both had awe of G-d and spent much time in meditative pursuit.

Dreams arise from our unconscious minds and therefore speak the language of the unconscious. The conscious mind is totally lost when it comes to understanding the unconscious. There is only one bridge that can unite these two divided halves of our minds. This is what the Bible calls the "spirit" of Elohim (G-d). Both Yosef and Daniel make mention of this being their secret tool when it comes to dream interpretation.

Yet, just what is this "spirit" and how can one cultivate it? Being that *"in a dream, in a vision of the night.... [G-d] opens the ears of men...that He may turn man aside from his conduct"* (Job 33:16, 17), it appears to be very important that we learn this skill.

The skill of cultivating a relationship with the spirit of Elohim (G-d) is discussed in numerous religious books, but the skill is not acquired through reading. A relationship with the spirit of G-d comes from only one place. It comes from the heart. This then is the secret of cultivating it.

When the Bible refers to one's heart, it is not referring to the organ in one's chest, but rather to an aspect of the human mind, that connects the conscious with the unconscious. The heart, therefore, is the "place" where thoughts and feelings merge. At this important juncture, the heart is the center of the body, specifically the spiritual body. This is why G-d commands us to love him with all our hearts and why His words are to be placed upon our hearts (Deut 6:5, 6). No reference to the head or intellect is mentioned here. G-d knows the severe limitations of the human intellect. When it comes to us experiencing G-d's "spirit" we need to experience it with an element within us more stable and grounded than our intellect.

The heart is everything when it comes to a discussion about anything spiritual or psychological. One cultivates strength of heart when one is passionate. The passion here that one must cultivate is a passion for G-d. This is best accomplished when one turns towards religion. However, just because someone is religious does not mean that they are passionate for G-d. Religion merely provides the vessels through which one's passion for G-d can be manifest.

Yosef was a passionate man who truly believed in G-d. Yosef lived centuries before the giving of the commandments on Mount Sinai. Nonetheless, without having to be commanded, he knew that to sleep with his master's wife was a mortal sin, one that he refused to do regardless the consequences (Gen 39). Yosef was falsely imprisoned for years. Nonetheless, he prospered in jail. Indeed, it was his being in jail that provided for him the opportunity to meet his destiny to become Viceroy of Egypt. Yosef's commitment to what he knew internally was right was his personal expression of his spiritual passion. This is how he observed his religion centuries before Mount Sinai.

Daniel is another example of passion towards G-d regardless of consequence (Dan 6). When faced with the choice to pray to G-d or an idol, Daniel ignored his own safety and did what he knew in his heart was right. He did not conceal his actions or make excuses for them. He boldly proclaimed his faith and his passion by his actions regardless the consequences. We all know what happened. Daniel was thrown into the lion's den. Yet, as Yosef prospered in jail, so did Daniel among the lions. Even in this age of exile, when no Temple stood in Jerusalem, when no miracles occur, one did occur for Daniel. The hungry man-eating lions did not harm Daniel. He was miraculously spared.

In order to be able to understand the language of dreams as did Yosef and Daniel one must cultivate a relationship of passion with the author of dreams, G-d. In this way when all sorts of conflicting imagery confuse one's mind, G-d can still speak to one's heart and place within it the meaning of the dream, over and above the interpretation of any dream symbolism.

This was Daniel's special gift. When King Nebuchadnezzar of Babylon forgot his dream, he threatened to kill all his wise men if one of them could not tell him his dream and its meaning. Although many tried, somehow the King felt inside himself that all their interpretations were false. Only when Daniel spoke did the unconscious of the King cry out from within him and confirm the truth of Daniel's words. Daniel first told Nebuchadnezzar what the dream was that he had forgotten and then proceeded to tell him what it meant. *"As for the mystery about which the king has inquired, neither wise men, astrologers, magicians nor diviners are able to declare it to the king. However, there is a G-d in Heaven who reveals secrets"* (Dan 2:26-28).

Daniel was not told these things in his head. Rather he felt them in his heart, and simply let his mouth speak from his heart as opposed to from his head. In this way alone, was Daniel proven correct, as was Yosef before him. The language of the heart is where conscious mind meets unconscious mind and speaks through the lips, often without the speaker being in control of what is said.

The most significant dreams always come along with their interpretations. No outside person will be able to tell you what your dream is or what it means. However deep down within each of us we somehow know what our dreams mean. When we are offered an interpretation, we either embrace it warmly as if we have always known it or reject it with a laugh as something foolish.

Passion of the heart, listening to one's inner voice, feeling G-d's word in the heart and not just thinking it in the head, these are what enables one to speak "spiritualeze". These steps are not impossible to take. Learning "spiritualeze" is like any other course of learning. It takes time and a whole lot of practice.

Chapter 26

The Power of True Love

I once heard an old saying that "the only thing that can return happiness to those who have lost it is love". Love is so much more than the attraction between human beings. Love is one of those ephemeral things that defies human definition and transcends life and death. Love is that rare element that lasts forever. As such, we can clearly recognize love as being an aspect of our Creator.

Love is such a spiritual thing. We so crave to experience human love that we spend our entire lives in pursuit of it. Many fail to find love and become bitter in its absence. Many fail to find love for a number of reasons. The primary reason why many do not find love is that they do not know how to recognize it when it comes.

So many things are called love that is not. Human love is all too often confused with biological, hormonal attraction. Yet, this type of attraction often masquerades as love and sometimes can house true love, but more often than not, biology and love are as different as is physical and spiritual.

When the confusion of mind succeeds and love is lost what is left is often depression and a sense of being lost and empty. Many who have experienced this feel that this precipice is a point of no return. We should all be thankful to our Creator that there is more to being human that mere physical attraction.

No matter how bad a situation appears and how lonely one feels, there is never a precipice too far out from which one cannot return. In other words, no matter how bad things are, they can always get a whole lot better, even to the point of the restoration of relative perfection. Yet, this restoration is not a miracle that happens because G-d waves His "magic wand". There are no such fantasies or miracles. Love can restore happiness to those who have lost it only when they are willing and open to receive it.

Herein lies the secret. True love is not something you find; it is something you give. True love is not what you feel; it is what you do. True love is not a state of mind; it is a state of being. True love transcends the limitations of physical life because it comes from a place out of this world. True love is a spiritual characteristic. It can only be experienced once a person has developed their spiritual side.

The Sages of old spoke to us about love and said, *"All love that is dependent upon a thing, when that thing is nullified so is the love. When love is not dependent upon a thing then it lasts forever"* (Avot 5:19).

Most of us do not know the real meaning of love. Granted love is a force of attraction. Yet, so are infatuation and lust. Every one of us at one time or another confuses these emotions with the true power and force of love.

There are two kinds of love – that which is dependent upon a thing and that, which is not. Both forms of love appear to be legitimate expressions of emotion and caring. Yet, of the two only one of them is eternal. The other form eventually fades with time. Love, therefore, can apparently exist on two different planes, between bodies and between souls. Unfortunately, often these two become confused.

Humans have longed learned that confusion of the mind is the worst problem that we can ever suffer from. Not only does it hinder our spiritual insights, it hinders our ability to feel and thus know things that are real. Mental confusion blurs our ability to distinguish between the real and the unreal, between that which lasts and that which does not.

When one has lost love one feels like their heart is broken. We all know this feeling. However, when one loses the love of one of the things of this world, the sadness thereof is short lived. Soon another something to love will come along and the first thing loved is soon forgotten. Thus, we go through the love of cars, homes, and platonic relationships. What can I say? Platonic is platonic. Platonic attachment is not deep. The pain in losing something platonic is not deep either.

This relaxed attitude is only true, however, when one is clear and able to differentiate between the platonic things of this world and the true attachments and bonds that bind us at the soul level. Sometimes we languish and miss the platonic things of this world as if they were the eternal things of spiritual origins. This misplaced attachment to the temporary causes us much anguish and pain. Yet, this type of pain is a result not of our loss but of our blurred vision that disables us to recognize the true from false in relationships.

Once one recognizes true love and knows that it never ends, then even with the death of a loved one or loss of a precious thing one is comforted.

When a spouse of many years passes away, somehow one knows inside oneself that the spouse is happy and in a better world. This inner knowledge is available because the spiritual connection between souls survives and transcends death. In other words, souls do not die. They just change from physical body to spiritual body. In their spiritual bodies, which reside in the abode we call Heaven; the souls of our loved ones are able to see us here in our physical world. They communicate with our souls, through our unconscious, often through dreams. They communicate with us their comfort and share it with us. In this way, in spite of our loss, we know that we are never truly alone.

Sometimes it happens however that a person never manages to find that one special love in life that awakens the spiritual within them. When this happens, depression often sets in and further hinders one's ability to find the true love out there that is the natural portion and right of every human being. It is in a case like this that we can become our own worst enemy and create for ourselves our own private hell.

Granted, depression is a biological illness that can be treated rather successfully with medication. Nonetheless, this does not mean that a person does not have good psychological reasons to be depressed. Herein lies the problem, what do we say to those people who have made poor choices in life and have locked themselves into situations that while not physically dangerous are nonetheless making them very unhappy?

The answer to this sometimes can be to change the situation, but more often than not this might be impossible. In such cases, and in many others as well, rather than changing one's situation, one should better work to change oneself. G-d sometimes dictates situations to us and whether we like them or not we are required by Higher decree to live through them. In these cases, many people begin to lose hope. They first lose hope in G-d, and then in themselves. These souls truly become lost and suffer in great pain. Yet, it is these very selfsame souls that can be healed the easiest, if only they are willing to be healed, not just in word, but in deed.

Remember that love is a spiritual element. It is a spark from G-d. A spark is a portion of light. No portion is whole separate from itself. No love is complete that does not include G-d at its center. The love of G-d is a healing for every soul. The love of G-d may or may not be emotional. No feelings are required in the love of G-d. What are required are the acts of love, the taking care of and the compassionate concern for G-d's creation. We are G-d's creation.

When we focus on the bigger picture and not on our own self-portrait, we will find love becomes much easier to give and all the more easily received. Many people feel broken of heart and bereft abandoned by G-d. Yet, these feelings are quite selfish. One is mourning one's own shortsightedness, instead of allowing oneself to be absorbed into the greater whole, the greater good.

One will find true love only outside of oneself. Therefore, rather than cry over one's failures in life, one should stop focusing on self and start focusing on others. By providing for others, we express our love for G-d. In this way, any broken heart begins to mend. One will find G-d and true happiness in the loving expressions of appreciation of those whom we help when they need us most.

Chapter 27

The Coming of the Mashiah

One of the apparently "hot" spiritual topics discussed today in many world religions is the idea of the coming of a Mashiah. According to the messianic idea, G-d is eventually going to run out of patience with mankind groping around in the spiritual darkness, causing harm to themselves and others. At some appointed time, unknown to man, G-d will send His human representative, the Mashiah, to set human affairs straight in accordance to the Divine plan.

Can you imagine what world reaction would be if someone were to claim that He is G-d's representative sent from Heaven to straighten out the world? Since the world's lunatic asylums are filled with so many who make this claim we may never know. Yet, of all the self-deluded souls who suffer such illusions of grandeur, there will still come one, who will not be delusional.

It is interesting to note that in all world religions the coming of Mashiah is never described as a peaceful event. The Mashiah comes to a world in turmoil and war. He comes to fight all of G-d's enemies and to impose upon the world a government ordained by Divine plan. Yet, the role of the Mashiah is not one of a religious dictator. Rather, the Mashiah is sent by G-d to usher in a new age of universal peace, prosperity, and spiritual evolution. He is called a savior, one whose role it is to teach us how to save ourselves from ourselves.

Granted the details of messianic teachings differ sharply between the religions. Yet, the details are not the issue. The issue is, if and when a Mashiah comes with an army of angels out of the sky as referred to in the Bible (Zech 14:5), how will the world interpret such an event?

Will the CNN and Fox News reporters covering Jerusalem look up into the sky and begin reporting that the long awaited Mashiah has finally come? How would they know that anyway? What does a Mashiah look like? All the more so, what does an army of angels look like?

Most likely if an army of angels were to suddenly appear in the sky with the mission of taking over the Earth, I do not believe that such an event would be welcomed as the long expected coming of the Mashiah. Rather, I can see the secular news reporters shouting out for all around the world to hear: INVASION! THE ALIENS HAVE COME!

In all due respect, angels are not portrayed in the Bible as blond haired, blue eyed, females in white robes, with wings and harps. This mythological image is best left in our children's storybooks. Real angels as described in the biblical book of Ezekiel look very otherworldly. They are said to have multiple faces, with animal like features, standing on a single leg, with numerous sets of wings reminiscent to Earthly insects. This is not exactly the type of being that we would like to have wake us up in the middle of the night, nor is it the type of being we would like to see invade the Earth.

If, all of a sudden, an army of these otherworldly beings were to appear in the skies over Jerusalem (and most likely simultaneously over other places around the world), who could blame the on-lookers from calling this an alien invasion. To be honest, it is.

Mind you, angels are not G-d. As we have learned, angels often do not act with what we consider our best interests. Angels have an agenda of their own. Therefore, if the prophecy proves correct and an army of angels does come to take over the Earth, I do not anticipate their coming and subsequent welcome to be anything less than hostile.

If the prophecies prove correct the Mashiah will come and usher in a new age of world "peace". Yet, Mashiah's vision and definition of such a "peace" might not be what the world governments had in mind. Somehow I do not believe the governments of the world will be so quick to relinquish their authority and system to an "alien" outsider.

Nonetheless, when you have an army of angels backing you up, the opinions, statements, beliefs, and actions of others will not really matter. Judging from biblical teachings, I do not foresee the Mashiah being very sympathetic to his political and religious opposition. The Bible states clearly that such opposition forces are to be killed by a plague.

In the Bible, the prophet Zechariah prophesied that in the future, after Mashiah comes, G-d will command all the nations of the world (or their representatives) to ascend once a year to Jerusalem to observe the annual holiday of Succot, the Holiday of the Tabernacles. Those nations that refuse this Divine command are to be severely punished. Apparently, the nations will still have the ability to refuse the Divine command, although the punishment for doing so is ominous.

The biblical scenario implies that the acceptance of the Mashiah and the messianic kingdom will be by force. His benevolence will only become apparent in time. In time, possibly generations, mankind will wake up to the fact that what has been imposed upon them actually is for their own good.

We must admit that no one knows exactly what the future holds. People of faith believe firmly that the Mashiah will come, when and how are points upon which no one agrees. However, these arguments do not matter. For if prophecy is true, then the Mashiah will come, in that way and in that manner as ordained from Above, regardless of human interpretation or misinterpretation. If prophecy is true the Mashiah will come, and the world will not be able to silence him by having him committed.

The real Mashiah will be a human being of flesh and blood, born of normal parents like you and me. Although he may come with an army of angels, this does not mean that he too is an extraterrestrial. He has to be human for who other than a fellow human could rule over and rectify humanity.

This then is the central and most crucial point about all messianic beliefs. The Mashiah is to come to make us more human and to teach us how to rise above our animalistic instincts. The Mashiah's role is to teach man how to make peace with G-d and to restore us to a "face" to "face" relationship with our Creator and the spiritual world.

There is an interesting mystical concept that states that all human souls are actually part of a greater super-soul, each of us being an individual part thereof. The soul of the Mashiah is said to be the chief soul, the head soul of the human race. Therefore, all mankind are, in essence, the individual parts of the greater super-soul of the Mashiah.

What this means is that we each have a spark of the messianic soul within us. Regardless of the mystical implications of this, the practical implications are profound. Rather than wait around for G-d to overwhelmingly intervene in human history, we can in the meantime actualize our inner messianic potentials and work together as a united mankind to make our world a better place.

The Mashiah does not have to come to a world in turmoil and war. If we are at peace within our own selves, within our own minds and hearts, we can make peace on a global scale. Inner peace leads to outer peace. The reverse does not work.

Mashiah will come to a world at war because the real war is being waged inside the human psyche, where we daily battle between our animalistic tendencies and our higher human aspirations. Mashiah will come to put an end to this war, and to all other wars along with it.

We can help speed up his coming by waging his war prior to his arrival. If we fight the inner messianic war against the inner evils of man, maybe we can avoid the Great War known to Jews as Gog and Magog and to the rest of the world as Armageddon. As always, we have free choice.

Chapter 28

The True Meaning of Being Religious

What does it mean to be religious? Most will answer and say that it means believing in the teachings of one's religion and being involved in the cultural/spiritual affairs of one's chosen congregation. This definition will more than not apply to most people and most religions. Yet, the most important elements in defining one being religious I purposely left out simply because most people unfortunately also leave them out of their religious lives. I am talking about morality and spirituality.

All too often we read stories about religious individuals; many time clergy (including Rabbis) who are caught involved with some of the worst types of human behavior. Whether it is perverse illicit sexual behavior, drug use, or dishonesty in business practices, the vices of secular society certainly have their following among religious observers.

This then is the problem. Religion is supposed to elevate its followers above the temptations of these vices. Yes, religious individuals, by definition, are supposed to be more moral and more righteous than their secular counterparts. What happens when they are not is that all religious persons are condemned as being hypocrites. The bad apples poison the whole barrel.

Worse than this, the secular community not only condemns the religious hypocrite; they also condemn religion as a whole. To add insult to injury, based upon the behavior of the religious hypocrite, many secularists even condemn G-d and become extremely anti-religious. In other words, the behavior of the religious hypocrite serves to reinforce the secularism of the secular and further turns them away from G-d.

There is at present a cultural war going on between those who adhere to religion, and those who do not. This battle is not limited to the State of Israel; it is also going on in Christian communities around the world, especially in the United States. Yet, this battle also rages in Islamic, Hindu, and other Oriental communities. Indeed, in every community that has an age-old spiritual or religious tradition, its adherents are under attack culturally, psychologically, and socially from the secular members of their relative communities. This is happening everywhere and no place is immune.

The question that we need to ask is why is there so much conflict? Mind you, the conflict is not so much over whether one believes in G-d or not, but rather, over which ways are better, the old "religious' ways or the new "secular" ways. The question is does the modern consumer oriented secular culture really offer a better alternative to the age-old traditions that people have followed for centuries?

We have to be careful how we answer this question because in truth modern culture does have many advantages over the old. The problem is that not enough people realize that the old ways still have many advantages over modern culture. Most individuals and societies have not yet been able to find a harmonious balance between the ways of old and the ways of new. This then is the greatest challenge facing us today: how to blend the best of both worlds (old and new) to create an even better future.

The modern secularist is absolutely convinced of the correctness of his ways in much the same way, as is the religionist. Much to the chagrin of the secularist but modern secularism has become as much a faith as any other religion.

Secularism is based upon certain principles and beliefs, many of which rely on scientific theory for their foundation. As we know, theories are simply educated guesses and not statements of fact.

Much of modern science and therefore, the secular culture defining itself by its discoveries are as much based on opinion and faith, as is any religion. The difference between the religions of old and today's "new" religion of secularism is that secularism takes full advantage of the media to present itself as the dominant and absolute truth.

With this conflict of religious versus secular cultures, it is no wonder that a number of religious individuals stray from the religious path. Many in religious circles fear the secular world and endeavor to build multiple walls of cultural and social separation to keep the religious adherents free from secular influence. Yet, as has been shown in numerous examples, the highest, and thickest of outside walls cannot protect someone from something that grows from within oneself. In other words, secularism can only affect the religious individual when said individual opens his/her heart to being influenced.

Everything revolves around what one has in his/her heart. Religious faith has little to do with doctrines and philosophies and a whole lot to do with morality and righteous behavior. One can adhere to all the doctrines and beliefs that one wishes and still, at the same time, act hypocritically against them. We recognize such a person as a hypocrite. Their actions proclaim his/her disregard for the doctrines and faith of their proclaimed religion.

When one is acting contrary to what one's religion teaches, one by definition is not being religious, regardless of how one dresses, what other religious activity one is involved in or what one professes. A hypocrite contradicts his/her entire religion, regardless of their adamant insistence that this is not true.

When we talk about hypocrisy, we must separate this application from the individual, who falls prey to his/her human inclinations and makes a one-time mistake. This descent is only human. While we do not condone such lacks of judgment, we understand them.

Every now and then a person is tempted and succumbs to temptation. Usually when a fall occurs, the religious individual is aware of the contrary nature of their deeds and seeks to rectify the situation. Such a person is to be lauded, for we all are human and have our weaknesses. We do not condemn the weak. On the contrary, we help them to become strong.

On the other hand, we do condemn the liar. The liar is not one who is weak, but rather one who follows a course of actions or a lifestyle contradictory to religion and at the same time tries to cover up said behavior by hiding out under the cloak of religious piety.

The weak person is embarrassed by a one-time mistake. The lying hypocrite never has such regrets in his/her heart. The liar hypocrite might express such remorse when his/her rotten behavior is publicly exposed. Yet, at this time it is too late to redeem the hypocrite. The damage such a one has done has been done. Many are disheartened with religion in general due to the rotten acts of a few rotten apples.

Religion boils down to one essential element and that is one's relationship with G-d. All too many religious individuals have a relationship with their religion. Of them very few have an active REAL relationship with G-d.

Many people have come to separate religion from spirituality because they do not find anything spiritual about being religious. This is the biggest contradiction, and at the same time, it is mostly true. This is a sad statement to make about the present state of religious affairs.

Nonetheless, we religious types should be motivated thereby to do the best we can to rectify the situation. This means that we must become ever more so spiritual individuals. We must deepen our relationship with our Creator and make our religion meaningful again to those who have lost their connection.

The best of the old ways are needed today now more than ever. Without them, mankind moves forward into the future like a sailboat at sea without a rudder. With nothing from the past to guide one, the course into the future is uncharted and could definitely be headed into dangerous waters. No worthy sea captain would ever take such a voyage. Why then do we not learn the lessons of wisdom from the wise and act accordingly.

Chapter 29

The Universal Laws for Everybody

So many spiritual traditions and religions have developed around the world over the centuries. Most religious worldviews are exclusive of one another and therefore exist side by side and in harmony with others. However, as human history has shown us, not all religious systems follow this "live and let live" motto.

As silly as it may sound, some religions actually compete with others. This has been going on for centuries. Each of the competitors is convinced that only they speak for G-d, and that only they possess the "real truth" of G-d's Word. While I believe that religious faith is a good thing, I also believe that religious extremism is a bad thing, a very bad thing.

When religious systems overlap, problems arise as to who is interpreting the mutually held beliefs and Scriptures correctly. Never mind who came first, the later religions say. "We have the truth and that is that. Follow it or else you will meet your destiny". I have always found religious threats appalling.

It is one thing if G-d Himself wishes to intervene in human history and speak to us through bona fide prophets. It is quite another thing when self-made prophets arise and inspire many to follow them in a path that brings great harm to large numbers of fellow human beings.

Granted the Bible is full of G-d's statements how He abhors unrighteousness. Yet, G-d's message to mankind in the Bible is never about doctrines of faith or beliefs. Rather G-d always repeats the same message to us over and over again. He simply wants us to behave with decency, care, respect, and compassion for one another. Apparently, G-d is not so much concerned about what we believe. However, the Bible clearly states that G-d does care about what we do.

Believe it or not, there are actually some religions that disagree with this view. These religions claim that G-d demands of us that we believe in the doctrines and principles of their respective faiths or we will all be damned to hell! Either proclaim the faith or spend eternity in hell. In addition, these religions, and their ministers, will tell you that your life in this world will be most difficult and painful because of G-d's dissatisfaction with you. It amazes me how many people buy into this message of fear, and intimidation.

I mean no disrespect to anyone or to anyone's beliefs. However, I can safely say, as a qualified biblical scholar, and ordained Rabbi, that nowhere in the Jewish Bible, (what others call the "Old" Testament) does it say that one will spend eternity in hell if one does not accept and profess a certain set of doctrines and beliefs.

Surprisingly while some Christian and Islamic doctrines damn non-believers, the religion from which they grew, Judaism has no such belief. Indeed, while Judaism believes that G-d gave His commandments to Israel at Mount Sinai, nowhere is it stated that those commandments should be preached to the world. Judaism does not believe that the whole world must become Jewish. Judaism believes that all mankind must rise up to our highest human potential: to live as beings created in the image of G-d.

The Bible teaches that Adam, father of all mankind, Jew and Gentile alike, ate of the forbidden fruit from the Tree of Knowledge. Consequently, all mankind became blemished in our knowledge. In other words, our ability to correctly perceive spiritual reality is severely limited. G-d is very well aware of our present human nature, and does not demand from us something that we are not able to give.

G-d does not ask of us to see spiritual matters correctly. G-d does not demand of mankind adherence to specific spiritual doctrines. G-d does not want us to concern ourselves with the invisible and the spiritual, other than when it connects with or interacts with our physical world. In other words, G-d wants us to focus on our behavior, in the here and now.

G-d wants us to worry about our lives and our character here in this world. G-d wants us to build up a safe, sound, and prosperous human society, here on Earth. G-d does not want us to become so Heavenly minded that we become no Earthly good. G-d does not want us to ascend to Heaven; he wants us to bring Heaven down to Earth.

There is an old Jewish tradition that centuries before G-d made a covenant with the nation of Israel, He first made a covenant with all mankind, initially with Adam and then after the flood with Noah. This initial covenant established certain universal religious and social principles that all mankind is required to follow. According to the tradition, these principles were seven in number. Today we consider these seven principles to be the bedrock of civilization.

The seven principles are that:

1. **One should believe in G-d** – that there is One true Supreme Power over everything.

2. **One should not blaspheme** – that one should be aware of and respect the Higher Power (not necessarily within the context of an established religion).

3. **One should act with morality**– no adultery, incest, and other forbidden sexual practice s.

4. **One should not murder** - to murder means to wrongly take a life, at the same time G-d ordained capital punishment as the penalty for murder.

5. **One should not steal** – the evil of theft is so great that it was considered the reason why G-d brought the flood in the days of Noah.

6. **One should establish courts of justice** – the bedrock of civilization, there must be laws and law enforcement to establish fairness and safety for all living in human society.

7. **One should not eat the limb of a living animal (prevention of cruelty to animals)** – one must recognize that man's obligations of humanity must also extend beyond himself to include the rest of G-d's creation.

These seven universal principles have been embraced by almost every civilization around the world throughout time. They are even well known to the leaders of the United States. On March 20, 1991, then President George Bush Sr. signed a congressional resolution (H.J. Resolution 104, Public Law 102-14, 1991) that the seven universal principles ordained by G-d and given to Adam and to Noah are "the bedrock of society from the dawn of civilization".

When we ask the age-old question what does G-d want from us, the answer is going to be found in our behavior. In other words, what G-d wants from us is to act like beings created in His image. As G-d is wise, and compassionate so are we to be. As G-d is sympathetic, yet disciplined, so are we to be. As G-d is just and at the same time giving, so are we to be. The comparisons do not stop here.

Religious beliefs are very well and good. Yet, ideas alone will never establish a stable human society. We can only live in peace and security when we all take responsibility for ourselves and look out for the needs and interests of others. Before we can have a stable society for us to live in, we each must first have stable and balanced minds and hearts. Before we can act humanly to others, we must first actualize humanity within ourselves and treat ourselves with respect and dignity.

If we abuse ourselves, we will certainly abuse others. With this behavior G-d is not pleased. When we hurt and harm others, whether psychologically, emotionally, even more so physically, G-d is not pleased. Remember the old saying, "what goes around, comes around". What you do to others will somehow, sometime, be done right back to you.

These are the universal laws that G-d gave to Noah (and to Adam before him) for all mankind to live by. By doing what G-d wants from us, we truly actualize what it means to be spiritual and created in the Divine Image. More so, we truly actualize what it means to be human.

If one wishes to be "right with G-d" then let one work on being the best human being that one can be. This is "real" religion and "real" spirituality. Anything short of this is simply an impostor.

Chapter 30

Conclusion: Mature Spirituality

All things, be they good or bad, must come to an end. It is simply the nature and cycle of life. So too, with this essay I conclude this work. We have covered many ideas and topics. I pray that I have given you enough points to think over and contemplate. In fact, this is the last point that I want to emphasize. We all need to spend more time thinking and contemplating the important issues in life.

G-d has placed us here on Earth for a purpose. That purpose is not just for the sake of refining of our spiritual souls. It is also for the sake of our day-to-day human existence. Unfortunately, this is where many religions and spiritual paths go awry. They fail to address the human; physical needs that we all share. Our physical needs are on the same level of importance and value, as our spiritual needs. G-d created both a spiritual realm and a physical realm for a reason. They are to be united as one; not one cast off in favor of the other.

G-d has placed us here on Earth to live in this world, and believe it or not, to enjoy it. He did not create all the pleasures and joys of life simply as temptations for us to stay away from. I believe that such an attitude of denial and abstinence is an opening to religious and physical abuse. At the same time, this does not mean that we pursue our physical desires with abandon.

Our physical world teaches us that there are limits and boundaries to everything. Sometimes we can expand our boundaries and sometimes we cannot. The definition of wisdom and maturity, therefore, is one who knows his/her boundaries and lives within them. This person will always be happy with their portion in life.

We have learned that we ourselves are masters of our own fate. At the same time, we have learned there are myriads of angelic beings watching us at every moment. Their job is to ever so subtly nudge us to do the right thing. They whisper ideas and thoughts into the "ears" of our unconscious minds, for good and evil. Although their influence is significant, it is ultimately we who have to make the decisions how to best live our lives.

Angelic influence can save us from disaster or bring disaster down upon our heads. We might not be able to do anything about that, but then again, our behavior does have an effect upon what G-d tells the angels regarding us. When it comes to angels, we are working outside the human plane of experience. We simply do not know what angels do or why G-d commands them as He does. Therefore, to place emphasis and time contemplating about angels is, frankly, a waste of time.

Rather than cultivate a relationship or spend time with the help (G-d's helpers, the angels), one should instead cultivate a relationship with the chairman and CEO, who in this case is the King of the universe. Learning to stand before G-d and having a relationship with Him in one's heart and head is one of today's most important challenges. A relationship with G-d may or may not include belonging to a religion. Yet, it must include belonging to the human race with its responsibilities and obligations.

It is easy to be religious on the outside. It is hard to be spiritual on the inside. Religion always talks about man's obligations to itself. Spirituality, on the other hand, talks about man's obligations to his fellow man. One cannot divorce one from the other. One cannot be said to be serving G-d without at the same time being of service to his/her fellow men. In other words, if you are truly religious, then you are truly moral. You help other people and provide for them because you are acting as G-d's agent for good.

Mind you, G-d does not need you to act as His agent for evil. He has the forces of nature and the myriads of angels to do that for Him. Our job is to look after and take care of one another. This message, more than any other, is what comes shouting forth from every single page of the Bible.

The greatest lesson facing anyone desiring to be spiritual, religious, or simply a normal regular guy/gal is learning to live life responsibly and maturely. Responsibility and maturity are the two key words that should guide all of our lives. G-d's spiritual purpose for us is the same as the physical purpose why we are here on Earth. We have to learn to act as mature adults and not as grown up children.

With all due respect to those who seek their "inner child," I suggest that they would better spend their time trying to find the "inner adult". Being an adult means living by Harry Truman's old motto, "the buck stops here".

Mature adults take responsibility for their actions and face life's adversities with stride. We are all masters of our fate, to some extent. Yet, when we reach the end of our personal abilities to influence our environment, when life happens to us instead of us making life happen, this is the test of the responsible and the mature. Many break down and cry when life deals one an unfair blow. Crying is OK and has its place. Yet, there is a time to cry and a time to stop crying. The mature are defined by what they do once they stop crying (for even the mature cry).

Recognizing that life's adversities are hurdles to overcome and not pits to fall into, this is maturity. Taking responsibility for one's life and to live one's life within the boundaries of one's limitations, this is maturity. Recognizing that love is what you do and not just what you feel, this is maturity. Recognizing that it is you who needs G-d and not Him who needs you, this is maturity. Recognizing that the world really is big enough to hold all of our individual different religious, philosophical and personal beliefs, this is maturity. Recognizing that there truly is something called right and wrong, good and evil, and that these definitions are universal and not individual in nature, this is maturity.

You want to know the secret of happiness in life? The answer is simple, live life with responsibility and maturity. You might not get everything you want, but you will be a whole lot happier with what you have. You might still miss what you do not have, but you will not be eaten up with envy and desire pushing you beyond your limits to achieve that which is unachievable.

At the same time, maturity dictates that one try to grow, expand, and broaden one's horizons. Life is not a plateau. At every moment one is either making progress in life or losing it. We are either moving forward or backwards at any given moment. True, we will never be able to stop all our backward movements. We will always make mistakes. That is the nature of life. What we must focus on is how we can avoid mistakes, for we are responsible for those mistakes that could have been avoided. Those mistakes that could not be avoided are there for us to learn from, not to repeat them in the future.

Life is short, and it should be sweet. Life does not have to be harsh. We do not need a devil to mess up our lives. We do a good enough job on our own without him. As difficult as the world around us is, we can create our own personal safe havens by making our inner security a priority. Being right with G-d means being right with others. This is a sure way to receive spiritual blessings whether one believes in that sort of thing or not.

So now, I conclude. I do not have any profound closing words. I have already said everything that I have wanted to say. I merely want to be able to look at you; my brother and sister human beings, created like me in the Image of G-d, and simply say, "Shalom".

That's it. No more. You know what you need to know. You know what you need to do. Now as one old Rabbi said, go and do it.

What better way to close this work that with the words of an old Jewish prayer *"may He who makes peace in His high heavens, make peace over us all... Amen".*

Part Four

The Disclosure Essays

Essay 1

Identifying the Dragon Masters of the Bible

The Torah portion Aharei, introduces us to the strange Yom Kippur ceremony of offering a goat to Azazel.

As with everything in Torah, there are a number of explanations offered to explain what this ceremony is all about. The gamut runs from the rational, which explains the ceremony and its psychological impact, to the mystical and magical, which explains the ceremony's cosmic, kabbalistic impact.

Again, as with everything in Torah, reality, and especially Torah interpretation, is essentially quantum in nature. The perception of the individual is what creates the subjective reality. Thus, how the Torah is to be interpreted is a matter that is in the eye of the beholder.

If we have a million souls, we'll have a million interpretations. And this is exactly what the Talmud, and the Kabbalah have always taught. The Sages have taught that the Torah has "seventy faces," but this is a symbolic number. The Kabbalists expand the number to all the souls of Israel, and expand this even further to state each soul has its own interpretations at each of the four levels of Torah understanding, in Hebrew called PaRDeS (pshat, remez, drash, and sod)

It has become the norm today for rabbis to write intellectual, and philosophical commentaries. Even many of my Kabbalist peers have fallen into this academic, non-experiential model. No wonder why we find so many words of Torah today, which have so very little to actually say, and reveal. Oh well!

Rather than impress you with pity academics, let me introduce you to a Kabbalistic wonder, that instead of just thinking about superficially in an academic way, I would want you to contemplate, and pursue deeper understanding, and possibly even meditative experience.

Let me introduce you to the Teli, the Dragon Masters of the Bible.

Yes, according to the Bible, there were (are) Dragons, and they are not animals, beasts, or the minions of evil. On the contrary the Dragons of the Bible are a holy, angelic race, who serve G-d in Heaven, and upon the Earth.

Centuries ago, one of the great medieval rabbis, Rabbi Menahem Tziyuni, wrote about these being in his *Sefer Tziyuni* on the Torah, for this week's Torah portion Aharei. He refers to the Dragon Masters, not by their Biblical names, but rather by the name given to them in the Kabbalistic classic, the *Sefer Yetzirah* (chapter 6). There they are called, the Teli.

"The Ministers ... that reside in the air, these are the Princes of the Teli...

The reason that they are called the Princes of the Teli is because to these Princes (of the Teli) belongs the leadership over all the hosts above.

By their mouths all the spheres of heaven go forth, and by their mouths, [all the spheres of heaven] stay still.

These Princes are the souls of the spheres, for each sphere vibrates, each has a separate intelligence that guides it in accordance to the secret of the emanation of the Name that radiates upon it.

The Princes of the Teli themselves are influenced from the angels above, these are the four Princes above, the angels of the Merkava."

The Teli Princes are in charge of *"the leadership over all the hosts above."* They are also thus in charge of all matters here on Earth. This authority is clearly outlined in the Bible itself. The Teli Dragon Masters were very well known in the Bible. Yet, they were called there by other names. In Daniel, they were called, "the Watchers."

"By the decree of the Watchers is the matter and by the word of the Holy Ones is the edict."

Daniel 4:14

The Watchers are the guardians of Earth. They serve G-d, and do His bidding. More than this, the Bible clearly, and properly identifies their Dragon nature, although centuries of interpretations (as referred to above), have almost completely erased their original identity. In Isaiah, the Teli Dragon Master are called "Seraphim."

"Seraphim stood above for Him, six wings, six wings to each one; with two he would cover his face, and with two he would cover his feet, and with two he would fly."

Isaiah 6:2

Seraphim are not "Sorefim/burning ones," they are Seraphs, which means "serpents."

The Serafim portrayed in Isaiah 6, are surrounding G-d, referred to there as ADONAI, and ADONAI is not in the Temple, normally called the Mikdash, or Mishkan. ADONAI is in the Hekhal.

The Name of G-d ADONAI, and the name Hekhal, used here in Isaiah 6, to describe the Temple, are terms understood in the Kabbalah to refer to the Olam (dimension) of Asiyah. Asiyah is the realm of our space/time continuum. As we saw above from R. Tziyuni, this Asiyatic domain itself is the domain of the Teli. Thus, we can definitively conclude that the Biblical Seraphim are none other than our holy Dragons, the Teli.

Now, we can understand why they are the Watchers, and why they have such incredible power over the affairs of our world.

In the *Sefer Yetzirah*, (Kaplan version, page 244), it says of the Teli that, *"The Teli in the universe, is like a king on his throne."* This is a powerful statement, which clearly indicates their authority, and dominion.

R. Aryeh Kaplan, in his commentary devotes most of his interpretation about the Teli to philosophical, and even astronomical matters, for the most part blurring their true identity (pages 234-236). But, to the rabbi's credit, he does eventually refer to the truth about them.

"Another important opinion is that of the practical Kabbalists. They write that the Teli is actually a place under the firmament of Vilon, and that it is inhabited by humanoid beings, which deport themselves in holiness and purity like angels. The divine mysteries are revealed to these beings, and they have the authority tto reveal these things to mortal humans. Methods are also given whereby these beings can be contacted."

Aryeh Kaplan, Sefer Yetzirah, pages 236-237

"Under the firmament of Vilon" is an ancient reference to what the later Kabbalists called, Olam HaAsiyah. The inhabitants of the Teli, he says are humanoid. Indeed, they are! They are the original Reptilians, and their original home was here on Earth. G-d created them here. They grew and matured, until eventually they became spiritual beings, serving now as our Watchers, and Guardians. The reason why they are here is because they have always been here. Earth is as much as their home, as it is ours. Essentially, the Teli are our older brothers/sisters.

The Teli will often interact with human beings. When they come to Earth, they take on human form, and become known to us as the human-like angels called the Ishim.

The Teli have been with us since the beginning. They were here long before the pre-Adamic human civilizations of the previous Shemitah (Atlantis/Lemuria?), and indeed worked with them, just like now they work with us.

There are many, many more secrets about the Teli. They are very active in human society today. They are very much a part of modern-day UFO, and Alien folklore. Essentially, the secret is that many so-called extraterrestrial encounters, are not extraterrestrial at all. They are often close-encounters with the Teli Dragon Masters, who disguise themselves in various forms, for reasons known only to them.

Like the immortal prophet Elijah (Eliyahu HaNavi), they come and go in human form, without anyone ever having a clue as to their authentic identity. Indeed, when Elijah was taken up into "Heaven," he was transformed into the angel, Sandalphon. Essentially, Elijah was taken by the Teli, and absorbed into their ranks. This is why he comes and goes, as they do!

The Dragons of the Bible are real. The Biblical ritual during Temple times to offer a goat to Azazel on Yom Kippur was very much directed by them.

No! There is no actual Devil, as believed in by other religions. Azazel is not Satan, regardless of midrashic metaphors that identify the two. It is always dangerous, and foolish to take literally that which is meant to be understood as symbolism, and metaphor.

The Biblical Yom Kippur ritual had its own wisdom and purpose, far removed from our reality, as we are far removed from its time period of thousands of years ago. What the ritual meant is today subject to the "seventy faces of Torah." So, take your pick as to which interpretation best suits your personal perception in our quantum universe.

Let it suffice for us to know that all our interpretations, like everything else here on Earth is under the watchful eye of the Watchers/Seraphim/Teli. They are doing their job in serving G-d. Let us learn from them, and focus on doing ours!

Essay 2

The Danger of Disclosure

Are the governments of the world united in a conspiracy to keep silent about what they know with regards to the reality of extraterrestrial life, and the equally real interactions those aliens have long had with us, here on Earth?

Officially speaking, no authoritative government source will acknowledge such alien life, or such encounters. Privately speaking, many have already acknowledged such things.

Off-the-record, many will make claims, the likes of which are not minor, or insignificant. The one thing that these off-the-record remarks seem to share in common is not so much that there are aliens, and that they are "visiting" us. Rather, these off-the-record remarks seem to share a very disturbing commonality. All seem to agree. Not only are aliens real, and here now, but they are dangerous, and we definitely have something to be worried about.

It seems consistent. Many private persons who claim to be in touch with aliens, seem to believe that the aliens are friendly, and nice. Many of these believe aliens will become some sort of saviors for humanity. Off -the-record government sources, who are the ones who have the ability to actually be in the front lines of actual alien encounters, tell a very different, and frightening story.

So, which is it? Are aliens our cutesy friends from outer space, or are they dangerous forces, whose intentions towards us are not cute, benign, or benevolent? What do our governments really know? What really is motivating them to clamp the lid of secrecy down so tight so as not to let slip the slightest amount of truth, whereas at the same time, allow whistleblowers, whose revelations do absolutely nothing to calm public concern, and distress.

Yes, our governments know something! Over the years they have learned many things through, what is now, decades of extraterrestrial contacts. What our governments know frightens them, and if we knew, would frighten us even more!

So, allow me to reveal some information here. What my readers will decide to do with with what I share will be entirely up to them. Let me reveal now why there will not be a public disclosure of the alien presence, not sooner, not later, and most likely, not ever!

Think about this! If the powers that be acknowledged that they picked up signals from an intelligent alien source hundreds, or thousands of light years away, what kind of impact would that have on our day-to-day affairs? Most likely not much. Granted, there would be a lot of curiosity, and entertainment, but nothing substantial would come of I to change the way we live on a daily basis.

Now, let's change the equation! What if the powers that be who are searching for E.T. all the way "out there" discovered them, but found that E.T. is not "out there" at all, but rather that they are much, much closer.

What if it was discovered that E.T. is actually from another dimensional plane, another dimension of our own planet Earth? What if E.T. is here now, and has always been here? What if E.T. can slide into, and out of, our dimension at will, using either a mechanical, and/or psychic form of transportation?

What if E.T. is, by our standards of definition, malevolent, and always has been? What if E.T. has the power to manipulate human cognitive perception, making us see them, (when we do see them), in any size, shape, or form of their own choosing?

What if we discovered all these things, and have already engaged E.T. in a war for the future of humanity? What if we are losing this war?

If all these things were true, what would our governments disclose? What could they disclose?

What could the powers in charge reveal along these lines without causing a global crisis of massive panic? What if such global panic, and crises, is exactly what negative E.T. really wants? Our governments would have to go to any extreme to prevent such global crises, societal panic, and collapse. Maybe this is why there is such a comprehensive conspiracy of silence. Maybe there has to be?

Think about this. Consider it fiction, it you will. Let us say that our human civilization is not the first technologically advanced civilization to have developed here on Earth. Let us say that thousands of years ago, there was another.

Let us say that this ancient civilization, let's just call it Atlantis and Lemuria, faced its own series of natural disasters, and in order to survive, a select few traveled in three directions, to the stars, to a parallel dimension, and to the inner recesses of the Earth (in accordance to the Hollow Earth theory).

Let us say that the survivors thrived, and that now thousands of years later, well entrenched in their new homes, they have no need to return to what is now, our Earth.

Nevertheless, these earlier Earthers still have an integral attachment to this planet. Indeed, it is very possible that they are the ones who have guided us through the centuries. Maybe they have an agenda to move us along a developmental path with the intent to eventually unite us with themselves. Maybe there is truth to all of this.

Now, what would happen if these early Earthers, technologically advanced as they are, were discovered by our modern scientists, and military authorities? What if they did not want their presence, their identities, their agenda, or their tools to accomplish said agenda known to us? What if they are the ones who the Bible calls, the Watchers?

If our world governments today were aware of these entities, and the potential, if not actual, threat they present to us, would it then be safe, or responsible for them to make known the E.T. presence? If our governments know full well that they cannot properly protect the public from what might be malevolent E.T. hands, is it responsible to make such a public confession?

Think about these things carefully. One might say that we all have the right to know the truth, regardless of how devastating that may be. But where do we draw the line? When do we say that public safety, and stability, outweighs the rights of the individual to have access to certain information?

If there is a real E.T. alien agenda, and it involves manipulating human current events, and there is nothing that we can do to influence this, then is it wise to reveal this, and thus allow public fear, and panic, to reign free? Maybe sometimes, it's best to hide a devastating truth until something can be done to neutralize any dangers?

Then again, maybe this is all speculation, and fantasy? Maybe these are all the thoughts of an imagination run wild? Maybe there are no aliens, or an alien agenda. Maybe! Or again, maybe not!

If there is a cause for alarm, then indeed, it would be the wise, and prudent thing for any government to reassure the public that all is well, in order to avoid what could very well become a global crises of fear.

Anything that can be considered a threat, but it still very, very far away is not so much a cause for alarm. If there are aliens far, far away from us in outer space, that might be exciting news, but it is not going to change our daily affairs. If, however, the aliens are much closer, closer to us in space, and closer to us in other ways, then maybe such a reality is not one the vast majority of individuals can handle.

Conspiracy theories run wild among us. Each one is more wild, and silly than another. People love to be entertained. People love to believe wild things. But, at the end of the day, there is a reassurance, that none of it is going to affect us personally, and intimately.

So, if there are E.T.s out there, far away, so what? But if the E.T.s are real, are dangerous, and out of our control, then it is best that the world governments guard this secret carefully, and fight a silent, secret war, for the sake of humanity's future.

Maybe this is what is really going on. And if this is too frightening a thought to consider, then dismiss it out of hand. Dismiss it as mere wild speculation. Go relax, go about your day, enjoy life, and forget about it. Maybe this is for the best. Maybe this is the way things need to be.

If there are going to be changes tomorrow, then let tomorrow come, and we'll deal with the changes then. As for today, let's get along with life, and be thankful for all that we have. If you are religious, and believe in a Higher Power, then pray to that Higher Power and ask for world peace, and personal protection.

G-d has His secrets, governments have thiers, and we each have our own. Let it be. If you seek hidden truths, so be it. But if you discover hidden truth, then take into consideration with whom that truth can be shared. You will discover for yourself that not everyone can handle every truth.

Essay 3

Angel Wars, Cause of Human Conflicts

There have always been wars here on Earth? Why? Why are we so self-destructive that we wipe out human life in the tens of millions?

We erase entire civilizations, ruthlessly murdering their entire populations. Why are we so devastatingly cruel?

Human-on-human violence seems to have been with humanity since the very beginnings of human civilization. The only other recorded human behavior present from the dawn of history is the presence of religion. Violence and religion seem to be the two most ancient human behaviors, and they certainly are no strangers to one another. Indeed, very often throughout history, violence and religion have gone hand in hand.

Religion usually involves the worship of this or that G-d(s). Often, religions themselves define certain behaviors that offend the G-d(s), the punishment for such an offense is usually death. This violence, for the most part, was still small in scale.

When, however, competing religions clash over who gets to decide what the reality of the universe looks like, then we have wars in the largest scale imaginable.

Today, again for the most part, our violent religious clashes take a second place to more modern expressions of radical faiths. Today's faiths are indeed religious in tone, in their psychological make-up, and in the influence they have on their believers, but more than not they leave G-d out of the equation.

The three most popular faiths today are not religions that revolve around a G-d in Heaven, but rather revolve around what is the right way for humanity to live here on Earth. These faiths, and yes, they are faiths, are the three philosophical, economical systems that have taken over almost every part of our planet. These three systems are capitalism, socialism, and communism.

This essay is not being written to discuss politics, or to compare, or weigh the pros and cons of the three political systems. Rather, my point is simple. In earlier times, when religions ruled the world, their minions regularly waged war one upon the other. Today, while some old time religions still embrace the path of violence, the greatest perpetrators of crimes against humanity are those who act with such wanton disregard for human life, all in the name of this or that country, or in the name of one of our three "new religions." Like, wise King Solomon said long ago, *"there's nothing new under the sun"* (Kohelet 1:9).

What causes all of our conflicts to be so ruthlessly violent? Is this due to some inherent flaw within human design that seeks our self-destruction? Or is there something much more sinister going on? The answer to this question, is found in Biblical, and later literature about angels. Read on with caution. You may not like what you are about to learn!

The Bible makes certain things very clear. G-d's definition of morality, and our human definition do not match!

G-d clearly states through the prophet:

"In order that they know from the shining of the sun and from the west that there is no one besides Me; I am the L-rd and there is no other. Who forms light and creates darkness, Who makes peace and creates evil; I am the L-rd, Who makes them all."

Isaiah 45:6-7

G-d is the creator of evil, there is no other! And G-d will use whatever He has created for whatever ends that He seems fit. Again, G-d speaks through the prophet:

"For My thoughts are not your thoughts, neither are your ways My ways," says the L-rd. As the heavens are higher than the earth, so are My ways higher than your ways and My thoughts [higher] than your thoughts."

Isaiah 55:8-9

G-d is certainly not apologetic for the Divine Way, nor for our lack of human understanding of the Divine Way. Human understanding is not required. This alone reveals to us much about the true nature of the Divine, first and foremost being that it certainly is not human!

According to the Bible, G-d is in charge of everything. Whatever transpires on Earth has its origins in the realms of Heaven. G-d actively involves Himself in human affairs, not always for one's personal betterment.

The example of Pharaoh in the days of the Exodus is well known:

"But I will harden Pharaoh's heart, and I will increase My signs and My wonders in the land of Egypt."

Exodus 7:3

Later, G-d turns against Ahab, King of Israel, and intentionally seeks to deceive him. The intent being that Ahab will act upon the deception being true, Ahab will be led to a terrible violent outcome.

"And he said, "Therefore, listen to the word of the L-rd. I saw the L-rd seated on His throne, and all the host of heaven were standing by Him on His right and on His left.

And the L-rd said, 'Who will entice Ahab so that he will go up and fall in Ramoth-Gilead?' One said in this manner and another one said in that manner. And a certain spirit came forth and stood before the L-rd and said, 'I will entice him,' and the L-rd said to him 'How?' And he said, 'I will go forth, and I will be a lying spirit in the mouth of all his prophets.'

And He said, 'You will entice and you will prevail. Go forth and do so.' And now, behold the L-rd has placed a lying spirit in the mouth of all these prophets of yours, whereas the L-rd spoke evil concerning you." I Kings 22:19-23

We may rightfully ask, by what right does G-d have, even if He is the Creator, to intentionally manipulate human minds? Why does He create evil, and as we see with regards to both Pharoah, and Ahab, so freely use it?

We all know the story of the Exodus. We all know that the final plague that led to the freedom of Israel from Egypt was the killing of the First-Born. If this really, literally happened, we must ask, was every victim of this terrible plague individually worthy of death? Wasn't there at least a single one of them who could have been innocent?

What about later with the parting of the Sea, which led to the destruction of the Egyptian army. Those men all went to their deaths following their Pharaohs orders. Like Alfred, L-rd Tennyson wrote in his Charge of the Light Brigade, *"Theirs not to make reply, Theirs not to reason why, Theirs but to do & die."*

Does anyone ever think about the devastating effects these actions had on the surviving family members of these men who were killed? Here, I am expressing human moral concern. But as we already know, *"My thoughts are not your thoughts, neither are your ways My ways," says the L-rd"* (Isaiah 55:8), and *"I am the L-rd... Who forms light and creates darkness, Who makes peace and creates evil; I am the L-rd, Who makes them all."* (Isaiah 45:6b-7).

Who am I, who are we, to challenge the morals of Heaven? According to the Bible, we are clearly all in the Hands of G-d, and subject to His "Higher Thoughts and Ways," regardless of whether those Thoughts or Ways agree with, or conform to, human moral standards.

G-d acts as G-d does. But G-d alone does not act in this way. G-d has delegated this authority, and power to His overseeing angels, those that direct human affairs on the Divine behalf.

"By the decree of the wakeful ones is the matter and by the word of the holy ones is the edict, in order that the living should know that the Most High rules over the kingdom of man, and to whom He wishes He gives it, and the lowest of men He sets upon it."

Daniel 4:14

As we saw with regards to Pharoah, and the prophets of Ahab, G-d manipulates human consciousness, to coerce individuals to act in accordance with the Divine edict. We might very well, at this point stop and ask about the extent of human free will. And although we may ask, and speculate about our answer, no answer at all seems to be coming to us from Heaven, and our Creator.

When Nebuchadnezzar was to be punished by Heaven for his sins, the angelic authorities chose not to strike down the King with violence. Rather, in the opinions of many, they did something much worse.

"They will change his heart from a man's, and the heart of a beast will be given him."

Daniel 4:13

Changing one's heart, in modern terms, would be called, inflicting the mind with mental illness. Essentially, the angels robbed Nebuchadnezzar of his sanity, and drove him insane, clinically so!

Now, if the angels themselves were to remain faithful to the Divine edict, and simply serve as executioners of the Divine Will, then we would have no one to blame, other than our Creator, G-d. But what if this is not the case? What if certain angels are taking matters into their own hands? What if angels are as corrupt as some human beings? If angels have the power over the minds of human beings, and they themselves are corrupt, how is this going to affect human affairs? We can return to the Bible for our answer.

While we might want to believe that all angels are holy servants, faithful to G-d, this might not be the case. While Daniel was praying to G-d, strangely an answer was not forthcoming. The reason for this delay, as outlined in the Bible is most peculiar. The angel who was sent by G-d with the answer to Daniel's prayer has this to say:

"And the prince of the kingdom of Persia has been standing against me for twenty-one days, and behold Michael, one of the first princes, has come to help, and I remained there beside the kings of Persia." *Daniel 10:13*

The Bible reveals a secret. Each nation has their angelic guardian. And each angelic guardian has an authority all his own. The angel may or may not choose to obey a Heavenly edict. Angels are in charge, and have tremendous powers over human beings, even over the faithful, righteous religious ones.

This subject is well understood by later Judaic writers of the Kabbalah. One of them summarized matters like this:

"Angels whose names end with "el" are the guardians of the nations, and they fight with one another like bucking rams."
Sodei Razia, R. Eliezer of Germiza

The Watchers, described in Daniel, are the angelic guardians of the Earth. In later Rabbinic literature the Watchers are referred to as the "Heavenly Sanhedrin."

Associating a collection of angels under the name "Sanhedrin" implies a level of holiness and purity, the likes of which was expected of the Sanhedrin, here on Earth. The Sanhedrin here on Earth served as the Supreme Court of the Jewish nation throughout the later period of the Second Temple, and a number of generations thereafter.

The Sages of the Sanhedrin would debate Biblical interpretations and pass Rabbinic legislation. We would expect a Heavenly Sanhedrin to be less contentious. However, we see that this is not the case. Indeed, we discover that the Heavenly Sanhedrin is far more contentious than its human counterpart ever was.

The Watcher Angels fight amongst themselves all the time. What happens among them shouldn't concern us but for the fact that when angels fight, they manipulate those nations under their dominion to also fight. Thus, human wars are psychologically influenced by the malicious influence of the Watcher Guardians on the human unconscious!

This matter is summed up well here:

"There is no nation or tongue that does not have its own "Sar" (angelic Prince) in the upper worlds. Being that these supernal

Princes have become corrupted they are constantly fighting, making war in Heaven. Therefore, there is a overwhelming great compulsion upon all their nations below to fight more and more [here] on Earth. This is why we have wars [here] on Earth, [it is] because of the Princes in Heaven."

Commentary to Sefer Temunah 3, Samekh

Just how do these "Princes" provoke wars, we cannot fully say. But we can learn from the Biblical examples how angels influence and control human minds, or better to say, human emotions.

Angels are telepathic beings. It is their nature to speak with human beings in dreams and visions, in a mind-to-mind style communication. As these compromised entities struggle and fight, all those under their spiritual dominion are subject to their spiritual influence. Thus, as they fight above, their energy disturbances cause human imbalances, leading us to fight as well, here on Earth.

This state of out-of-control harmful angelic influence is referred to in Kabbalistic literature as "Galut," the mystical understanding of exile. Essentially, as long as Divine Consciousness is blocked from human minds, the corrupting influence of fallen angels influences us all.

In religions around the world enlightenment is sought as a goal to escape the pain and sufferings of everyday life. In the Torah tradition, we pray daily for "Geulah," (redemption). Essentially, we too seek to raise global consciousness to recognize the harmful, negative influences that can overwhelm us from within our own minds, and hearts.

Real religion is never about competing, or conflicting ideas, or beliefs. Real religion has to proclaim a singular message: human unity, as part of the greater universal unity. This is the unity of that which we call G-d.

The best way to overcome negative spiritual influences is to not give in to the negative ideas, and beliefs that divide. Each individual must struggle within oneself to overcome the tendency that seeks division, and thus to harm another.

When we embrace unity within ourselves, we will have overcome those forces that seek our harm. This, in my opinion, is real religion, and the most important thing before us to accomplish
.

Essay 4

Native Earthers vs. Space Brothers, The Other Side of the Story

The war started long ago. Invaders came from outer space. Their intentions, so they claim, were to repair a broken world, to fix a fallen race, to raise the vibrations of souls that have fallen out of sync with the higher universe. The invaders came, they say, to serve man!

Who would not want their help? Who would not want to reach out, and join with the space brothers in their noble efforts? Who wouldn't want to get right with the universe? The space brothers came to help us, why shouldn't we trust them, surrender to them, and to do what they tell us to do? The space brothers, after all, are not really invaders, they came, so they say, to serve man!

Long ago, the space brothers came. They came here to Earth, this Earth, our Earth! Earth had been devastated by natural disasters. The great civilization that had lasted here for millennia was now shattered, and destroyed. The death toll was catastrophic. The destruction was almost complete. Yet, there remained a remnant, a band of consolidated survivors.

The surviving few saw in advance the disasters to come. They prepared. They saved the best of their civilization. They saved the best of their arts, and sciences. This band of devoted and women and men were determined to rebuild all that which had been lost.

After all, this was their Earth, their beloved Earth. Who more than them had the determination, and the right to rebuild, and to restore all that which had been lost? But the space brothers didn't see it in this way. The space brothers were from a higher dimensional plane, or so they claimed. The space brothers saw the devastation and proclaimed that the disaster, although natural, was caused because of a misalignment of natural forces. The space brothers, of course, knew about such things. They were, after all, from a higher dimensional plane.

The space brothers came from their higher dimension, and proclaimed to the survivors of Earth, that their intervention was necessary. Without the intervention of the space brothers to properly realign higher dimensional energies, there would continue to be natural disaster after natural disaster, until eventually the entire planet Earth would be consumed, and destroyed. No one would then survive. No one would be left. The space brothers thus came to help us help ourselves. This is what they claimed, this is what they said. Who were the survivors of Earth to challenge this, who were they to disagree?

So the space brothers came, and set up shop. They came to fix the broken, and to repair the devastation. They approached the valiant native Earthers, and invited them to join in, so together, they could embrace the future. But the space brothers brought with them aside from tools for rebuilding, a new code of ethics, and morals. The space brothers came to tell the native Earthers what was wrong with their ancient society, and what was needed to repair its energetic weaknesses.

Needless to say, the native Earthers did, and did not, appreciate what the space brothers had to say. Yes, their help in rebuilding was much appreciated, and indeed, needed. But all this talk about realigning energy patterns to properly correlate with the higher dimensions, it sounded all right, and good, but what the space brothers were asking meant a total change from what was before. The space brothers wanted to completely invert Earther society, and recreate it in their own image.

What could the Earthers do? How could they take advantage of all the good that the space brothers offered, and at the same time, resist their attempts to recreate Earth in their own space brother image? And thus the struggle began. Ancient Earther versus space brothers.

This struggle was not a military one. There were no armies. The goal was not to repel the space brothers entirely, but merely to thwart their efforts to recreate Earth in their space brother image.

And so the war began. Yet, this war was fought with weapons of mind, and of heart. Weapons were energetic, not physical. Earther resistance was not violent, rather, it was cunning. The Earthers wanted the space brothers to stay, but to stay in accordance to the rules that they, the Earthers, were to lay out. After all, this is their Earth.

Unable to resist the wave of the future, the native Earthers surrendered to the space brothers, and joined in their endeavors. But this was only pretense. They had to get closer to the space brothers, to understand them, and to learn their weaknesses. If there was a weakness to exploit they would discover it, and use it. After all, they did not actually want to harm the space brothers, they didn't even want them to leave. All the native Earthers wanted was to rebuild their lost world as it was, and not in the new image of the space brothers.

So, the native Earthers were shrewd. Rather than outright oppose the space brothers they chose instead to challenge their higher dimensional energetic alignments. After all, this was their Earth, and the native Earthers also knew about energetic alignments. These so-called higher dimensional alignments were things the native Earthers did not know, and were not certain if they were real. But one thing was certain, these higher dimensional alignments would be the end of the ways of Old Earth, and this is something that the native Earthers would fight to save.

And so a representative of the native Earthers was chosen to represent them to the space brothers. The representative would work with the space brothers, and together they would rebuild broken Earth. The representative was very wise, and very shrewd.

His mission, mind you, was not to harm the space brothers, but rather simply to compromise their mission, to make it palatable to the position, and the culture of the native Earthers.

And so the representative set out about his tasks. In the end, he did succeed. The space brothers were indeed compromised. The space brothers lost their connection with their native higher energetic dimension, but did not lose their tools of mind and heart, with which they could rebuild fallen Earth.

And so it came to pass that the space brothers themselves fell, and became entrapped here on Earth. Now, the native Earthers had a new problem to deal with. What were they to do with the now fallen space brothers? The now fallen space brothers could not be driven out, on the contrary, the now fallen space brothers had become the New Earthers. The Old Earthers were now stuck with the New Earthers, and integration was not going to be easy. Indeed, for most, it was not even desirable. And so, the struggle between Old Earther and their ways, and New Earther and their ways, raged.

And so now, you know the story. You see how it all began. We, yes, you and me, we are the children of the fallen space brothers. We are the New Earthers. Human history, especially from the Biblical point of view tells the story from the space brother/New Earther point of view. It is we who are not originally of this Earth.

Adam and Eve are the "space brothers," the representatives of the higher dimensional plane called YHWH. The Biblical serpent, the Nahash (enchanter), is the original humanoid, reptilian Old Earther. He represents the dimensional plane referred to Biblically as ELOHIM. Since the beginning, the Biblical message has been to unite ELOHIM (nature), with YHWH (the higher dimensional planes). But the message has been blurred, and the mission has been compromised!

To every story, there is always more than one side, more than one way of looking at what happened. We seldom take into account the views of the original, ancient, Old Earthers. Most of us do not even know that they existed, and that they still exist to this day.

So, let the truth be told! We are the original invaders. Our true essence, our souls, that which makes us "space brothers" is not indigenous to this Earth. Our true essence is what we call our Adamic (neshama) souls. Native Earthers also had/have souls, but their energetic vibrations emanate from one place (ELOHIM/nature), whereas our energetic vibrations emanate from a higher dimensional plane (YHWH/Atzilut), from which we have been cut off.

Our Adamic mission here on Earth was to rise up, and repair a fallen world (Tikun of the Fallen Kings). We have only partially been successful. Then again, the Old Earthers have also only been partially successful. They were never able to repair old Earth in the image of what once was (the pre-Adamic civilization). And we have never been able to rebuild Earth in alignment with the higher dimensional planes (the future Messianic era).

The struggle between "us" (new) and "them" (old) continues to this day. "We" still want to move forward. "They" still want to move backwards. And so human civilizations and societies rise and fall, moving forwards and back.

We were given help (Sinai). Reconnection with our higher dimensional plane was established (Torah). We were told what to do, and how to do it. Now, all that is left to do, is to listen to what we've been told, and to do it. But not too many are listening. And because we never succeeded in addressing the old energetic imbalances, they are still here with us.

Just as in the past, natural disasters arose because of the energetic misalignments of the Native Earthers, so too is it with us today. Nasty business having to deal with energetic misalignments, but somebody has got to do it. That is the reason, after all, why we came to Earth in the first place. And so now you know the rest of the story.

Essay 5

The Reason for the Coverup, Modern Masks for Ancient Visitors

For those seeking the truth about disclosure, about what our governments truly know about extraterrestrial, and ultra-terrestrial life, one needs to first understand why there would be such an overwhelming need for such a serious conspiracy of cover-up.

Governments are not stupid. If there is something to hide, you can rest assured that there is good reason to keep hidden what needs to be kept hidden. So, rather than turn to modern governments for answers, that, to be blunt, will not be forthcoming, one can instead turn to ancient literature, specifically the teachings of the Kabbalah, that will indeed shine some very needed light on this subject.

The masters of the Torah Kabbalah have been at the very center of the extraterrestrial/ultraterrestrial phenomena since the days of the receiving of the Torah at Mt. Sinai. This event was most likely one of, if not, the largest close encounter event of its kind. In spite of what the written word says in the Bible, and that centuries of Rabbinic lore have added and augmented, I for one, do not believe that any of us truly and fully understand the nature of the Sinai event, and the later prophetic tradition that grew up out of it in ancient Israel, and into modern times.

For the most part, modern-day Kabbalah and Kabbalists are nothing more than metaphysical philosophers, who read books and very rarely ever understand them fully. In centuries gone by, indeed, not to long ago, the majority of Kabbalists also practiced a number of different forms of prophetic meditative techniques that enabled them to train their minds, and to expand consciousness, thus enabling them to access, and to interact with the extraterrestrials, and ultraterrestrials.

The original prophetic Kabbalists continued the connection with the prophetic schools of ancient Israel that have been with us since Biblical times. These Kabbalists interacted with entities who were never identified as aliens from another planet. In those days, long gone by, those entities may very well have been associated with specific planets, but they were then called angels, not aliens. And this is an important point that helps us identify the true identity of the so-called extraterrestrials.

Yes, the Kabbalists have had many close encounters. Some had intense close encounters on a regular basis. But these experiences were believed to be in the realm of the holy, and the religious. No one in those days would have associated a secular scientific meaning to the nature of those experiences.

In ancient times, the Kabbalists could call upon the great archangels Metatron, or Sandalphon, and they would come. They could call for a visitation from the immortal prophet Elijah, and he too would appear. Now, don't you think that we should ask, if there really are angels like Metatron and Sandalphon, and if the immortal prophet Elijah really is immortal, and he too pops up from time to time, then where exactly are they coming from? Then again, who exactly are these entities for real? If we say that they are angels, then we have to ask ourselves, what exactly are angels, and how do they fit into our modern understanding of extraterrestrials?

We see from ancient examples, right up to present times, that whether we speak of angels or extraterrestrials, one thing that the two have in common is their interactions with humanity. In ancient times we had angels popping in and out of human affairs. Today, only the religious claim to see, or to experience angels, everyone else, even some of the religious, see and experience extraterrestrials. Our reports about other-worldly beings have changed, but have these other-worldly beings themselves changed? Maybe we are dealing with the same bunch of entities, but that they have been modernized, and been given new identities, to keep them up to date with the times?

Maybe the angels and demons of old are indeed the extraterrestrials of today. If this is indeed so, then maybe we can begin to erase the imaginary line that has long been used to separate religious beliefs from scientific ones. If the angels and demons of old are the E.T.s of today, then we can start answering our questions about their origins, and intent, using religious content to help us answer modern scientific questions.

Certain texts of Kabbalistic literature reveal an extensive amount of information about the pre-Adamic civilizations that rose and fell here on Earth. It can even be understood from some of these texts that there were numerous such civilizations. One thing that can be extrapolated from the texts is that the earlier civilizations were not necessarily human.

Ancient, authoritative Torah sources reveal that the stories in the beginning of Genesis were never meant to be understood literally, as so many today mistakenly believe. The beginning of Genesis was not written to relate history. Rather, the stories therein are coded messages which reveal a tremendous amount of information about our ancient past. The stories of creation, the Garden of Eden, of Adam, Eve, and the Serpent are actually all metaphors to describe events, not from any physical point of view, but rather from what we have come to call "the spiritual." One of these bits of information is that what we have come to call, "the spiritual," actually has a tangible reality, a reality that intersects with, and sometimes, overlaps our own.

In previous essays I have introduced you to the Teli, the Dragon Masters of the Bible, who are referred to as the Watchers in Daniel, and as the Seraphim in Isaiah. Let us discuss more about their specific origins.

This humanoid/reptilian race of the Teli are, in relationship to us, a higher, more advanced, more spiritual, and more technological species. They are reptilian, yet they are very spiritual, and as the Bible attests, they are very close to G-d.

In western culture, we have associated everything reptilian with being evil, demonic, and of the "Devil." But, of course, as is clear from the Bible itself, (reference Job 1), the actual Biblical character of the "Devil" is nothing more than a faithful ministering angel before the Divine.

The so-called Devil is not the evil, anti-G-d monster as described in certain world religions. The actual angel itself, is not any different from the other angels of its species. The Hebrew word, "Satan," actually is not a proper name, it is used more as an adjective of description.

In Hebrew, the correct form is "HaSatan." This properly means, "The Accuser." We can see that this is a title, not a name. It indicates something similar to being a prosecutor in a trial. This entity, like all of its race, are reptilian Teli. These are the ones who stand before G-d, and cry out "holy, holy, holy." Yet, due to our human racial fear of this one specific entity, we now ascribe fear to its entire race, regardless of the fact that this one Teli alone, of all its race, is responsible for what it does, while the others are not. We have blurred the lines of clarity in this issue, and have thus lost our perception, insight, and understanding.

So, according to the Bible, and later Kabbalistic literature, there really are ancient and advanced reptilian races "out there." In spite of some Biblical and later references to anything reptilian being bad, this is not an all-inclusive conclusion. We have spoken here about the Teli. They are the ancient race that developed here on Earth, who have evolved beyond physical form, and now serve G-d as Heaven's messengers. Their relationship with our Earth, and with us should be self-evident. This is their Earth as well, and we are like their younger siblings.

Just as life developed here on Earth, is directed by Divine design, and by Heavenly decree, so too has life developed on other planets, in this dimensional plane, and on other worlds not of this dimensional plane. Essentially, our universe(s) are packed with all forms of life, both ancient and new, both (by our standards) good and evil. Although the Bible and later Kabbalistic literature do not say verbatim which other planets house which other life forms, we cannot look at the literary silence about this topic, to be a statement of denial of the realities therein.

Kabbalisic literature is full of stories of encounters between human beings and all sorts of other entities. In religion, we call most of the entities either angels, or demons. Yet, these descriptions are far too vague, and essentially mythological, to be of any serious value to help us properly identify who these entities actually are, and from where do they really come. In modern times we speak about extraterrestrials, and more recently ultraterrestrials (other dimensional beings). Yet, for a number of reasons, mostly because of a lack of information and knowledge, we often do not connect the dots to draw, and thus see the bigger picture. Essentially, what the big picture reveals is a very ancient image, dressed up in modern garb.

Essentially, the aliens of today, for the most part, but not entirely, are the angels and demons of old. Yet, what we know about the E.T.s today must be applied to what we do not know about the reality of the ancient angels and demons. Many still make the mistake of thinking about E.T.s in scientific terms, and the angels and demons in religious/spiritual terms. We must correct this error, and start thinking about angels and demons, and where they fit into the scientific domain.

The Kabbalists of old have long told the story of our pre-Adamic times. They spoke of the worlds that G-d created, and destroyed before our world. Using Bible verses, they symbolically spoke about "kings of Edom" who reigned prior to there being a "king in Israel." All this talk explains much about the pre-Adamic worlds, what each was like, and how each fell. These religious teachings must be examined so as to extract from them their true, concealed meanings. It will be from these revelations that we will identify not only our present ultra-terrestrial "visitors," but we will also be able to identify their agenda.

So, we do not fear mythological creatures such as a devil, or demons. But we do become keenly aware that there are other life forms out there that have as strong a connection to our Earth, as do we. And many of these life forms, very bluntly, do not like humanity in its present form. In their eyes, Adamic souls are the extraterrestrial invaders, the space brothers of the previous essay. They want nothing more than for us to fail in our mission here, and then for us to return to whatever dimension from which we came. According to Torah and Kabbalah, this would, of course, thwart the plan of YHWH, the Creator. But that does not seem to disturb these entities, for in their eyes they are faithful to ELOHIM, the Creator, and like Pharaoh in ancient Egypt, they do not care too much for YHWH, and what "He" (It!) represents.

Yet, the Torah's message has always been consistent. "And you shall know today, and contemplate in your heart that YHWH is THE ELOHIM, in the Heavens above, and on the Earth beneath, there is no other." (Deut 4:39). This is the "space brother's" message, a message which proclaims that the previous epochs, were indeed destroyed by Higher Spiritual Forces, and not just by happenstance natural disasters. The old ways were imbalanced, and due to their own shortcomings created the situations that led to their own downfalls. YHWH sent the Adamic Collective Neshama Soul to correct this state of affairs. This struggle between the old and the new is the inner source, and "spiritual" cause of all the strife and upheaval that human civilization has faced for millennia.

The revelations that are to come in the future are ready to be found in the Kabbalistic literature from the past. Our modern governments already know this. They recognize the nature of the entities with whom we are dealing. Such recognition has made it certain that absolutely no authentic disclosure can be made at present. Frankly, for most, the truth is just too much to handle. Our governments are correct to conceal the truth. It is for the good of the many.

Now, there are those out there who, indeed, can handle the truth. And indeed, they are most worthy to know the truth. Yet, no government can cater to the fit minority, when the future of the unprepared majority is at stake. No revelation will be forthcoming from any government about the reality of the extraterrestrial/ultraterrestrial presence here on Earth. Therefore, if you want to know the truth, then look for it where it can be found. This is why these essays are being written, to point ready souls in the proper direction.

The rest, of course, is up to you.

Courses Offered Through the KosherTorah School

Available through our website www.koshertorah.com

The following is a selection of courses available at the present time from the KosherTorah School. All course lessons are in audio MP3 for easy downloading and access. Fees and instructions for acquiring the courses are included herein. Please go to our website: www.koshertorah.com for a much larger selection of courses, and classes on many topics in the Bible, Judaism, Kabbalah, Meditation.

1. The Hebrew book of Enoch
Sefer Hanokh also known as, The Ascent of R. Ishmael

A Seventeen (17) Lesson Audio Course Taught by Ariel B. Tzadok

Course Outline

Lesson 1, Chapter 1. **An overall introduction into the experience of *Merkava* ascent.** Ascent is a psychological, astral phenomena. This is why the ascent is properly called a "descent," meaning a descent into the deepest levels of the unconscious, and from there, astrally traveling outside. **This series is geared towards explaining the practical realities of such travels**, with pointers from my personal experiences. The meaning of the Gates and the Guardians, and how their appearances change in accordance to the eye of the beholder (*especluria sh'ayna me'ira/kilpah*). This is not a class just about academic or philosophical ideas and concepts. The connection between the spiritual, psychological and extraterrestrial is fully explained. For those seeking actual spiritual experience and guidance, this is the class for you.

Lesson 2, Chapters 2 – 4. **Secret of the Metatron Race.** Identifying the different races of extraterrestrials that we call angels. How these entities view the human race with disdain. Why Enoch is called Metatron and "Youth". The 70 names of Metatron (and G-d), how each is understood and perceived differently by all the nations of the world. The race of the Metatrons, preexisting the universe, and where they are now, and what they are doing. How Enoch joined the already existing race of Metatrons, and who they really are. Secrets of the pre-Adamic dragon race, the *Teli*. Secrets of Atlantis, and the fall in Eden, secret of the *Nahash*/Serpent. The objection to Enoch's ascent, and how this led to a rebellion in *Rakia*.

This lesson is the source material of many later *midrashic* teachings. It discusses the great Heavenly plan, and emphasizes why astral ascents of this nature are so vital to one's personal spiritual growth and for the betterment of the entire race.

Lesson 3, Chapters 5 – 7. **The Fallen Angels & the Origins of Idolatry.** Secrets of the tangible life-force energy field called the *Shekhina* / Chi / Orgone / Vril / *Nefesh*. It was an actual energy source that connected ancient Earth to its source world *Aravot Rakia*. After the expulsion of the Adamic race from Eden, human beings searched for a different source of energy and technology in order to run the planet. They tapped into other natural forces. They were taught how to do these things (technologies) by angelic entities who disagreed with G-d's plan and direction for experiment Earth. Rather than surrendering to the Divine plan, humanity decided instead to forge their own plan, and entities from above assisted them in this effort (both in the past, and in the present). This then is the true form of idolatry. Enoch was taken up to Heaven to serve as witness and proof that project humanity could be successful and that Adamic souls can be successfully integrated into homo sapien bodies. Just how Enoch was genetically transformed for life off Earth will be the topic of the next lesson.

Lesson 4, Chapters 8 – 11. **Genetic Transformations & the Secret of the YHWH Princes.** Enoch was prepared to be altered from a homo sapien human being into whatever form he became. Enoch was placed at the gates of *Aravot*, the place of connection between what the later Kabbalah would call the *Beriatic* and *Yetziratic* universes. In other words, Enoch sat in the 7th Heaven at the veil that conceals the higher 8 – 10 levels of Heaven. Many terms and numbers are referred to which clearly are some kind of code, which to this day, seems unbreakable. Enoch/Metatron serves YHWH as His Divine representative in the lower worlds. *Mashiah* Ben Aharon & the heavenly High Priest. Michael/Metatron. Enoch/Metatron serves as the *Zeir Anpin* (using the later term). There are however Higher Princes, angels who also share the Name YHWH with their Creator. This class discusses the secret relationship of YHWH, Adam and Torah, and concludes with a brief discussion as to what really is the Torah, and what exactly are its secrets.

Lesson 5, Chapters 12 – 14. **Enoch/Metatron, the Little YHWH, Who is Not G-d!** Enoch becomes Metatron, and Metatron is called the Little YHWH, but this does not make him to be YHWH Himself. Metatron can bear G-d's authority, but not G-d's essence. G-d's name is IN Metatron (as in the angel of the L-rd, in Exodus), but he is not G-d. This relationship between Enoch/Metatron and the

Son of Man discussed in Daniel, and First Enoch, became the foundation of the Christian belief that Yeshu was somehow G-d incarnate. This class explains the history of this concept, how it began, and how it became what it is today. Enoch/Metatron's authority is over all the Heavens and Earth, that which the later Kabbalah calls the realms of *Asiyah* and *Yetzirah*. All in these domains are under Metatronic authority, and this includes Samael, and all the powers charged by G-d to test humanity. This class continues to reveal more about the Metatronian race, and humanity's relationship to it, at present, and in the future.

Lesson 6, Chapters 15 – 16. **Metatron, Moshe and Elisha Aher.** We begin with the nature of Enoch's transformation into another life-form capable of permanent existence in his new realm. We also reference Elijah and how his ascent was different. Enoch is Metatron, Elijah is Sandalphon, Metatron in *Yetzirah*, Sandalphon is *Asiyah*, and what this all practically means. Moshe ascended above in astral form. Upon appearing "above," he too is confronted as was Enoch before him. Metatron is dispatched to defend Moshe, but this is not their first meeting. They met earlier at the burning bush, when Metatron served as "the angel of the L-rd". Later, Aher ascends. Seeing Metatron, he proclaims that there are two "gods". What he meant was that there appeared to be two different sets of rules as to how the universe operates, the rules of Heaven (under the name YHWH), and the rules of Earth (under the name *Elohim*). Aher is corrected, but makes a terrible choice, requiring the Sages to disavow him because of this choice. More about Aher is discussed in our Legends of the Talmud series, in the class about the Four who ascend Above (from Tractate *Hagigah*). We conclude with practical and relevant lessons about religious extremism.

Lesson 7, **The Seven Heavens & their Angels.** How Rabbinic Judaism is as much a descendant of the Essene school, as it is the Pharisee school. References from the books, *Shoreshei Shemot* and *Malakhei Elyon*, on the names of angels, and how our list in Hebrew Enoch is unique, and not found in later literature. How it is strange that the angels and heavens, as discussed in the Zohar, do not always coincide with the Enoch sources. This class emphasizes the fundamental differences between systems based on personal experience, and those based upon philosophical speculations. Examples are made from the Talmud *Hagigah*, and an episode from Rabbi Yaakov of Merush, who would communicate with angels, and ask them what Heaven says about Jewish ritual law practices. References are also made to Josephus, Qumran, the laws of teaching *Ma'aseh Merkava*, and the difference between the original *Sitrei Torah* (secrets of the

Torah), and the later Kabbalah (Jewish mysticism). Introduction into the 72 Angelic Princes over the nations, and their relationship to the planets.

Lesson 8, **The Angelic Hierarchy, Introduction into the Galactic Government.** First, we discuss the age-old controversy, are angels all incorporeal, or are there those that are physical. We see from the text that their physicality is definitely implied. These entities travel by some means of transportation device, herein called, "horses". Angelic authorities form a strict hierarchy, each with their individual realm of authority and responsibility. Many angel names given herein are not found anywhere else, and may be words in a language that we humans cannot identify. Many angels names are codes, and others are titles, describing the entities field of responsibility. Then come the YHWH angels. These are above *Aravot*, and using the language of the later Kabbalah, reside in *Olam HaBeriah*. Above these stand the one angel, who is two. One over life, and the other over death. We conclude this lesson with deep secrets about the relationship between Metatron and Samael, bringing us an understanding about the Devil and evil as it is revealed through the *Hekhalot* and the Torah.

This class also includes the most direct, and practical full instructions on how *merkava* ascent and astral travel is to be performed.

Lesson 9, Chapters 19-21, **Angel Tech of the *Merkava* Chariot.** Rekhaviel, Hayaliel and the *Hayot*. This lesson indicates that the *Merkava*/chariot (as recorded in Ezekiel) is something more than just a mere form of transportation device. Individual "angelic" entities are responsible for specific parts of its operations, and these entities are endowed with tremendous power and authority. **This class discusses the actual nature of what is the *merkava*/chariot, and what insights we can glean from our text to reveal what its actual function and workings might be.** *The merkava is a life-force, life-giving "machine". It is inter-dimensional, whose function is the sustenance and maintenance of life in existence.* The entity "angels" associated with it at the different levels therein are both individual beings and machines both at the same time. While we read their names in Hebrew, these names are only titles for our present understanding. This class explains more about the visualization/meditative exercises used to glimpse a view of the psychic *merkava*, and how this can be accessed within human consciousness. We also discussed the Golden Spiral, the Fibonacci sequence, and how this fits into, and possibly helps explain, the actual function of the *merkava* living machine.

Lesson 10, Chapter 22, **Secrets of Keruviel YHWH, and the *Cherubim*.** Mission of the *Cherubim*, Crossing the Bridges of Fire. We open with a review of the difference between theoretical religious knowledge and direct spiritual experience. Hebrew Enoch is a book written in code that describes actual, direct experiences with higher realities. We discuss the differences between astral projection (*haluka d'rabbanan*), and seeing higher worlds in expanded consciousness. *Cherubim* are not little babies, but something entirely foreign, and frightening. They serve as part of the *Merkava* machine. We discuss Keruviel YHWH as a *Beriatic* being, and then proceed to describe and identify *Cherubim* from the *Merkava* vision of Ezekiel, chapters 1 and 10. Also mentioned is Ezekiel 9, and the "X" mark placed on the righteous, in the past (and the future). Keruviel YHWH as a *Beriatic* being is a *Neshama*, not a *Malakh*. As such he is one of "Israel" above. What "Israel" above is discussed and how it differs from Israel below. *Cosmic Torah are the laws of nature. Torah on Earth (halakha/the commandments) are how human souls align themselves with the cosmic polarities.*

The *Cherubim* are the entities which, as part of the *Merkava*, serve as the conduit transferring Divine energy and directives from above to below. This is why their form is on the Ark of the Covenant, and why it is specifically a *Cherub*, with a sword of fire, that guards the way to the Garden of Eden. We briefly discuss the Inner Earth Temple, and how the Ark is there being serviced by modern-day Zadokite priests.

We conclude with a discussion of the bridges of fire, and how they are the pathways of psychic/astral ascent, and how each of us, individually, is destined and required to walk this path, no matter how long it takes for us to do so.

Lesson 11, Chapter 26, **The Original Purpose of Apocalypse.** Seraphiel, the *Seraphim* and the Satan. We open with an understanding of the poetic nature of angelic descriptions, and how the original Hebrew texts are used as chants to attempt a personal visual experience of the realities of the individual entities described. How experiential literature (prophetic/*merkava*), starting with Ezekiel and Daniel in the Bible, continued throughout the Temple period and into the Talmudic period, and where this genre of literature is today. The relationship of *Beriatic* angels to souls, souls to the Name YHWH, and how these both relate to *Yetziratic* entities. How there are human souls and "Israel" in every world, on every planet, regardless of dimension or galaxy. The *Seraphim* are the higher *Teli*, the *Beriatic* entities of fire. Their function is to burn the tablets of the Satan, written by Samael and Dubiel that recounts the sins of

Israel. It is clear that Satan is not Samael. These three, Seraphiel, Samael and Dubiel correspond above the triad below of Rome, Israel and Persia. These powers exist on our planet as part of the great Divine plan for the evolution of our world. This is discussed in some detail. *Readings from the book Malakhei Elyon by Rabbi Reuben Margolis showing a relationship between Seraphiel and Adam. Readings from the book Shoreshei Shemot by Rabbi Moshe Zacuto showing a magical formula using the angel Seraphiel.*

Lesson 12, Chapters 28-31. **The Watchers & the Heavenly Court, the Princes of YHWH.** We begin with a discussion about understanding natural law and how everything in the universe requires natural balance. We then review how existence operates under specific parameters and how conscious, sentient entities are part of the fabric of everything to ensure that the Supernal Mind is manifest properly in all its multiple parts. There are a chain of Watchers, from the highest in *Aravot* to the *Teli* here on Earth. We briefly discuss the history of the ancient, holy dragons, and the ones who broke from them in the fall. We discuss how all the individual nations of the world each have equal access to, and relationship with Heaven, each in their own way. How judgment of a soul actually occurs and why. Judgment, including mercy is part of natural law, and part of the operations of the great "machine" of creation. The Princes of YHWH are the members of the Heavenly Supreme Court, who are each called by the name of YHWH. They are part of the collective. We explain what a Throne is, what judgment is, and how it is a natural, ongoing process of alignment of all integral parts into the greater whole which is YHWH. Perspectives of the *sefirot*, internal or external, and why this is important.

Lesson 13. Chapters 43-44. **Journeys Around the Afterlife with Metatron & R. Yishmael.** This class begins with an introduction about the true nature of souls, and the realities they experience outside of human bodies. How the afterlife is perceived as a projections of one's thoughts during life. The *Gan Eden* of Earth and *Gehinom* are considered to be physical locations in Inner Earth, where souls reside all the while that they no longer inhabit human bodies. The nature of souls trapped here on Earth, and what is needed for them to be freed. Righteousness and sin are both calibrations of life force energy, pro and con respectively. Those who calibrate towards righteousness align with life, and ascend, and vice versa for the opposite souls. The reality of the Throne of Glory and the *Beriatic* realm. Newborn souls (*beriatic*) that will only be born once *Mashiah* comes. The nature of disincarnate intermediate souls and how they are rectified. A brief discussion about possessions and exorcisms. The nature of

Divine Justice and the foundation of existence, prayers for mercy and redemption, what delays redemption, and what we must practically do to assist in the great scheme of things to help bring redemption closer. Mention of a meditative exercise to assist one in discovering one's true inner identity.

Lesson 14, Chapters 45 – 46. **The Generations of Man & the Souls of the Stars.** Secret relationship of space/time and consciousness. The invisible universe above ours, the invisible mind (unconscious) within us, and the invisible order and structure that guides them all. The Higher Torah, the natural, universal way, how it existed before Sinai, and how, even now, this Torah exists everywhere. Every nation has this Torah and every nation has its prophets. All is structured and ordained in accordance to quantum probabilities, and in accordance to reverse time, where the future marches backwards into the past. The vortex of meeting when the future past meets the past future is the time when *Mashiah* dawns in our world. The source of astrology, the souls of the stars. Readings from RaMBaM (Maimonides). Stars are alive, living, sentient, self-aware beings. Our future relationship with stars. The natural, way according to Higher Torah, how to understand Jewish Law, through Gemara study.

Lesson 15, Chapters 47 – 48a. **Souls of the Angels, G-d's Right Hand & the Coming of *Mashiah*.** Angels do have souls. These souls descend into forms for the sake of being conduits of life-force energy. Yet, sometimes these forms are improper, and the "song" they "sing" is wrong. Their forms (bodies) are then deconstructed in the *Nehar Dinur* (River of Fire) that separates the higher and lower dimensional planes. G-d's Right Hand, a metaphor for the *sefirotic Partzuf Zeir Anpin* (ZA), who is in a state of *dormita* (concealment) during the time of exile. This is symbolically called G-d's right Hand being tied up behind his back. The redemption begins in this state. Human righteousness contributes. Righteous human consciousness projects into the collective mind seeds of influence to "speed" things up if possible. Yet, the redemption comes "in its time". When redemption comes there will be a comprehensive transformation of human consciousness and the dimensional planes in which it exists. Reference is made to many messianic prophecies. Secret of Inner Earth, the *Kan Tzippur* (Bird's Nest), the age and birth date of *Mashiah* ben David, and the secret identity of the army that supports *Mashiah* in his establishment of the Kingdom of Heaven upon the Earth. Reference is also made to many current events, including the purpose of the existence of the present State of Israel

Lesson 16, Chapter 48b. **Enoch's Ascent & Metatron's Authority.** A review of the entire Enoch legend. How and why a human being was chosen from Earth to ascend to realms beyond, to serve in a position of authority over already existing higher races of beings. The necessity of understanding science and natural truth, and how these themselves are Torah. Therefore, whatever be truth, and wherever it is found, this is Torah. There is thus no separation whatsoever between science and real religion. The scientific understanding of life transforming from one form into another, or how exactly could Enoch be translated from a human being into a being of either pure energy, or into another form that we cannot imagine, and most likely could not even recognize as a life-form.

The race of Metatrons, and where Enoch the former human fit into them, and into G-d's greater plan for humanity and our planet. Metatron as general over his army of lesser ranked messengers (angels). Metatron in charge of the Watchers (Daniel), and how the Watcher interact with him, and how they can (and do) equally fight with one another. Metatron's relationship with human souls, and the true nature of repentance, how Hebrew *Teshuva*, and eastern Karma differentiate. The fate of the souls of human children who die before having fulfilled their Earth missions.

Lesson 17, **The Seventy Names and Identities of Metatron.** In this final lesson of the series, I summarize and reveal all the secrets of how Metatron is known to all the different nations of the world, (and to citizens of other planets), each by a name and context unique to their individual cultures and religions. We discuss specific names Yahuel, Eved, Ruah Piskonit, the little YHWH, Na'ar, Taftafyah, and clear up the garbled forms of the angel Zagnugael, who appeared to Moshe in the burning bush.

We discuss Moshe' ascent into heaven in his astral body, and how in that body consciousness shifts into astral consciousness, maybe this being what we today call theta and delta brain waves. When he descends back into his body, he forgets the Torah because in the flesh he is back in his alpha-beta mind. Moshe was thus altered to be able to use all four together in perfect harmony. This gave him the ability to read G-d's Mind, and thus making Moshe, chief of all prophets.

Quantum Torah was given on Sinai, the entire Torah is its primordial, non-physical state. This is the universal Torah, the Torah of *Mashiah*, the true secrets of the Torah. All have access to this Torah, whereas Israel alone embraces the Torah of Moshe.

The importance of *Halakha*, the living flow of the living Torah. Who alone has the right to be called a *Rav*, a teacher of Torah. The argument in Heaven between Metatron who taught Moshe the Torah and the angels who were angry at him for doing so. **The healing tradition of Torah, and how it is similar today to that found in certain aspects of traditional Chinese medicine (TCM). The Jewish connection between Native American beliefs and peoples, and Chinese beliefs.** The secret order of using the seventy names from the book *Sefer Heshek*, by R. Eliezer of Worms. This is the order found on my Metatron *Shiviti*.

Course Details
The cost of the course is $340.00.

To purchase this course: Log on to our KosherTorah School website. Click on any one of the links that say "support" or "donate". This will bring to you to our generic payment page. Make payment in the proper amount.
Upon checkout make sure that you note in the "comments box" which course you are purchasing. Write: **"for the _____ Course".** Once your payment has been received you will receive in turn via email a PDF document that includes the class outlines, as well as the links to the online classes.

2. The Kabbalah of Spiritual Contact
The Cultivation of Expanded Consciousness and Extra Sensory Perceptions in the Torah Tradition
Based on the Kabbalistic classic, The Gates of Holiness (Sha'arei Kedusha), Section Three by Hayim Vital. A seventeen (17) lesson audio course taught by Ariel B. Tzadok

Course Outline

Lesson 1 – Chapter 1A. **An overall review of the worlds we call YHWH**
We begin with readings from *Sefer Ba'al Shem Tov* (*V'et'hanan* 71, 69, 66) to establish that our discussion about the supernal worlds is indeed a discussion about the psychological worlds inside us.
All references to worlds, *sefirot*, emanations and the like must be understood metaphorically, and symbolically. We do not associate to them any literalness at all.

There is the Supernal Emanator and then there is the Emanated. The Emanated is YHWH, which is the pattern of all the worlds in existence.

There is a difference between emanation and creation. Discussion explains the relationship of G-d manifest (YHWH) and the Unmanifest (*Eyn Sof*).

This class outlines the existence of the four/five worlds and their relationship to the ten *sefirot*, which again, are understood a levels of consciousness within the human psyche.

This first class lays the foundations for everything that we will build in the following classes of this course.

Lesson 2 – Chapter 1B. **The Seven Heavens & Extraterrestrial Life**
An overall review of the Seven Heavens understood to be varying degrees of physicality in the universe.

An extended discussion of extraterrestrial life, and the forms that it may take. Relationship of these forms to traditional religious understandings, with reference examples to modern science fiction.

All life follows the general pattern of the worlds, and *sefirot*, therefore, all forms of life to be found on other worlds while physically different, will share similar qualities of consciousness.

Speculations with regards to the subdivisions of *sefirot* levels within *Asiyah/Malkhut* and their relationship to modern discoveries of Dark Matter, and Dark Energy. Comments on the mistake of Geocentrism, and why according to Torah such a belief, while at one time acceptable, (and the norm), is no longer acceptable, or even tolerable. The levels of soul, and how even Maimonides understood that planets and stars were actually sentient life forms, with self-awareness, and cosmic consciousness.

Lesson 3 – Chapter 2A. **The Purpose of Humanity in the Universe, and on Earth**
Why was humanity created in the form of body and soul? Why do we have inclinations towards the highest good, and at the same time, the lowest evil? What is our relationship to other sentient species, those who we call angels? These are the questions R. Vital raises as we begin this chapter.

We review the order of the worlds, emphasizing their psychological nature, and not their metaphysical reality. We speculate about the nature of higher domains in relationship to matter and the speed of light. Levels of consciousness are what define our humanity, and these levels, psychological as they are, also reside in their own domains, which very well may be higher dimensional planes, each being its own independent universe.

We introduce the concept of YHWH of 45 (*MAH*), as it is a reference to "Man" above, and to the many "images" of "Man" below.

We outline the "image of Man," as it refers to the domain of the *sefirot/Atzilut/*Creator, and the lower worlds together called creation/the Tree of Knowledge. We elaborate many details regarding this biblical metaphor.

Lesson 4 – Chapter 2B – **The Kabbalah of Human Essence**

The inner domains of the human being, with startling revelations of how the individual and collective unconscious is influenced by specific other-worldly intelligence who definitely do not share human moral values. This is the secret of the "dark light" that masks the angelic races who direct the forces underlying the physical universe. Reference to Daniel's Watchers, the *Teli* dragons, and those of their number who came to Earth with powers and abilities far beyond those of mortal men, and who yet do not at all share human moral values. The forces of life and consciousness that R. Vital takes from traditional Greek philosophical teachings.

Lesson 5 – Chapter 2C – **Human Potential, and the Fifth Element**

All life-forms are conscious sentient beings. Yet, some levels of life have higher levels of consciousness than others. This class reviews the five level, with emphasis on humanity, and the minority within humanity that forms a fifth element, not based on ethnicity or religion, but rather on consciousness, crossing all cultural divides.

The nature of human enlightenment, and its relationship to prophecy and the messianic age.

Lesson 6 – Chapter 2D – **Souls, Angels, Humans**

This lesson describes the relationship between our true Adamic reality as parts of a greater collective which transcends individuality, and every finite physical form. Adamic entities can exist in any form in any dimension, including other physical worlds, and still contain "the soul of man".

What exactly is "the soul of Man (Adam)".

The intermediary function of entities whose role it is to serve as conduits from the collective source of things down to the individual forms in the finite plane. How these intermediary forms are clearly superior to that which is beneath them, but inferior to that which is above them. How and why these intermediary forms exist.

Further discussions explaining levels of consciousness and how these apply to different levels of soul.

Lesson 7 – Chapter 2E – **The Purpose of Good and Evil**

The relationship of the *Neshama* higher Self to the *Nefesh* lower self is explained in detail with the psychological application to the relationship between the conscious mind, and the personal unconscious.

The two inclinations, the *Yetzer HaTov*, and the *Yetzer HaRa* are explained to be emotional factors used to properly calibrate and correlate the *Nefesh* to the *Neshama*.

Good and evil exist within the subjective context of application. The concepts of good and evil are then extended to collective proportions is relationship to the requirements directing human social behavior, and the need for commandments.

This class addresses many relevant, modern issues about religion, tolerance, extremism, and explains many deep theological concepts in a easy to grasp way.

Lesson 8 – Chapter 2F – **The Purpose of Human Incarnation on Earth.**

This lesson is a comprehensive review of everything that Torah, Kabbalah, prophecy, and our KosherTorah School teaches about the truth of human existence, potential, and future.

A comprehensive realistic, and psychological understanding of the "five worlds," what they really mean, and how they are experienced in normal life.

The purpose and practice of meditation and spirituality. The expansion of human consciousness includes intellectual revelation, emotional balance, and all its relevant physical applications, including technological development.

The actual meaning of the messianic era, and the role of future technologies.

Lesson 9 – Chapter 3, **The Hindrances that Block Prophecy.**

Prophecy is the expansion of human consciousness that brings a widening imaginative faculty into strong alignment with the rational mind. When the two are in complete harmony, and communication, consciousness can expand to perceive greater, deeper levels of reality. Such awareness always is attached to some form, object, or things. These become symbolic messengers from one's higher self. These then are one's personal angel, spiritual guide, and guardian angel.

The hindrances are anything from whatever cause, intellectual, emotional, or physiological, that causes confusion in the mind and heart, and/or congestion in the physical anatomy.

Religion is meant to serve as an archetypal expression that gives form to inner, deeper psychological truths, which are the foundation of our humanity.

Religious sin is understood in its proper context as psychological imbalances. This class addresses relevant social, and political issues in light of their affect upon the collective unconscious.

Lesson 10 – Chapter 5, **The Levels of Consciousness, 1**

All souls form a singularity. The path of meditation is to expand individual awareness into higher realms of thought, and perception. The path is for one to discover one's unique individual place. This path is the way of discovery to reveal "the spark of *Mashiah*" within the soul of each of us.

Lesson 11 – Chapter 5, **The Levels of Consciousness, 2**

The differences between dreams, meditation, and astral travel.

When does the soul leave the body to travel into other realms? When does the mind/soul stay put, and instead of ascending into Heaven, bring Heaven down to Earth?

The active and passive nature of developing psychic abilities of the mind.

The power of the imaginative faculty, the point of union between rationalist philosophy, and prophetic Kabbalah meditation.

Practical examples of meditative experiences, with references to Eastern meditative practices, to emphasize the psychological nature of this topic, and thus its global appeal.

Lesson 12 – Chapter 5, **The Levels of Consciousness, 3**

Prophecy and Clairvoyance. The practical development of psychic abilities according to the Torah/Kabbalah and Psychology.

R. Hayim Vital, like Abulafia and Maimonides before him, accepts the belief (originating from the Greek philosophers) that psychic development (in Judaism called prophecy) is a natural development of the refined individual. Psychic powers are not a gift, but can be acquired by anyone who cultivates them. Discussion of using mental constructs to provide forms for higher realities to manifest within the conscious mind. Example of tarot cards and how they are properly read.

The ascent up the *Sefirotic* Tree of Life, and how this image forms the general pattern that enables us to seek internal emotional balance.

The importance of passion (*yesod*) in accomplishing psychic development. Practical examples about sexual attraction, and marital relationships.

Lesson 13 – Chapter 7 – **Prophetic Consciousness in Modern Times**

Understanding the psychological nature of spiritual practices.

Orthodox Judaism is a path for Orthodox Jews, but it is not (and has never been) a path for everyone. The Torah path is a subjective path, it is one of many that leads to the development of the mind, and through this to the development of psychic abilities, which in earlier days were called Prophecy and *Ruah HaKodesh* (Divine inspiration). Reference the teaching of the *Tana D'vei Eliyahu*.

This lesson is geared towards dispelling the myth of the importance of external paths, as opposed to internal paths.

Lesson 14 – Chapter 7 – **Psychic Phenomena in the Kabbalistic Tradition**

There are all kinds of Kabbalistic methods for making spiritual contact. Most are misunderstood in the imagination. This class explains the reality underlying the legends to expose the actual para-psychological parameters of those Kabbalists well-trained enough to experience them.

What it means to experience Elijah the Prophet, and other ancient masters.

The true nature of human inspiration, and its relationship to "Divine" inspiration.

The experience of "cosmic/G-d" consciousness, and how it differs from experiencing spiritual insights through a mentally conceived form.

The internal power of integrated beliefs, devotion, and righteous behavior.

Also, the commonality of Torah-based experiences with those of various other religions, what we call the sparks of the exiled Torah.

Lesson 15 – Gate 6 – **The Levels of Extra Sensory Perception**

This lesson begins the concluding section of this course, and reviews the four worlds, and ten *sefirot*, and how they are to be viewed psychologically, with emphasis on practical embrace, and experience.

Numerous psychological examples are given to show how the Kabbalistic system actually works.

Emphasis on understanding the realms of the *Klipot*, and a discussion about one addressing one's personal sub-conscious emotional issues.

The ascent through the Palaces and the Gates, the meanings of archetypes, and how they are constructively used.

Again, this lesson makes regular reference to other spiritual traditions to emphasize the psychological reality underlying the Kabbalah of Spiritual Connection.

Lesson 16 – Gate 6 – **Ezekiel's Chariot & the Heavenly Palaces.**

A realistic overview of the ancient practice of *Hekhalot* ascent. All ascent is experienced psychologically, in what I refer to as a mental technology. Palaces, guardians, and angels are all archetypal experiences, not limited to the individual imagination, although that is where each is visualized, and experienced.

Mental constructs are individualized, active imagination, prophetic vision unique to the individual.

An involved discussion about the realm of the *klipot*, the sub-conscious, and the importance of coming to peace with one's own internal emotional turmoil.

What is and is not an actual extraterrestrial encounter, and how these can be physical, mental or a combination of both.

Lesson 17 – Gate 6. **Kabbalistic Magic and Angelic Encounters.**

What is the actual nature of magic. What is the difference between the fantasy of magic, and its actual psychological, and para-psychological parameters. Discussion of herbology, magic wands, and other ancient forms.

Magical beliefs in society and politics, mention of the Nazi Thule, and the British Golden Dawn, (and of course, Harry Potter).

The levels of prophecy, and the unique nature of the experience of Moshe, who, in my opinion was genetically altered in his actual, and physical close encounter on Mt. Sinai. This is what differed in the nature of his prophetic experience from the later prophets. Explanation of what is means to prophecy through *Beriah* and *Yetzirah*. The world of Metatron, and the race of the Metatrons. What really happened to the four who entered the *Pardes*, and why such endeavors are psychologically dangerous.

What exactly is *Kabbalah Ma'asit*, and how it differs from prophetic meditation, and the usage of holy names, and the like.

The class concludes with an understanding of the nature of Earth spirits and why they are not be disturbed by human invocation soliciting their support, in contradiction to the nature of their missions.

Course Details
The cost of the course is $340.00.

To purchase this course: Log on to our KosherTorah School website. Click on any one of the links that say "support" or "donate". This will bring to you to our generic payment page. Make payment in the proper amount.

Upon checkout make sure that you note in the "comments box" which course you are purchasing. Write: **"for the _____ Course"**. Once your payment has been received you will receive in turn via email a PDF document that includes the class outlines, as well as the links to the online classes.

3. Sefer HaBahir
The book of Brilliance An Ancient Guide To Experiencing Spiritual Truths
A Fifteen (15) Lesson Audio Course Taught by Ariel Bar Tzadok

Course Outline

Class 1

Introduction into the book, its author(s) and its methods. Grecian methods of learning, and how they have become fully entrenched in Judaic literature. Two contradictory verses, with a third that comes to reconcile them. Thesis, antithesis and synthesis. This comes to teach us the Torah fundamental principle that all comes from G-d, be it good and evil, light and darkness, day and night. The importance of understanding contradictory realities. Quantum reality. The five elements of *Tohu* and *Bohu*.

Class 2

Sections 3 & 4. The meaning of blessing. It is never enough to understand Torah as religion, it must be understood as science. Relationship of the invisible to the visible, white fire to black fire, parallel universe to our universe, dark matter to seen matter. Torah is all around us, laws of Torah are the laws of nature. One does not see the King until one enters His house. One does not get to see YHWH before one enters *Elohim*. *Elohim* is the study of natural law, and science. Science/nature/*Elohim* is the path to YHWH. Zohar says that the gates of wisdom opened in the year 5600, this is technological advancement. This will assist us to bring about the messianic age.

Class 3

Sections 5 – 9. Torah Cosmology. How was the universe created. Biocentrism, readings from the book by Dr. Robert Lanza. Life before creation, not life from creation. Life's source is the unseen, our universe, the seen vessel for Life. How was it divided between the seen and the unseen. What is the relationship of these two, what is their future. First, there was creation, then 730 million years later, something else happened that revealed the Torah from its concealed state to its revealed state. This class will discuss literal cosmology in light of the Kabbalistic metaphorical worlds, of *Asiyah*, *Yetzirah* and *Beriah*.

Class 4

Sections 10 – 14. Cosmic Evolution and the Development of Consciousness.
Evolution occurs both within the cosmic universe and equally within the collective mind of humanity. The invisible (dark) part of our universe that surrounds us forms a unique relationship with the visible universe. This relationship is what the Bible referred to as *Bohu* and *Tohu*. These cosmic dimensions are the source of what we humans call good and evil. We define good as complete and evolved, whereas evil as defined as the incomplete and the evolving. More readings from Biocentrism, by Dr. Robert Lanza. We will also discuss the metaphor of the shapes of Hebrew letters.

Class 5

Sections 15-20. The Hebrew Letters, Poetic Metaphors for the Cosmos.
References from the Talmud *Sanhedrin*, and the *Sefer Baal Shem Tov*. A brief review of the different Hebrew scripts, Paleo-Hebrew, Assyrian script (modern block form), Rashi (*Sephardi*) and modern cursive (*Ashkenazi*). In which script was the Torah given to Moshe on Sinai. Primordial Torah prior to human events. The metaphorical meaning of the letters Alef, Bet and Gimel, and how they relate to the upper triad of *sefirot*, *Keter*, *Hokhma* and *Binah*. Using the symbols of the shapes of the letters to describe the development of the evolution of consciousness.

Class 6

Sections 21-25. The Creation of the Angels, the First Ones and the Second Ones. Relationship of the first evolved entities, the original collective of the Metatrons, the First Ones. Then as evolution progressed into forming this world other races evolved and became the Second Ones, creating a chain of command for the manifestation of the Singular Divine Will. Lessons about lower-case "g" gods, earth spirits, angels and archangels, what they are, and how they view us. Humanity's purpose, why our universe exists, and what purpose it serves.

Class 7

Sections 26-31. Evolution of Mind, the Universe, and Religious Thought.
Religious ideas develop and evolve over time. Secret meanings of the Hebrew word *Ish* (Man) and how this applies to G-d. This lesson shows the original forms of the teachings about the Small Face of G-d (*Zeir Anpin*, ZA). Three levels in creation, the higher realm (Hey), lower realm (lower Hey) and the bridge that connects the two (Vav). Many Zoharic and Lurianic lessons have their basis in these Bahiric teachings. Secrets of the Fallen Hey. Secrets of the Rectification

(Ascending Light, *Ohr Hozer*). Concluding lesson about the secrets of *Mashiah* in the Garden of Eden in Inner Earth.

Class 8

Sections 32-35. The Sacred Triad, G-d & the Invisible and Visible Universe. Not only are there the "*DU Partzufim*" of parallel worlds, there is also the third realm of the Divine that is separate and above them. This lesson introduces us to the idea of the triad, the sacred pyramid. We discuss its development and relationship to the universe in general, the mind of man in specific, and even reference how this idea was adopted into Christianity as the foundation of the concept of the Trinity. Brief mention is made between this idea and the concept of the *sefirot*. Also discussed is the relationship of the Divine source world to our visible universe, and we are designed to evolve and grow.

Class 9

Sections 36-39. Secrets of the Vowels. The vowels used in Hebrew prove that *Sefer Bahir* is a text of a much later period than either Temple or Talmudic times. The vowels are used to describe the relationship between the visible and invisible worlds referred to in later Kabbalah as the *Du Partzufim*. Earlier Torah based mysticism was based on actual experience and ascent into the invisible realm(s). As these practices were being replaced by the theoretical school of mysticism, called Kabbalah, the older experiences had to be explained, because most could no longer experience them. This lesson explains this relationship.

Class 10

Sections 40-46. Original Teachings of the Seven Lower *Sefirot*. Secrets of the Voice of G-d, the Great Fire and the Word of G-d. The *sefirotic* pattern is not a theoretical construct, rather it is an expression of the Universal Mind (G-d) as It manifests from concealed to revealed, and is received by that created in Its Image, that being the mind of man. At Sinai, the Voice above went forth, emanating through the Life Force (*Nefesh*/Chi) energy that permeates all matter, including the human mind/brain, and was there received and interpreted as Words. Thus the revelation of Sinai was telepathic in nature. This still occurs today in the form of the *Bat Kol*. This is also how communication was received via the Ark of the Covenant, through the High Priest's breastplate and the mysterious *Urim* and *Tumim*. All this is discussed in this lesson.

Class 11

Sections 47-50. The Partial Image of the Voice. A discussion about the different levels of Divine consciousness, the masks (*Partzufim*) of G-d. What actually happened at Mt. Sinai. Reading from Maimonides, Guide to the Perplexed, about the telepathic nature of Torah reception. Relationship of the Metatron class of angels to the Name of G-d, YHWH. The upper triad of *sefirot* and their relationship to the Heavenly Holy of Holies discussed in the ancient text, 2nd Enoch. *Hokhma, Binah,* and the nature of physical movement when the operations of reception (Kabbalah) are operational.

Class 12

Sections 51-55. Secrets of the Upper & Lower Waters, Gold & Silver. Referencing biblical metaphors to describe the nature and relationship of the physical/visible universe with the spiritual/invisible universe. How these universes are accessed. What is their place in the mind and in our experiences. A discussion about the ancient *Pesher* method of personalized biblical interpretations. Also discussed is how the Torah can either be an elixir of life or the elixir of death, all depending upon how one comes to approach it.

Class 13

Sections 63, 92-94. Secret of 32, the 72 Names of G-d and the Mechanics of Creation. The 32 is heart. This is a symbol for the mechanical operations of creation under the direction of various races of angels. The blue (*tekhelet*) in *tzitzit* represents the life force energy of biocentric consciousness (*nefesh*) that serves as the sign that G-d is the author and director of the system. This class explains the actual nature of the relationship between the dimensional planes, and how they actually operate in what I call a "mechanical" order. We discuss higher life forms, dimensional and planetary travel, and shape-shifting for the sake of intergalactic relocation (Enoch, Elijah).

Class 14

Sections 95-96, 98-99. Secrets of the Guardians of the Universe. The quantum universe operates in accordance to laws in three dimensions, space, time and consciousness. These are ruled over by three levels of "administrators" (angels). Human consciousness is a necessary component for discovering the proper "theory of everything". Light matter and dark matter. *Ophanim*, Dragons (*Teli*), *Hayot, Cherubim.* How other entities direct the universe, and direct human consciousness through direct (and indirect) telepathic contact. The heart, the purpose of Israel in the human race. The inner Garden of Eden.

Dangers of violating the laws of time, and space. Together with Class 13, these two lessons reveal a tremendous amount of secrets about things that are popularly questioned today.

Class 15

Sections 101-112. Secrets of the *Teli*. The secret identity of the Holy Servants of G-d in control of space, time and consciousness in a quantum universe. Their relationship to the *Merkava*, and Gavriel, Mikhael and Uriel. Their relationship to righteousness and the 36 righteous in each generation (the *Lamed-Vav*). The secret of the cosmic spiral where left and right turn and reverse, the secret of the Ouroboros. The secret of the Aharonic blessing, the three Names YHWH and the vowels to be used for its projection as a blessing. Secrets of projecting into the collective consciousness the powers of good and change, or evil and destruction, the warning of what goes around comes around. The secret Twelve Names of the Ascent through which one makes contact with the *Teli* and requests of them that which is to be requested. This class, along with classes 13 and 14 in the *Bahir* series form a triad which reveals secrets and meditative techniques that I have never previously discussed.

Course Details
The cost of the course is $300.00.

To purchase this course: Log on to our KosherTorah School website. Click on any one of the links that say "support" or "donate". This will bring to you to our generic payment page. Make payment in the proper amount.
Upon checkout make sure that you note in the "comments box" which course you are purchasing. Write: **"for the _____ Course".** Once your payment has been received you will receive in turn via email a PDF document that includes the class outlines, as well as the links to the online classes.

4. The Holy Names & their Usages

Jewish "Magic" a Ten-Hour Audio Course with R. Ariel B. Tzadok

Course Outline

Class 1 – **The 72 Triad Name of G-d, Lesson 1,** from *Pardes Rimmonim* of Rabbi Moshe Cordevero. The origins of the 72 triad name. The Zoharic explanation of its boustrophedon structure. The *sefirotic* relationships. Two different sets of vowels. Relationship of the *pasukim*, triads and letters. The meaning of the number 72. An overall explanation of how the name is understood in the theoretical school of Kabbalah, to distinguish this understanding from our following lessons showing the magical/prophetic properties of the name in Raziel, Abulafia, Vital and Zacuto.

Class 2 – **The 72 Triad Name of G-d, Lesson 2,** from the writings of R. Eliezer of Worms. *Sefer HaShem*, the book of the Name, and a special formula for using the Names in a ritual for healing. *Sefer Raziel HaMalakh*, the three orders of the Names and how in groups of 7 they are used for individual purposes, included are the Names, the invocations, and hints as to the proper hours and days when each is to be used. This lesson clearly shows the contrast between the theoretical school and the magical school.

Class 3 – **The 72 Triad Name, Lesson 3** from the writings of Avraham Abulafia and Hayim Vital. An overview and comparison from Rabbi Vital's *Shaarei Kedusha* and original insights from Rabbi Abulafia's works, *Hayei Olam HaBa* and *Sefer Heshek*. An overall usage of the 72 Name as a meditative tool, with the two Rabbis describing two differing forms for its usage. This class is an excellent review of the Abulafia techniques, which include active imagination and cultivating inner dialogue with one's higher self and spiritual guide.

Class 4 – **The 72 Triad Name, Lesson 4** from the book *Shoreshei HaShemot* of Rabbi Moshe Zacuto. Rabbi Zacuto was a secularly trained cosmopolitan Rabbi in the 17th century, living mostly in Amsterdam and Venice. Yet, as a Kabbalist, he authored this text which is unique as it serves as an encyclopedia for all holy names known at the time. In review of the 72 Name, Rabbi Zacuto references traditional material from Cordevero (covered in class 1), and some material from Vital (covered in class 3). The Rabbi then strikes out and adds outright magical material from sources not named. He includes various usages for each name, with angelic associations. He then proceeds to outline other forms of combining the three verses that construct the name and gives magical formulas for their usage. We conclude with looking at yet another name of 72 made up from three different verses from the first chapter of Ezekiel.

Class 5 – *Ana B'koah,* **the Name of 42, Lesson 1** from *Pardes Rimmonim, Sefer HaKana* and the *Shoreshei Shemot*. The similarities and differences between these three texts. This Name is unlike the 72. It is not mechanical, it is authentically alien. Like the 72, the 42 corresponds to angelic names, but unlike the 72, the 42 has two sets of names, one of which are familiar *"el"* names, and then another set of stranger, unfamiliar names. How these names are used, how the 42 is merged with YHW and not YHWH as is the 72. This is the name associated with creation, how this is so. The secret of the vessels, angels, *Elohim* that brought forth this universe.

Class 6 – *Ana B'koah*, **Lesson 2,** magical uses of the individual names from *Sefer Shoreshei Shemot.*

Class 7 – **The 22 Letter Name** from *Birkat Kohanim* in *Pardes Rimonim*, the 12 letter Name from *Sefer Refuah vhayim mYerushalayim,* the name on the staff of Moshe. From Rabbi Nehuniah ben Hakana in *Pardes Rimonim*, the names of Heaven and Earth in the *Hekhalot* tradition, *Araritah* and *Ahoy.*

Class 8 – **Alphabetical List of Other Names,** including *Malakhim* from *Sefer Shoreshei Shemot.* The psychology of psychic projection that makes these types of activities actually work. The secret of the "prince of the cup". Gazing into a full cup to seek images that will communicate hidden knowledge. This was the practice of the magical cup ascribed to the biblical Yosef.

Class 9 – **The Alphabet of the Angels.** Selections of Names and Practices from *Shoreshei Shemot.* Select Names include Dikarnosa, Taftafya, Tzamarkad and others. Also covered is the pendulum meditation, in full details. Review of angelic letters, paleo-Hebrew and their relationship. Readings from *Sanhedrin* 21, with regards to what was the original script of the Torah. According to Rashi, it might have been angelic script. Using the *Mezuzah* as an amulet of protection.

Class 10 – **Laws of Using *Kabbalah Ma'asit*.** Readings from Rabbi Hayim Vital. *Sha'arei Kedusha*, Section 3, Chapter 6 defines for us what is *Kabbalah Ma'asit*, and thus also defines what it is not. We see that *Kubbalah Ma'asit* does not include the usages of Holy Names. *Sha'ar HaMitzvot, Shemot* also repeats the warnings of the *Sha'arei Kedusha*, but adds an important detail. One who meets a certain criteria as outlined in the Talmud, (*Avodah Zara* 35b) can and should use Holy Names. We review this Talmud for clear elucidation. We then proceed to review Rabbi Hayim's own use of *Kabbalah Ma'asit*. We learn how to call upon the dead to come to one in a dream (*Sefer Peulot*). We see the original "body of G-d" *Shiur Komah* in Rabbi Hayim's commentary to the magical text *Brit Menuha*, and we conclude with Rabbi Hayim's references to which angels perform which function, and how they are called upon. This is the final class in Semester 3.

Course Details
The cost of the course is $200.00.

To purchase this course: Log on to our KosherTorah School website. Click on any one of the links that say "support" or "donate". This will bring to you to our generic payment page. Make payment in the proper amount.
Upon checkout make sure that you note in the "comments box" which course you are purchasing. Write: **"for the _____ Course"**. Once your payment has been received you will receive in turn via email a PDF document that includes the class outlines, as well as the links to the online classes.

About Ariel Bar Tzadok
& the KosherTorah School

Rabbi Ariel proudly welcomes to the KosherTorah School all peoples, of all backgrounds, who wish to learn about the authentic and original Biblical world outlook.

KosherTorah is not just about the Bible.

KosherTorah is not just about Judaism.

KosherTorah is not just about religion.

KosherTorah is not just about G-d.

KosherTorah is about us!

KosherTorah is about building bridges!

KosherTorah is about becoming a more decent human being!

KosherTorah is about common sense, simple living, righteous behavior, and liberty and respect for all.

For over thirty years, Rabbi Ariel has been a world renowned expert of the authentic, Biblical "Secrets of the Torah" teachings, that many today simply call "Kabbalah."

Rabbi Ariel teaches the sulam aliyah (ladder of ascent) school of Kabbalah, which consists of the Biblical teachings of the works of Ezekiel's chariot (Ma'aseh Merkava), and the prophetic meditative techniques passed down through the centuries.

The purpose of these teachings is to cultivate actual, authentic, and personal spiritual experiences, the likes of which are psychological, and transformational. The purpose of spirituality is to explore one's inner self, and to discover, and unleash one's inner, latent potentials. To this task is the KosherTorah School dedicated.

While knowledgeable of the theoretical/philosophical schools taught by others, Rabbi Ariel places special emphasis on teaching the "other schools" which most today are unaware of, or not qualified to teach. These specifically are the prophetic/meditative and so-called "magical" schools. Rabbi Ariel teaches others HOW-TO practice these ancient methods for each individual to acquire their own unique spiritual experiences.

The KosherTorah School focuses on teaching Biblical, and later mystical literature in a rational way to enable the student to extract their universal teachings from their numerous layers of myth and metaphor. The school proudly serves the educational needs of a global audience, and welcomes students from all walks of life.

Born and raised on Long Island, New York, Ariel Bar Tzadok studied abroad in Israel for a number of years. He studied in Jerusalem at the premier Sephardic institute, Yeshivat Porat Yosef (Old City), and later in Kollel Hekhal Pinhas. While studying for his rabbinic ordination, he was blessed to become the private student of the renowned Kabbalist, Rabbi Meir Levi, *obm*, the foremost student of the leading Kabbalist of Jerusalem, Rabbi Mordechai Sharabi *obm*.

In June 1983, Rabbi Ariel received his rabbinic ordination (Haredi/Orthodox) from Rabbi Ya'akov Peretz, Rosh Yeshiva (Dean) of Kollel Hekhal Pinhas, and Beit Midrash Sephardi in the Old City of Jerusalem.

Rabbi Ariel augmented his religious education with studies in the other religions of the world, esoteric studies and practices, philosophies and psychological systems, particularly studying Jungian psychology at the Jungian Center in New York.

In 1992, after teaching privately for many years, Rabbi Ariel officially established his school (with the original Hebrew name Yeshivat Benei N'vi'im) to address the growing concerns of spiritual misguidance, and misinformation that is pervasive in the Jewish community at large. Since then, while staying faithful to his Orthodox Torah origins, Rabbi Ariel has expanded the KosherTorah School to meet the needs of an ever widening audience.

Rabbi Ariel is a regular featured guest on the popular TV program Ancient Aliens. He also appears in other TV programs, speaks on radio talk shows, and is published in scholarly journals and newspaper articles. His YouTube page hosts hundreds of his videos and he regularly teaches live public classes on Facebook. He has spoken before religious congregations, university groups and lectures around the country.

Made in the USA
Las Vegas, NV
06 December 2024